CCNA Routing and Switching
Portable Command Guide
Third Edition

Scott Empson

Cisco Press

800 East 96th Street

Indianapolis, IN 46240

CCNA Routing and Switching Portable Command Guide

Third Edition

Scott Empson

Copyright© 2013 Cisco Systems, Inc.

Published by:
Cisco Press
800 East 96th Street
Indianapolis, IN 46240 USA

ISBN-13: 978-1-58720-430-2

ISBN-10: 1-58720-430-4

Library of Congress Control Number: 2013939799

Printed in the United States of America 4 5 6 7 8 9 0

Fourth Printing: May 2015

Trademark Acknowledgments

Warning and Disclaimer

Corporate and Government Sales

The publisher offers excellent discounts on this book when ordered in quantity for bulk purchases or special sales, which may include electronic versions and/or custom covers and content particular to your business, training goals, marketing focus, and branding interests. For more information, please contact:

U.S. Corporate and Government Sales
1-800-382-3419
corpsales@pearsontechgroup.com

For sales outside of the U.S. please contact:

International Sales
international@pearsoned.com

Feedback Information

At Cisco Press, our goal is to create in-depth technical books of the highest quality and value. Each book is crafted with care and precision, undergoing rigorous development that involves the unique expertise of members from the professional technical community.

Readers' feedback is a natural continuation of this process. If you have any comments regarding how we could improve the quality of this book, or otherwise alter it to better suit your needs, you can contact us through e-mail at feedback@ciscopress.com. Please make sure to include the book title and ISBN in your message.

We greatly appreciate your assistance.

Publisher	Paul Boger
Business Operation Manager, Cisco Press	Jan Cornelssen
Associate Publisher:	Dave Dusthimer
Executive Editor	Mary Beth Ray
Senior Development Editor	Christopher A. Cleveland
Managing Editor	Sandra Schroeder
Copy Editor	Keith Cline
Project Editor	Mandie Frank
Technical Editor	Elan Beer
Editorial Assistant	Vanessa Evans
Proofreader	Debbie Williams
Cover Designer	Mark Shirar
Composition	Trina Wurst

Americas Headquarters
Cisco Systems, Inc.
San Jose, CA

Asia Pacific Headquarters
Cisco Systems (USA) Pte. Ltd.
Singapore

Europe Headquarters
Cisco Systems International BV
Amsterdam, The Netherlands

Cisco has more than 200 offices worldwide. Addresses, phone numbers, and fax numbers are listed on the Cisco Website at www.cisco.com/go/offices.

CCDE, CCENT, Cisco Eos, Cisco HealthPresence, the Cisco logo, Cisco Lumin, Cisco Nexus, Cisco StadiumVision, Cisco TelePresence, Cisco WebEx, DCE, and Welcome to the Human Network are trademarks; Changing the Way We Work, Live, Play, and Learn and Cisco Store are service marks; and Access Registrar, Aironet, AsyncOS, Bringing the Meeting To You, Catalyst, CCDA, CCDP, CCIE, CCIP, CCNA, CCNP, CCSP, CCVP, Cisco, the Cisco Certified Internetwork Expert logo, Cisco IOS, Cisco Press, Cisco Systems, Cisco Systems Capital, the Cisco Systems logo, Cisco Unity, Collaboration Without Limitation, EtherFast, EtherSwitch, Event Center, Fast Step, Follow Me Browsing, FormShare, GigaDrive, HomeLink, Internet Quotient, IOS, iPhone, iQuick Study, IronPort, the IronPort logo, LightStream, Linksys, MediaTone, MeetingPlace, MeetingPlace Chime Sound, MGX, Networkers, Networking Academy, Network Registrar, PCNow, PIX, PowerPanels, ProConnect, ScriptShare, SenderBase, SMARTnet, Spectrum Expert, StackWise, The Fastest Way to Increase Your Internet Quotient, TransPath, WebEx, and the WebEx logo are registered trademarks of Cisco Systems, Inc. and/or its affiliates in the United States and certain other countries.

All other trademarks mentioned in this document or website are the property of their respective owners. The use of the word partner does not imply a partnership relationship between Cisco and any other company. (0812R)

About the Author

Scott Empson is the chair of the Bachelor of Applied Information Systems Technology degree program at the Northern Alberta Institute of Technology in Edmonton, Alberta, Canada, where he teaches Cisco routing, switching, network design, and leadership courses in a variety of different programs (certificate, diploma, and applied degree) at the postsecondary level. Scott is also the program coordinator of the Cisco Networking Academy Program at NAIT, an Area Support Centre for the province of Alberta. He has a Masters of Education degree along with three undergraduate degrees: a Bachelor of Arts, with a major in English; a Bachelor of Education, again with a major in English/Language Arts; and a Bachelor of Applied Information Systems Technology, with a major in Network Management. He currently holds several industry certifications, including CCNP, CCDP, CCAI, CIEH and Network+. Before instructing at NAIT, he was a junior/senior high school English/language arts/computer science teacher at different schools throughout Northern Alberta. Scott lives in Edmonton, Alberta, with his wife, Trina, and two children, Zachariah and Shaelyn.

About the Technical Reviewer

Elan Beer, CCIE No. 1837, is a senior consultant and Cisco instructor specializing in data center architecture and multiprotocol network design. For the past 25 years, Elan has designed networks and trained thousands of industry experts in data center architecture, routing, and switching. Elan has been instrumental in large-scale professional service efforts designing and troubleshooting internetworks, performing data center and network audits, and assisting clients with their short- and long-term design objectives. Elan has a global perspective of network architectures through his international clientele. Elan has used his expertise to design and troubleshoot data centers and internetworks in Malaysia, North America, Europe, Australia, Africa, China, and the Middle East. Most recently, Elan has been focused on data center design, configuration, troubleshooting, and service provider technologies. In 1993, Elan was among the first to obtain the Cisco Certified System Instructor (CCSI) certification, and in 1996, Elan was among the first to attain Cisco System's highest technical certification, the Cisco Certified Internetworking Expert. Since then, Elan has been involved in numerous large-scale data center and telecommunications networking projects worldwide.

Dedications

As always, this book is dedicated to Trina, Zach, and Shae.

Acknowledgments

Anyone who has ever had anything to do with the publishing industry knows that it takes many, many people to create a book. It may be my name on the cover, but there is no way that I can take credit for all that occurred to get this book from idea to publication. Therefore, I must thank:

The team at Cisco Press. Once again, you amaze me with your professionalism and the ability to make me look good. Mary Beth, Chris, Mandie: Thank you for your continued support and belief in my little engineering journal.

To my technical reviewer, Elan: Thanks for keeping me on track and making sure that what I wrote was correct and relevant.

Contents at a Glance

Introduction   xx

Part I   TCP/IP v4

CHAPTER 1   How to Subnet   1

CHAPTER 2   VLSM   15

CHAPTER 3   Route Summarization   25

Part II   Introduction to Cisco Devices

CHAPTER 4   Cables and Connections   31

CHAPTER 5   The Command Line Interface   37

Part III   Configuring a Router

CHAPTER 6   Configuring a Single Cisco Router   45

Part IV   Routing

CHAPTER 7   Static Routing   57

CHAPTER 8   EIGRP   63

CHAPTER 9   Single-Area OSPF   73

CHAPTER 10   Multi-Area OSPF   83

Part V   Switching

CHAPTER 11   Configuring a Switch   91

CHAPTER 12   VLANs   101

CHAPTER 13   VLAN Trunking Protocol and Inter-VLAN Communication   107

CHAPTER 14   Spanning Tree Protocol and EtherChannel   121

Part VI   Layer 3 Redundancy

CHAPTER 15   HSRP and GLBP   137

Part VII   IPv6

CHAPTER 16   IPv6   153

CHAPTER 17   OSPFv3   163

CHAPTER 18   EIGRP for IPv6   171

Part VIII Network Administration and Troubleshooting

CHAPTER 19 Backing Up and Restoring Cisco IOS Software and Configurations   177

CHAPTER 20 Password-Recovery Procedures and the Configuration Register   187

CHAPTER 21 Cisco Discovery Protocol (CDP)   193

CHAPTER 22 Remote Connectivity Using Telnet or SSH   195

CHAPTER 23 Verifying End-to-End Connectivity   199

CHAPTER 24 Configuring Network Management Protocols   203

CHAPTER 25 Basic Troubleshooting   207

CHAPTER 26 Cisco IOS Licensing   213

Part IX   Managing IP Services

CHAPTER 27 Network Address Translation   219

CHAPTER 28 Dynamic Host Configuration Protocol (DHCP)   227

Part X   WANs

CHAPTER 29 Configuring Serial Encapsulation: HDLC and PPP   233

CHAPTER 30 Establishing WAN Connectivity Using Frame Relay   239

CHAPTER 31 Configuring Generic Routing Encapsulation (GRE) Tunnels   249

CHAPTER 32 Configuring Point-to-Point Protocol over Ethernet (PPPoE)   251

Part XI Network Security

CHAPTER 33 Managing Traffic Using Access Control Lists (ACL)   257

Part XII Appendixes

APPENDIX A Binary/Hex/Decimal Conversion Chart   271

APPENDIX B Create Your Own Journal Here   296

Table of Contents

Introduction   xx

Part I   TCP/IP v4

CHAPTER 1   How to Subnet   1

Class A–E Addresses   1

Converting Between Decimal Numbers and Binary   2

Subnetting a Class C Network Using Binary   2

Subnetting a Class B Network Using Binary   5

Binary ANDing   9

So Why AND?   10

Shortcuts in Binary ANDing   11

The Enhanced Bob Maneuver for Subnetting (or How to Subnet
Anything in Under a Minute)   12

CHAPTER 2   VLSM   15

IP Subnet Zero   15

VLSM Example   16

Step 1 Determine How Many H Bits Will Be Needed to Satisfy
the *Largest* Network   16

Step 2 Pick a Subnet for the Largest Network to Use   17

Step 3 Pick the Next Largest Network to Work With   18

Step 4 Pick the Third Largest Network to Work With   20

Step 5 Determine Network Numbers for Serial Links   21

CHAPTER 3   Route Summarization   25

Example for Understanding Route Summarization   25

Step 1: Summarize Winnipeg's Routes   26

Step 2: Summarize Calgary's Routes   27

Step 3: Summarize Edmonton's Routes   27

Step 4: Summarize Vancouver's Routes   28

Route Summarization and Route Flapping   30

Requirements for Route Summarization   30

Part II   Introduction to Cisco Devices

CHAPTER 4   Cables and Connections   31

Connecting a Rollover Cable to Your Router or Switch   31

Using a USB Cable to Connect to Your Router or Switch   31

Terminal Settings   32

LAN Connections   33

Serial Cable Types   33

Which Cable to Use?   35

568A Versus 568B Cables   35

CHAPTER 5   The Command Line Interface   37

Shortcuts for Entering Commands   37

Using the [Tab⇄] Key to Complete Commands   37

Console Error Messages   38

Using the Question Mark for Help   38

enable Command   39

exit Command   39

disable Command   39

logout Command   39

Setup Mode   39

Keyboard Help   40

History Commands   41

terminal Commands   41

show Commands   42

Using the Pipe Parameter (|) with the show Command   42

Part III   Configuring a Router

CHAPTER 6   Configuring a Single Cisco Router   45

Router Modes   45

Entering Global Configuration Mode   46

Configuring a Router Name   46

Configuring Passwords   46

Password Encryption   47

Interface Names   47

Moving Between Interfaces   50

Configuring a Serial Interface   50

Configuring a Fast Ethernet Interface   51

Configuring a Gigabit Ethernet Interface   51

Creating a Message-of-the-Day Banner   51

Creating a Login Banner   51

Setting the Clock Time Zone   52

Assigning a Local Host Name to an IP Address   52

The no ip domain-lookup Command   52

The logging synchronous Command   52

The exec-timeout Command   53

Saving Configurations   53

Erasing Configurations   53

show Commands   53

EXEC Commands in Configuration Mode: The do Command   54

Configuration Example: Basic Router Configuration   54

Boston Router   55

Part IV Routing

CHAPTER 7   Static Routing   57

Configuring a Static Route on a Router   57

The permanent Keyword (Optional)   58

Static Routes and Administrative Distance (Optional)   58

Configuring a Default Route on a Router   59

Verifying Static Routes   59

Configuration Example: Static Routes   60

Boston Router   60

Buffalo Router   61

Bangor Router   61

CHAPTER 8   EIGRP   63

Configuring Enhanced Interior Gateway Routing Protocol (EIGRP)   63

EIGRP Auto-Summarization   65

EIGRP Manual Summarization   65

Passive EIGRP Interfaces   65

Equal-Cost Load Balancing: Maximum Paths   66

Unequal-Cost Load Balancing: Variance   66

Bandwidth Use   67

Authentication   67

Verifying EIGRP   68

Troubleshooting EIGRP   69

Configuration Example: EIGRP   69

Austin Router   70

Houston Router   71

CHAPTER 9   Single-Area OSPF   73

Configuring OSPF   73

Using Wildcard Masks with OSPF Areas   74

Loopback Interfaces   75

Router ID   75

DR/BDR Elections   76

Modifying Cost Metrics   76

OSPF auto-cost reference-bandwidth   77

Authentication: Simple   77

Authentication: Using MD5 Encryption   78

Timers   78

Propagating a Default Route 78
Verifying OSPF Configuration 79
Troubleshooting OSPF 79
Configuration Example: Single Area OSPF 80
    Austin Router 80
    Houston Router 81
    Galveston Router 82

CHAPTER 10 Multi-Area OSPF 83

Configuring Multi-Area OSPF 83
Passive Interfaces 84
    Route Summarization 84
Configuration Example: Multi-Area OSPF 85
    ASBR Router 86
    ABR-1 Router 87
    ABR-2 Router 88
    Internal Router 89

Part V Switching

CHAPTER 11 Configuring a Switch 91

Help Commands 91
Command Modes 91
Verifying Commands 92
Resetting Switch Configuration 92
Setting Host Names 92
Setting Passwords 93
Setting IP Addresses and Default Gateways 93
Setting Interface Descriptions 94
The mdix auto Command 94
Setting Duplex Operation 95
Setting Operation Speed 95
Managing the MAC Address Table 95
Configuring Static MAC Addresses 95
Switch Port Security 96
Verifying Switch Port Security 96
Sticky MAC Addresses 97
Configuration Example 97

CHAPTER 12 VLANs 101

Creating Static VLANs 101
    Using VLAN Configuration Mode 101
    Using VLAN Database Mode 102

Assigning Ports to VLANs   102

Using the range Command   103

Verifying VLAN Information   103

Saving VLAN Configurations   103

Erasing VLAN Configurations   104

Configuration Example: VLANs   104

CHAPTER 13   VLAN Trunking Protocol and Inter-VLAN Communication   107

Dynamic Trunking Protocol   107

Dynamic Trunking Protocol (DTP)   108

Setting the Encapsulation Type   108

VLAN Trunking Protocol (VTP)   109

Verifying VTP   110

Inter-VLAN Communication Using an External Router: Router-on-a-
Stick   110

Inter-VLAN Communication on a Multilayer Switch Through a Switch
Virtual Interface   111

Removing L2 Switchport Capability of a Switch Port   111

Configuring Inter-VLAN Communication   111

Inter-VLAN Communication Tips   112

Configuration Example: Inter-VLAN Communication   112

ISP Router   113

CORP Router   114

L2Switch2 (Catalyst 2960)   116

L3Switch1 (Catalyst 3560)   118

L2Switch1 (Catalyst 2960)   119

CHAPTER 14   Spanning Tree Protocol and EtherChannel   121

Spanning Tree Protocol   121

Enabling Spanning Tree Protocol   121

Configuring the Root Switch   122

Configuring a Secondary Root Switch   122

Configuring Port Priority   123

Configuring the Path Cost   123

Configuring the Switch Priority of a VLAN   123

Configuring STP Timers   124

Verifying STP   124

Optional STP Configurations   125

Changing the Spanning-Tree Mode   126

Extended System ID   126

Enabling Rapid Spanning Tree   127

Troubleshooting Spanning Tree   127

Configuration Example: STP   127

EtherChannel   129
    Interface Modes in EtherChannel   130
    Guidelines for Configuring EtherChannel   130
    Configuring Layer 2 EtherChannel   131
    Verifying EtherChannel   131
    Configuration Example: EtherChannel   132

Part VI   Layer 3 Redundancy

CHAPTER 15   HSRP and GLBP   137
    Hot Standby Router Protocol   137
    Configuring HSRP on a Router   138
    Configuring HSRP on an L3 Switch   138
    Default HSRP Configuration Settings   139
    Verifying HSRP   139
    HSRP Optimization Options   139
        Preempt   140
        HSRP Message Timers   140
        Interface Tracking   141
    Multiple HSRP   141
    Debugging HSRP   142
    Virtual Router Redundancy Protocol   143
    Configuring VRRP   143
    Verifying VRRP   144
    Debugging VRRP   145
    Gateway Load Balancing Protocol   145
        Configuring GLBP   145
    Verifying GLBP   147
    Debugging GLBP   148
    Configuration Example: GLBP   148
        DLS1   149
        DLS2   150

Part VII   IPv6

CHAPTER 16   IPv6   153
    Assigning IPv6 Addresses to Interfaces   153
    IPv6 and RIPng   154
    Configuration Example: IPv6 RIP   155
        Austin Router   155
    IPv6 Tunnels: Manual Overlay Tunnel   157
        Juneau Router   157
        Fairbanks Router   158

Static Routes in IPv6   159
Floating Static Routes in IPv6   160
Default Routes in IPv6   160
Verifying and Troubleshooting IPv6   160
IPv6 Ping   162
IPv6 Traceroute   162

CHAPTER 17   OSPFv3   163

IPv6 and OSPFv3   163
Enabling OSPF for IPv6 on an Interface   163
Enabling an OSPF for IPv6 Area Range   164
Enabling an IPv4 Router ID for OSPFv3   165
Forcing an SPF Calculation   165
Verifying and Troubleshooting IPv6 and OSPFv3   165
Configuration Example: OSPFv3   166
R3 Router   166
R2 Router   167
R1 Router   168
R4 Router   169

CHAPTER 18   EIGRP for IPv6   171

IPv6 and EIGRP   171
Enabling EIGRP for IPv6 on an Interface   171
Configuring the Percentage of Link Bandwidth Used by EIGRP   172
Configuring Summary Addresses   172
Configuring EIGRP Route Authentication   172
Configuring EIGRP Timers   172
Logging EIGRP Neighbor Adjacency Changes   173
Adjusting the EIGRP for IPv6 Metric Weights   173
Verifying and Troubleshooting EIGRP for IPv6   173
Configuration Example: EIGRP for IPv6   174
R3 Router   174
R2 Router   175
R1 Router   176

Part VIII Network Administration and Troubleshooting

CHAPTER 19   Backing Up and Restoring Cisco IOS Software and
Configurations   177

Boot System Commands   177
The Cisco IOS File System   178
Viewing the Cisco IOS File System   178
Commonly Used URL Prefixes for Cisco Network Devices   178

Deciphering IOS Image Filenames   179

Backing Up Configurations to a TFTP Server   180

Restoring Configurations from a TFTP Server   180

Backing Up the Cisco IOS Software to a TFTP Server   181

Restoring/Upgrading the Cisco IOS Software from a TFTP Server   181

Restoring the Cisco IOS Software from ROM Monitor Mode Using
   Xmodem   182

Restoring the Cisco IOS Software Using the ROM Monitor
   Environmental Variables and tftpdnld Command   184

CHAPTER 20   Password-Recovery Procedures and the Configuration
Register   187

The Configuration Register   187

     A Visual Representation   187

     What the Bits Mean   187

     The Boot Field   188

     Console Terminal Baud Rate Settings   188

     Changing the Console Line Speed: CLI   189

     Changing the Console Line Speed: ROM Monitor Mode   189

Password-Recovery Procedures for Cisco Routers   190

Password Recovery for 2960 Series Switches   191

CHAPTER 21   Cisco Discovery Protocol (CDP)   193

Cisco Discovery Protocol   193

CHAPTER 22   Remote Connectivity Using Telnet or SSH   195

Configuring a Device to Accept a Remote Telnet Connection   195

Using Telnet to Remotely Connect to Other Devices   196

Verifying Telnet   197

Configuring the Secure Shell Protocol (SSH)   197

Verifying SSH   198

CHAPTER 23   Verifying End-to-End Connectivity   199

ICMP Redirect Messages   199

The ping Command   199

Examples of Using the ping and the Extended ping Commands   200

The traceroute Command   201

CHAPTER 24   Configuring Network Management Protocols   203

Configuring SNMP   203

Configuring Syslog   204

Syslog Message Format   204

Syslog Severity Levels   205

Syslog Message Example   205
Configuring NetFlow   206
Verifying NetFlow   206

CHAPTER 25   Basic Troubleshooting   207
Viewing the Routing Table   207
Clearing the Routing Table   208
Determining the Gateway of Last Resort   208
Determining the Last Routing Update   208
OSI Layer 3 Testing   208
OSI Layer 7 Testing   209
Interpreting the show interface Command   209
Clearing Interface Counters   209
Using CDP to Troubleshoot   209
The traceroute Command   209
The show controllers Command   210
debug Commands   210
Using Time Stamps   210
Operating System IP Verification Commands   211
The ip http server Command   211
The netstat Command   211
The arp Command   211

CHAPTER 26   Cisco IOS Licensing   213
Cisco Licensing Earlier Than IOS 15.0   213
Cisco Licensing for the ISR G2 Platforms: IOS 15.0 and Later   215
Verifying Licenses   215
Cisco License Manager   215
Installing a Permanent License   216
Installing an Evaluation License   217
Backing Up a License   217
Uninstalling a License   217

Part IX   Managing IP Services

CHAPTER 27   Network Address Translation   219
Configuring Dynamic NAT: One Private to One Public Address
Translation   219
Configuring PAT: Many Private to One Public Address Translation   221
Configuring Static NAT: One Private to One Permanent Public Address
Translation   222
Verifying NAT and PAT Configurations   223
Troubleshooting NAT and PAT Configurations   224

Configuration Example: PAT   224

   ISP Router   224

   Company Router   225

CHAPTER 28   Dynamic Host Configuration Protocol (DHCP)   227

Configuring a DHCP Server on an IOS Router   227

Verifying and Troubleshooting DHCP Configuration   228

Configuring a DHCP Helper Address   228

DHCP Client on a Cisco IOS Software Ethernet Interface   229

Configuration Example: DHCP   229

   Edmonton Router   229

   Gibbons Router   231

Part X   WANs

CHAPTER 29   Configuring Serial Encapsulation: HDLC and PPP   233

Configuring HDLC Encapsulation on a Serial Line   233

Configuring Point-to-Point Protocol (PPP) on a Serial Line (Mandatory
   Commands)   233

Configuring PPP on a Serial Line (Optional Commands):
   Compression   234

Configuring PPP on a Serial Line (Optional Commands): Link
   Quality   234

Configuring PPP on a Serial Line (Optional Commands):
   Multilink   234

Configuring PPP on a Serial Line (Optional Commands):
   Authentication   234

Verifying and Troubleshooting a Serial Link/PPP Encapsulation   235

Configuration Example: PPP with CHAP Authentication   236

   Boston Router   236

   Buffalo Router   237

CHAPTER 30   Establishing WAN Connectivity Using Frame Relay   239

Configuring Frame Relay   239

   Setting the Frame Relay Encapsulation Type   239

   Setting the Frame Relay Encapsulation LMI Type   239

   Setting the Frame Relay DLCI Number   240

   Configuring a Frame Relay map Statement   240

   Configuring a Description of the Interface (Optional)   240

   Configuring Frame Relay Using Subinterfaces   240

Verifying Frame Relay   241

Troubleshooting Frame Relay   242

Configuration Example: Point-to-Point Frame Relay Using
   Subinterfaces and OSPF   242

Houston Router   242

Austin Router   244

Galveston Router   244

Laredo Router   245

Configuration Example: Point-to-Multipoint Frame Relay Using
Subinterfaces and EIGRP   246

R1 Router   246

R2 Router   247

R3 Router   248

CHAPTER 31   Configuring Generic Routing Encapsulation (GRE) Tunnels   249

Configuring a GRE Tunnel   249

Branch Router   249

HQ Router   250

Verifying a GRE Tunnel   250

CHAPTER 32   Configuring Point-to-Point Protocol over Ethernet (PPPoE)   251

Configuring a DSL Connection using PPPoE   251

Step 1: Configure PPPoE (External Modem)   252

Step 2: Configure the Dialer Interface   253

Step 3: Define Interesting Traffic and Specify Default
Routing   253

Step 4: Configure NAT Using an ACL   254

Step 5: Configure NAT Using a Route Map   254

Step 6: Configure DHCP Service   255

Step 7: Apply NAT Programming   255

Step 8: Verify a PPPoE Connection   255

Part XI   Network Security

CHAPTER 33   Managing Traffic Using Access Control Lists (ACL)   257

Access List Numbers   257

Using Wildcard Masks   258

ACL Keywords   258

Creating Standard ACLs   259

Applying Standard ACLs to an Interface   260

Verifying ACLs   260

Removing ACLs   260

Creating Extended ACLs   261

Applying Extended ACLs to an Interface   262

The established Keyword (Optional)   262

Creating Named ACLs   262

Using Sequence Numbers in Named ACLs   263

Removing Specific Lines in Named ACLs Using Sequence
    Numbers   264
Sequence Number Tips   264
Including Comments About Entries in ACLs   265
Restricting Virtual Terminal Access   265
Tips for Configuring ACLs   266
ACLs and IPv6   266
Configuration Examples: ACLs   267

Part XII Appendixes

APPENDIX A   Binary/Hex/Decimal Conversion Chart   271

APPENDIX B   Create Your Own Journal Here   279

Command Syntax Conventions

The conventions used to present command syntax in this book are the same conventions used in the IOS Command Reference. The Command Reference describes these conventions as follows:

- **Boldface** indicates commands and keywords that are entered literally, as shown. In actual configuration examples and output (not general command syntax), boldface indicates commands that are manually input by the user (such as a show command).

- *Italics* indicate arguments for which you supply actual values.

- Vertical bars (|) separate alternative, mutually exclusive elements.

- Square brackets [ ] indicate optional elements.

- Braces { } indicate a required choice.

- Braces within brackets [{ }] indicate a required choice within an optional element.

Introduction

Welcome to CCNA Routing and Switching! This book is the result of a massive redesign by Cisco of their entry-level certification exams to more closely align with industry's need for networking talent as we enter into the era of "the Internet of Everything." The success of the previous two editions of this book prompted Cisco Press to approach me with a request to update the book with the necessary new content to help both students and IT professionals in the field study and prepare for the new CCNA Routing and Switching exam. For someone who originally thought that this book would be less than 100 pages in length and limited to the Cisco Networking Academy program for its complete audience, I am continually amazed that my little engineering journal has caught on with such a wide range of people throughout the IT community.

I have long been a fan of what I call the "engineering journal," a small notebook that can be carried around and that contains little nuggets of information—commands that you forget, the IP addressing scheme of some remote part of the network, little reminders about how to do something you only have to do once or twice a year (but is vital to the integrity and maintenance of your network). This journal has been a constant companion by my side for the past 15 years; I only teach some of these concepts every second or third year, so I constantly need to refresh commands and concepts and learn new commands and ideas as they are released by Cisco. My journals are the best way for me to review because they are written in my own words (words that I can understand). At least, I had better understand them, because if I can't, I have only myself to blame.

My first published engineering journal was the *CCNA Quick Command Guide*; it was organized to match to the (then) order of the Cisco Networking Academy program. That book then morphed into the *Portable Command Guide*, the third edition of which you are reading right now. This book is my "industry" edition of the engineering journal. It contains a different logical flow to the topics, one more suited to someone working in the field. Like topics are grouped together: routing protocols, switches, troubleshooting. More-complex examples are given. New topics have been added, such as OSPFv3 and EIGRPv6 for IPv6, multi-area OSPF, PPPoE, GRE tunnels, and Cisco IOS Version 15. The popular "Create Your Own Journal" appendix is still here (blank pages for you to add in your own commands that you need in your specific job). We all recognize the fact that no network administrator's job can be so easily pigeonholed as to just working with CCNA topics; you all have your own specific jobs and duties assigned to you. That is why you will find those blank pages at the end of the book. Make this book your own; personalize it with what you need to make it more effective. That way your journal will not look like mine.

Networking Devices Used in the Preparation of This Book

To verify the commands in this book, I had to try them out on a few different devices. The following is a list of the equipment I used when writing this book:

- C2821 ISR with PVDM2, CMME, a WIC-2T, FXS and FXO VICs, running 12.4(10a) IPBase IOS

- WS-C2960-24TT-L Catalyst switch, running 12.2(25)SE IOS

- WS-C2950-12 Catalyst switch, running Version C2950-C3.0(5.3)WC(1) Enterprise Edition software

- C1941 ISRG2 router with WIC 2T and HWIC-4ESW, running Version 15.1(1)T Cisco IOS with a technology package of IPBaseK9

Those of you familiar with Cisco devices will recognize that a majority of these commands work across the entire range of the Cisco product line. These commands are not limited to the platforms and Cisco IOS Software versions listed. In fact, these devices are in most cases adequate for someone to continue his or her studies into the CCNP level, too.

Private Addressing Used in this Book

This book makes use of RFC 1918 addressing throughout. Because I do not have permission to use public addresses in my examples, I have done everything with private addressing. Private addressing is perfect for use in a lab environment or in a testing situation because it works exactly like public addressing, with the exception that it cannot be routed across a public network. That is why you will see private addresses in my WAN links between two routers using serial connections or in my Frame Relay cloud.

Who Should Read This Book

This book is for those people preparing for the CCNA Routing and Switching exam, whether through self-study, on-the-job training and practice, or through study within the Cisco Networking Academy program. There are also some handy hints and tips along the way to make life a bit easier for you in this endeavor. It is small enough that you will find it easy to carry around with you. Big, heavy textbooks might look impressive on your bookshelf in your office, but can you really carry them all around with you when you are working in some server room or equipment closet somewhere?

Optional Sections

A few sections in this book have been marked as optional. These sections cover topics that are not on the CCNA Routing and Switching certification exam, but they are valuable topics that I believe should be known by someone at a CCNA level. Some of the optional topics might also be concepts that are covered in the Cisco Networking Academy program courses.

Organization of This Book

This book follows what I think is a logical approach to configuring a small to mid-size network. It is an approach that I give to my students when they invariably ask for some sort of outline to plan and then configure a network. Specifically, this approach is as follows:

Part I: TCP/IP v4

- **Chapter 1, "How to Subnet"**—An overview of how to subnet, examples of subnetting (both a Class B and a Class C address), the use of the binary AND operation, the Enhanced Bob Maneuver to Subnetting

- **Chapter 2, "VLSM"**—An overview of VLSM, an example of using VLSM to make your IP plan more efficient

- **Chapter 3, "Route Summarization"**—Using route summarization to make your routing updates more efficient, an example of how to summarize a network, necessary requirements for summarizing your network

Part II: Introduction to Cisco Devices

- **Chapter 4, "Cables and Connections"**—An overview of how to connect to Cisco devices, which cables to use for which interfaces, and the differences between the TIA/EIA 568A and 568B wiring standards for UTP

- **Chapter 5, "The Command-Line Interface"**—How to navigate through Cisco IOS Software: editing commands, keyboard shortcuts, and help commands

Part III: Configuring a Router

- **Chapter 6, "Configuring a Single Cisco Router"**—Commands needed to configure a single router: names, passwords, configuring interfaces, MOTD and login banners, IP host tables, saving and erasing your configurations

Part IV: Routing

- **Chapter 7, "Static Routing"**—Configuring static routes in your internetwork

- **Chapter 8, "EIGRP"**—Configuring and verifying EIGRP

- **Chapter 9, "Single Area OSPF"**—Configuring and verifying single-area OSPF

- **Chapter 10, "Multi-Area OSPF"**—Configuring and verifying multi-area OSPF

Part V: Switching

- **Chapter 11, "Configuring a Switch"**—Commands to configure Catalyst 2960 switches: names, passwords, IP addresses, default gateways, port speed and duplex; configuring static MAC addresses; managing the MAC address table; port security

- **Chapter 12, "VLANs"**—Configuring static VLANs, troubleshooting VLANs, saving and deleting VLAN information.

- **Chapter 13, "VLAN Trunking Protocol and Inter-VLAN Communication"**—Configuring a VLAN trunk link, configuring VTP, verifying VTP, inter-VLAN communication, router-on-a-stick, subinterfaces, and SVIs.

- **Chapter 14, "Spanning Tree Protocol and EtherChannel"**—Verifying STP, setting switch priorities, and creating and verifying EtherChannel groups between switches

Part VI: Layer 3 Redundancy

- **Chapter 15, "HSRP and GLBP"**— Configuring HSRP, interface tracking, setting priorities, configuring GLBP.

Part VII: IPv6

- **Chapter 16, "IPv6"**— Transitioning to IPv6; format of IPv6 addresses; configuring IPv6 (interfaces, tunneling, static routing)

- **Chapter 17, "OSPFv3"**— Configuring OSPF to work with IPv6,

- **Chapter 18, "EIGRP for IPv6"**— Configuring EIGRP to work with IPv6.

Part VIII: Network Administration and Troubleshooting

- **Chapter 19, "Backing Up and Restoring Cisco IOS Software and Configurations"**—Boot commands for Cisco IOS Software, backing up and restoring Cisco IOS Software using TFTP, Xmodem, and ROMmon environmental variables

- **Chapter 20, "Password-Recovery Procedures and the Configuration Register"**—The configuration register, password recovery procedure for routers and switches

- **Chapter 21, "Cisco Discovery Protocol (CDP)"**—Customizing and verifying CDP

- **Chapter 22, "Remote Connectivity Using Telnet or SSH"**—Commands used for Telnet and SSH to remotely connect to other devices

- **Chapter 23, "Verifying End-to-End Connectivity"**—Commands for both **ping** and extended **ping**; the **traceroute** command

- **Chapter 24, "Configuring Network Management Protocols"**—Configuring SNMP, working with syslog, Severity Levels, Configuring NetFlow

- **Chapter 25, "Basic Troubleshooting"**—Various **show** commands used to view the routing table; interpreting the **show** interface command; verifying your IP settings using different operating systems

- **Chapter 26, "Cisco IOS Licensing"**— Differences between licensing pre- and post-Cisco IOS Version 15, installing permanent and evaluation licenses, backing up and uninstalling licenses

Part IX: Managing IP Services

- **Chapter 27, "Network Address Translation"**—Configuring and verifying NAT and PAT

- **Chapter 28, "Dynamic Host Configuration Protocol (DHCP)"**—Configuring and verifying DHCP on a Cisco IOS router

Part X: WANs

- **Chapter 29, "Configuring Serial Encapsulation: HDLC and PPP"**—Configuring PPP, authentication of PPP using CHAP, compression in PPP; multilink in PPP, troubleshooting PPP, returning to HDLC encapsulation

- **Chapter 30, "Establishing WAN Connectivity Using Frame Relay"**—Configuring basic Frame Relay, Frame Relay and subinterfaces, DLCIs, verifying and troubleshooting Frame Relay

- **Chapter 31, "Configuring Generic Routing Encapsulation (GRE) Tunnels"**—Configuring and verifying GRE tunnels

- **Chapter 32, "Configuring Point-to-Point Protocol over Ethernet (PPPoE)"**—Configuring a DSL connection using PPPoE

Part XI: Network Security

- **Chapter 33, "Managing Traffic Using Access Control Lists (ACL)"**—Configuring standard ACLs, wildcard masking, creating extended ACLs, creating named ACLs, using sequence numbers in named ACLs, verifying and troubleshooting ACLs, ACLs and IPv6

Part XII: Appendixes

- **Appendix A, "Binary/Hex/Decimal Conversion Chart"**—A chart showing numbers 0 through 255 in the three numbering systems of binary, hexadecimal, and decimal

- **Appendix B, "Create Your Own Journal Here"**—Some blank pages for you to add in your own specific commands that might not be in this book

Did I Miss Anything?

I am always interested to hear how my students, and now readers of my books, do on both certification exams and future studies. If you would like to contact me and let me know how this book helped you in your certification goals, please do so. Did I miss anything? Let me know. Contact me at ccnaguide@empson.ca or through the Cisco Press website, http://www.ciscopress.com.

CHAPTER 1

How to Subnet

Class A–E Addresses

Class	Leading Bit Pattern	First Octet in Decimal	Notes		Formulae	
A	0xxxxxxx	0–127	0 is invalid 127 reserved for loopback testing		2^N Where N is equal to number of bits borrowed	Number of total subnets created
B	10xxxxxx	128–191			$2^N - 2$	Number of valid subnets created
C	110xxxxx	192–223			2^H Where H is equal to number of host bits	Number of total hosts per subnet
D	1110xxxx	224–239	Reserved for multicasting		$2^H - 2$	Number of valid hosts per subnet
E	1111xxxx	240–255	Reserved for future use/ testing			

Class A Address	N	H	H	H
Class B Address	N	N	H	H
Class C Address	N	N	N	H

N = Network bits
H = Host bits
All 0s in host portion = Network or subnetwork address
All 1s in host portion = Broadcast address
Combination of 1s and 0s in host portion = Valid host address

Converting Between Decimal Numbers and Binary

In any given octet of an IP address, the 8 bits can be defined as follows:

2^7	2^6	2^5	2^4	2^3	2^2	2^1	2^0
128	64	32	16	8	4	2	1

To convert a decimal number into binary, you must turn on the bits (make them a 1) that would add up to that number, as follows:

187 = 10111011 = 128+32+16+8+2+1

224 = 11100000 = 128+64+32

To convert a binary number into decimal, you must add the bits that have been turned on (the 1s), as follows:

10101010 = 128+32+8+2 = 170

11110000 = 128+64+32+16 = 240

The IP address 138.101.114.250 is represented in binary as

10001010.01100101.01110010.11111010

The subnet mask of 255.255.255.192 is represented in binary as

11111111.11111111.11111111.11000000

Subnetting a Class C Network Using Binary

You have a Class C address of 192.168.100.0 /24. You need nine subnets. What is the IP plan of network numbers, broadcast numbers, and valid host numbers? What is the subnet mask needed for this plan?

You cannot use N bits, only H bits. Therefore, ignore 192.168.100. These numbers cannot change.

Step 1. Determine how many H bits you need to borrow to create nine valid subnets.

$2^N - 2 \geq 9$
N = 4, so you need to borrow 4 H bits and turn them into N bits.

Start with 8 H bits	HHHHHHHH
Borrow 4 bits	NNNNHHHH

Step 2. Determine the first valid subnet in binary.

0001HHHH	Cannot use subnet 0000 because it is invalid. Therefore, you must start with the bit pattern of 0001
0001**0000**	All 0s in host portion = subnetwork number
0001**0001**	First valid host number
.	
.	
.	
0001**1110**	Last valid host number
0001**1111**	All 1s in host portion = broadcast number

Step 3. Convert binary to decimal.

00010000 = 16	Subnetwork number
00010001 = 17	First valid host number
.	
.	
.	
00011110 = 30	Last valid host number
00011111 = 31	All 1s in host portion = broadcast number

Step 4. Determine the second valid subnet in binary.

0010HHHH	0010 = 2 in binary = second valid subnet
0010**0000**	All 0s in host portion = subnetwork number
0010**0001**	First valid host number
.	
.	
.	
0010**1110**	Last valid host number
0010**1111**	All 1s in host portion = broadcast number

Step 5. Convert binary to decimal.

00100000 = 32	Subnetwork number
00100001 = 33	First valid host number
.	
.	
.	
00101110 = 46	Last valid host number
00101111 = 47	All 1s in host portion = broadcast number

Step 6. Create an IP plan table.

Valid Subnet	Network Number	Range of Valid Hosts	Broadcast Number
1	16	17–30	31
2	32	33–46	47
3	48	49–62	63

Notice a pattern? Counting by 16.

Step 7. Verify the pattern in binary. (The third valid subnet in binary is used here.)

0011HHHH	Third valid subnet
00110000 = **48**	Subnetwork number
00110001 = **49**	First valid host number
.	
.	
.	
00111110 = **62**	Last valid host number
00111111 = **63**	Broadcast number

Step 8. Finish the IP plan table.

Subnet	Network Address (0000)	Range of Valid Hosts (0001–1110)	Broadcast Address (1111)
0 (0000) invalid	192.168.100.**0**	192.168.100.**1**–192.168.100.**14**	192.168.100.**15**
1 (0001)	192.168.100.**16**	192.168.100.**17**–192.168.100.**30**	192.168.100.**31**
2 (0010)	192.168.100.**32**	192.168.100.**33**–192.168.100.**46**	192.168.100.**47**
3 (0011)	192.168.100.**48**	192.168.100.**49**–192.168.100.**62**	192.168.100.**63**
4 (0100)	192.168.100.**64**	192.168.100.**65**–192.168.100.**78**	192.168.100.**79**
5 (0101)	192.168.100.**80**	192.168.100.**81**–192.168.100.**94**	192.168.100.**95**
6 (0110)	192.168.100.**96**	192.168.100.**97**–192.168.100.**110**	192.168.100.**111**
7 (0111)	192.168.100.**112**	192.168.100.**113**–192.168.100.**126**	192.168.100.**127**
8 (1000)	192.168.100.**128**	192.168.100.**129**–192.168.100.**142**	192.168.100.**143**

Subnet	Network Address (0000)	Range of Valid Hosts (0001–1110)	Broadcast Address (1111)
9 (1001)	192.168.100.**144**	192.168.100.**145**– 192.168.100.**158**	192.168.100.**159**
10 (1010)	192.168.100.**160**	192.168.100.**161**– 192.168.100.**174**	192.168.100.**175**
11 (1011)	192.168.100.**176**	192.168.100.**177**– 192.168.100.**190**	192.168.100.**191**
12 (1100)	192.168.100.**192**	192.168.100.**193**– 192.168.100.**206**	192.168.100.**207**
13 (1101)	192.168.100.**208**	192.168.100.**209**– 192.168.100.**222**	192.168.100.**223**
14 (1110)	192.168.100.**224**	192.168.100.**225**– 192.168.100.**238**	192.168.100.**239**
15 (1111) invalid	192.168.100.**240**	192.168.100.**241**– 192.168.100.**254**	192.168.100.**255**
Quick Check	**Always an even number**	**First valid host is always an odd # Last valid host is always an even #**	**Always an odd number**

Use any nine subnets—the rest are for future growth.

Step 9. Calculate the subnet mask. The default subnet mask for a Class C network is as follows:

Decimal	Binary
255.255.255.0	11111111.11111111.11111111.00000000

1 = Network or subnetwork bit
0 = Host bit
  You borrowed 4 bits; therefore, the new subnet mask is the following:

11111111.11111111.11111111.**1111**0000	255.255.255.**240**

NOTE You subnet a Class B or a Class A network with exactly the same steps as for a Class C network; the only difference is that you start with more H bits.

Subnetting a Class B Network Using Binary

You have a Class B address of 172.16.0.0 /16. You need nine subnets. What is the IP plan of network numbers, broadcast numbers, and valid host numbers? What is the subnet mask needed for this plan?

You cannot use N bits, only H bits. Therefore, ignore 172.16. These numbers cannot change.

Step 1. Determine how many H bits you need to borrow to create nine valid subnets.

$$2^N - 2 \geq 9$$

N = 4, so you need to borrow 4 H bits and turn them into N bits.

Start with 16 H bits	HHHHHHHHHHHHHHHH (Remove the decimal point for now)
Borrow 4 bits	**NNNN**HHHHHHHHHHHH

Step 2. Determine the first valid subnet in binary (without using decimal points).

0001HHHHHHHHHHHH	
0001**000000000000**	Subnet number
0001**000000000001**	First valid host
.	
.	
.	
0001**111111111110**	Last valid host
0001**111111111111**	Broadcast number

Step 3. Convert binary to decimal (replacing the decimal point in the binary numbers).

0001**0000.00000000** = 16.0	Subnetwork number
0001**0000.00000001** = 16.1	First valid host number
.	
.	
.	
0001**1111.11111110** = 31.254	Last valid host number
0001**1111.11111111** = 31.255	Broadcast number

Step 4. Determine the second valid subnet in binary (without using decimal points).

0010HHHHHHHHHHHH	
0010**000000000000**	Subnet number
0010**000000000001**	First valid host
.	
.	
.	
0010**111111111110**	Last valid host
0010**111111111111**	Broadcast number

Step 5. Convert binary to decimal (returning the decimal point in the binary numbers).

00100000.00000000 = 32.0	Subnetwork number
00100000.00000001 = 32.1	First valid host number
.	
.	
.	
00101111.11111110 = 47.254	Last valid host number
00101111.11111111 = 47.255	Broadcast number

Step 6. Create an IP plan table.

Valid Subnet	Network Number	Range of Valid Hosts	Broadcast Number
1	16.0	16.1–31.254	31.255
2	32.0	32.1–47.254	47.255
3	48.0	48.1–63.254	63.255

Notice a pattern? Counting by 16.

Step 7. Verify the pattern in binary. (The third valid subnet in binary is used here.)

0011HHHHHHHHHHHH	Third valid subnet
00110000.00000000 = 48.0	Subnetwork number
00110000.00000001 = 48.1	First valid host number
.	
.	
.	
00111111.11111110 = 63.254	Last valid host number
00111111.11111111 = 63.255	Broadcast number

Step 8. Finish the IP plan table.

Subnet	Network Address (0000)	Range of Valid Hosts (0001–1110)	Broadcast Address (1111)
0 (0000) invalid	172.16.**0.0**	172.16.**0.1**–172.16.**15.254**	172.16.**15.255**
1 (0001)	172.16.**16.0**	172.16.**16.1**–172.16.**31.254**	172.16.**31.255**
2 (0010)	172.16.**32.0**	172.16.**32.1**–172.16.**47.254**	172.16.**47.255**

Subnet	Network Address (0000)	Range of Valid Hosts (0001–1110)	Broadcast Address (1111)
3 (0011)	172.16.**48.0**	172.16.**48.1**–172.16.**63.254**	172.16.**63.255**
4 (0100)	172.16.**64.0**	172.16.**64.1**–172.16.**79.254**	172.16.**79.255**
5 (0101)	172.16.**80.0**	172.16.**80.1**–172.16.**95.254**	172.16.**95.255**
6 (0110)	172.16.**96.0**	172.16.**96.1**–172.16.**111.254**	172.16.**111.255**
7 (0111)	172.16.**112.0**	172.16.**112.1**–172.16.**127.254**	172.16.**127.255**
8 (1000)	172.16.**128.0**	172.16.**128.1**–172.16.**143.254**	172.16.**143.255**
9 (1001)	172.16.**144.0**	172.16.**144.1**–172.16.**159.254**	172.16.**159.255**
10 (1010)	172.16.**160.0**	172.16.**160.1**–172.16.**175.254**	172.16.**175.255**
11 (1011)	172.16.**176.0**	172.16.**176.1**–172.16.**191.254**	172.16.**191.255**
12 (1100)	172.16.**192.0**	172.16.**192.1**–172.16.**207.254**	172.16.**207.255**
13 (1101)	172.16.**208.0**	172.16.**208.1**–172.16.**223.254**	172.16.**223.255**
14 (1110)	172.16.**224.0**	172.16.**224.1**–172.16.**239.254**	172.16.**239.255**
15 (1111) invalid	172.16.**240.0**	172.16.**240.1**–172.16.**255.254**	172.16.**255.255**
Quick Check	**Always in form even #.0**	**First valid host is always even #.1 Last valid host is always odd #.254**	**Always odd #.255**

Use any nine subnets—the rest are for future growth.

Step 9.   Calculate the subnet mask.The default subnet mask for a Class B network is as follows:

Decimal	Binary
255.255.0.0	11111111.11111111.00000000.00000000

1 = Network or subnetwork bit
0 = Host bit

You borrowed 4 bits; therefore, the new subnet mask is the following:

11111111.11111111.**1111**0000.00000000	255.255.**240**.0

Binary ANDing

Binary ANDing is the process of performing multiplication to two binary numbers. In the decimal numbering system, ANDing is addition: 2 and 3 equals 5. In decimal, there are an infinite number of answers when ANDing two numbers together. However, in the binary numbering system, the AND function yields only two possible outcomes, based on four different combinations. These outcomes, or answers, can be displayed in what is known as a truth table:

0 and 0 = 0

1 and 0 = 0

0 and 1 = 0

1 and 1 = 1

You use ANDing most often when comparing an IP address to its subnet mask. The end result of ANDing these two numbers together is to yield the network number of that address.

Question 1

What is the network number of the IP address 192.168.100.115 if it has a subnet mask of 255.255.255.240?

Answer

Step 1. Convert both the IP address and the subnet mask to binary:

192.168.100.115 = 11000000.10101000.01100100.01110011

255.255.255.240 = 11111111.11111111.11111111.11110000

Step 2. Perform the AND operation to each pair of bits—1 bit from the address ANDed to the corresponding bit in the subnet mask. Refer to the truth table for the possible outcomes:

192.168.100.115 = 11000000.10101000.01100100.01110011

255.255.255.240 = 11111111.11111111.11111111.11110000

ANDed result   = 11000000.10101000.01100100.01110000

Step 3. Convert the answer back into decimal:

11000000.10101000.01100100.01110000 = 192.168.100.112

The IP address 192.168.100.115 belongs to the 192.168.100.112 network when a mask of 255.255.255.240 is used.

Question 2

What is the network number of the IP address 192.168.100.115 if it has a subnet mask of 255.255.255.192?

(Notice that the IP address is the same as in Question 1, but the subnet mask is different. What answer do you think you will get? The same one? Let's find out!)

Answer

Step 1. Convert both the IP address and the subnet mask to binary:

192.168.100.115 = 11000000.10101000.01100100.01110011

255.255.255.192 = 11111111.11111111.11111111.11000000

Step 2. Perform the AND operation to each pair of bits—1 bit from the address ANDed to the corresponding bit in the subnet mask. Refer to the truth table for the possible outcomes:

192.168.100.115 = 11000000.10101000.01100100.01110011

255.255.255.192 = 11111111.11111111.11111111.11000000

ANDed result   = 11000000.10101000.01100100.01000000

Step 3. Convert the answer back into decimal:

11000000.10101000.01100100.01110000 = 192.168.100.64

The IP address 192.168.100.115 belongs to the 192.168.100.64 network when a mask of 255.255.255.192 is used.

So Why AND?

Good question. The best answer is to save you time when working with IP addressing and subnetting. If you are given an IP address and its subnet, you can quickly find out what subnetwork the address belongs to. From here, you can determine what other addresses belong to the same subnet. Remember that if two addresses are in the same network or subnetwork, they are considered to be *local* to each other and can therefore communicate directly with each other. Addresses that are not in the same network or subnetwork are considered to be *remote* to each other and must therefore have a Layer 3 device (like a router or Layer 3 switch) between them to communicate.

Question 3

What is the broadcast address of the IP address 192.168.100.164 if it has a subnet mask of 255.255.255.248?

Answer

Step 1. Convert both the IP address and the subnet mask to binary:

192.168.100.164 = 11000000.10101000.01100100.10100100

255.255.255.248 = 11111111.11111111.11111111.11111000

Step 2. Perform the AND operation to each pair of bits—1 bit from the address ANDed to the corresponding bit in the subnet mask. Refer to the truth table for the possible outcomes:

$$192.168.100.164 = 11000000.10101000.01100100.10100100$$
$$255.255.255.248 = 11111111.11111111.11111111.11111000$$
$$\text{ANDed result} \quad = 11000000.10101000.01100100.10100000$$
$$= 192.168.100.160 \text{ (Subnetwork \#)}$$

Step 3. Separate the network bits from the host bits:

255.255.255.248 = /29 = The first 29 bits are network/subnetwork bits; therefore, *11000000.10101000.01100100.10100*000. The last three bits are host bits.

Step 4. Change all host bits to 1. Remember that all 1s in the host portion are the broadcast number for that subnetwork:

*11000000.10101000.01100100.10100*111

Step 5. Convert this number to decimal to reveal your answer:

11000000.10101000.01100100.10100111 = 192.168.100.167

The broadcast address of 192.168.100.164 is 192.168.100.167 when the subnet mask is 255.255.255.248.

Shortcuts in Binary ANDing

Remember when I said that this was supposed to save you time when working with IP addressing and subnetting? Well, there are shortcuts when you AND two numbers together:

- An octet of all 1s in the subnet mask will result in the answer being the same octet as in the IP address.

- An octet of all 0s in the subnet mask will result in the answer being all 0s in that octet.

Question 4

To what network does 172.16.100.45 belong, if its subnet mask is 255.255.255.0?

Answer

172.16.100.0

Proof

Step 1. Convert both the IP address and the subnet mask to binary:

172.16.100.45 = 10101100.00010000.01100100.00101101

255.255.255.0 = 11111111.11111111.11111111.00000000

Step 2. Perform the AND operation to each pair of bits—1 bit from the address ANDed to the corresponding bit in the subnet mask. Refer to the truth table for the possible outcomes:

172.16.100.45 = 10101100.00010000.01100100.00101101

255.255.255.0 = 11111111.11111111.11111111.00000000

10101100.00010000.01100100.00000000

= 172.16.100.0

Notice that the first three octets have the same pattern both before and after they were ANDed. Therefore, any octet ANDed to a subnet mask pattern of 255 is itself! Notice that the last octet is all 0s after ANDing. But according to the truth table, anything ANDed to a 0 is a 0. Therefore, any octet ANDed to a subnet mask pattern of 0 is 0! You should only have to convert those parts of an IP address and subnet mask to binary if the mask is not 255 or 0.

Question 5

To what network does 68.43.100.18 belong, if its subnet mask is 255.255.255.0?

Answer

68.43.100.0 (There is no need to convert here. The mask is either 255s or 0s.)

Question 6

To what network does 131.186.227.43 belong, if its subnet mask is 255.255.240.0?

Answer

Based on the two shortcut rules, the answer should be

131.186.???.0

So now you only need to convert one octet to binary for the ANDing process:

227   = 11100011

240   = 11110000

11100000 = 224

Therefore, the answer is 131.186.224.0.

The Enhanced Bob Maneuver for Subnetting (or How to Subnet Anything in Under a Minute)

Legend has it that once upon a time a networking instructor named Bob taught a class of students a method of subnetting any address using a special chart. This was known as the Bob Maneuver. These students, being the smart type that networking students usually are, added a row to the top of the chart, and the Enhanced Bob Maneuver was born. The chart and instructions on how to use it follow. With practice, you should be able to subnet any address and come up with an IP plan in under a minute. After all, it's *just* math!

The Bob of the Enhanced Bob Maneuver was really a manager/instructor at SHL. He taught this maneuver to Bruce, who taught it to Chad Klymchuk. Chad and a coworker named Troy added the top line of the chart, enhancing it. Chad was first my instructor in Microsoft, then my coworker here at NAIT, and now is one of my Academy instructors— I guess I am now his boss. And the circle is complete.

The Enhanced Bob Maneuver

	192	224	240	248	252	254	255	Subnet Mask
128	64	32	16	8	4	2	1	Target Number
8	7	6	5	4	3	2	1	Bit Place
	126	62	30	14	6	2	N/A	Number of Valid Subnets

Suppose that you have a Class C network and you need nine subnets.

Step 1. On the bottom line (Number of Valid Subnets), move from *right* to *left* and find the closest number that is *bigger* than or *equal* to what you need:

Nine subnets—move to 14.

Step 2. From that number (14), move up to the line called Bit Place.

Above 14 is bit place 4.

Step 3. The dark line is called the *high-order line*. If you cross the line, you have to reverse direction.

You were moving from right to left; now you have to move from left to right.

Step 4. Go to the line called Target Number. Counting *from the left*, move over the number of spaces that the bit place number tells you.

Starting on 128, moving 4 places takes you to 16.

Step 5. This target number is what you need to count by, starting at 0, and going until you hit 255 or greater. Stop before you get to 256:

0

16

32

48

64

80

96

112

128

144

160

176

192

208

224

240

256 Stop—too far!

Step 6. These numbers are your network numbers. Expand to finish your plan.

Network #	Range of Valid Hosts	Broadcast Number
0 (invalid)	1–14	15
16	17–30 (17 is 1 more than network # 30 is 1 less than broadcast#)	31 (1 less than next network #)
32	33–46	47
48	49–62	63
64	65–78	79
80	81–94	95
96	97–110	111
112	113–126	127
128	129–142	143
144	145–158	159
160	161–174	175
176	177–190	191
192	193–206	207
208	209–222	223
224	225–238	239
240 (invalid)	241–254	255

Notice that there are 14 subnets created from .16 to .224.

Step 7. Go back to the Enhanced Bob Maneuver chart and look above your target number to the top line. The number above your target number is your subnet mask.

Above 16 is 240. Because you started with a Class C network, the new subnet mask is 255.255.255.240.

CHAPTER 2

VLSM

Variable-length subnet masking (VLSM) is the more realistic way of subnetting a network to make for the most efficient use of all of the bits.

Remember that when you perform classful (or what I sometimes call classical) subnetting, all subnets have the same number of hosts because they all use the same subnet mask. This leads to inefficiencies. For example, if you borrow 4 bits on a Class C network, you end up with 14 valid subnets of 14 valid hosts. A serial link to another router only needs 2 hosts, but with classical subnetting, you end up wasting 12 of those hosts. Even with the ability to use NAT and private addresses, where you should never run out of addresses in a network design, you still want to ensure that the IP plan that you create is as efficient as possible. This is where VLSM comes in to play.

VLSM is the process of "subnetting a subnet" and using different subnet masks for different networks in your IP plan. What you have to remember is that you need to make sure that there is no overlap in any of the addresses.

IP Subnet Zero

When you work with classical subnetting, you always have to eliminate the subnets that contain either all zeros or all ones in the subnet portion. Hence, you always used the formula $2^N - 2$ to define the number of valid subnets created. However, Cisco devices can use those subnets, as long as the command **ip subnet-zero** is in the configuration. This command is on by default in Cisco IOS Software Release 12.0 and later; if it was turned off for some reason, however, you can re-enable it by using the following command:

```
Router(config)#ip subnet-zero
```

Now you can use the formula 2^N rather than $2^N - 2$.

2^N	Number of total subnets created	
2^{N-2}	Number of valid subnets created	No longer needed because you have the **ip subnet-zero** command enabled
2^H	Number of total hosts per subnet	
$2^H - 2$	Number of valid hosts per subnet	

VLSM Example

You follow the same steps in performing VLSM as you did when performing classical subnetting.

Consider Figure 2-1 as you work through an example.

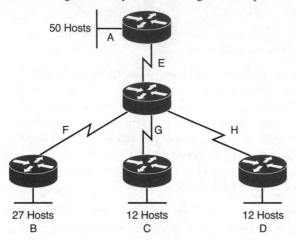

Figure 2-1   Sample Network Needing a VLSM Address Plan

A Class C network—192.168.100.0/24—is assigned. You need to create an IP plan for this network using VLSM.

Once again, you cannot use the N bits—192.168.100. You can use only the H bits. Therefore, ignore the N bits, because they cannot change!

The steps to create an IP plan using VLSM for the network illustrated in Figure 2-1 are as follows:

Step 1. Determine how many H bits will be needed to satisfy the *largest* network.

Step 2. Pick a subnet for the largest network to use.

Step 3. Pick the next largest network to work with.

Step 4. Pick the third largest network to work with.

Step 5. Determine network numbers for serial links.

The remainder of the chapter details what is involved with each step of the process.

Step 1 Determine How Many H Bits Will Be Needed to Satisfy the *Largest* Network

A is the largest network with 50 hosts. Therefore, you need to know how many H bits will be needed:

If $2^H - 2 =$ Number of valid hosts per subnet

Then $2^H - 2 \geq 50$

Therefore H = 6 (6 is the smallest valid value for H)

You need 6 H bits to satisfy the requirements of Network A.

If you need 6 H bits and you started with 8 N bits, you are left with 8 − 6 = 2 N bits to create subnets:

Started with: NNNNNNNN (these are the 8 bits in the fourth octet)

Now have: NNHHHHHH

All subnetting will now have to start at this reference point, to satisfy the requirements of Network A.

Step 2 Pick a Subnet for the Largest Network to Use

You have 2 N bits to work with, leaving you with 2^N or 2^2 or 4 subnets to work with:

NN = 00HHHHHH (The Hs = The 6 H bits you need for Network A)

01HHHHHH

10HHHHHH

11HHHHHH

If you add all zeros to the H bits, you are left with the network numbers for the four subncts:

00**000000** = .0

01**000000** = .64

10**000000** = .128

11**000000** = .192

All of these subnets will have the same subnet mask, just like in classful subnetting.

Two borrowed H bits means a subnet mask of

11111111.11111111.11111111.11000000

or

255.255.255.192

or

/26

The /x notation represents how to show different subnet masks when using VLSM.

/8 means that the first 8 bits of the address are network; the remaining 24 bits are H bits.

/24 means that the first 24 bits are network; the last 8 are host. This is either a traditional default Class C address, or a traditional Class A network that has borrowed 16 bits, or even a traditional Class B network that has borrowed 8 bits!

Pick *one* of these subnets to use for Network A. The rest of the networks will have to use the other three subnets.

For purposes of this example, pick the .64 network.

00000000 =	.0	
01000000 =	.64	Network A
10000000 =	.128	
11000000 =	.192	

Step 3 Pick the Next Largest Network to Work With

Network B = 27 hosts

Determine the number of H bits needed for this network:

$$2^H - 2 \geq 27$$

$$H = 5$$

You need 5 H bits to satisfy the requirements of Network B.

You started with a pattern of 2 N bits and 6 H bits for Network A. You have to maintain that pattern.

Pick one of the remaining /26 networks to work with Network B.

For the purposes of this example, select the .128/26 network:

10000000

But you need only 5 H bits, not 6. Therefore, you are left with

10N00000

where

10 represents the original pattern of subnetting.

N represents the extra bit.

00000 represents the 5 H bits you need for Network B.

Because you have this extra bit, you can create two smaller subnets from the original subnet:

10**000000**

10**100000**

Converted to decimal, these subnets are as follows:

10**000000** =.128

10**100000** =.160

You have now subnetted a subnet! This is the basis of VLSM.

Each of these sub-subnets will have a new subnet mask. The original subnet mask of /24 was changed into /26 for Network A. You then take one of these /26 networks and break it into two /27 networks:

10**000000** and 10**100000** both have 3 N bits and 5 H bits.

The mask now equals:

11111111.11111111.11111111.11100000

or

255.255.255.224

or

/27

Pick one of these new sub-subnets for Network B:

10**000000** /27 = Network B

Use the remaining sub-subnet for future growth, or you can break it down further if needed.

You want to make sure the addresses are not overlapping with each other. So go back to the original table.

00**000000** =	.0/26	
01**000000** =	.64/26	Network A
10**000000** =	.128/26	
11**000000** =	.192/26	

You can now break the .128/26 network into two smaller /27 networks and assign Network B.

00**000000** =	.0/26	
01**000000** =	.64/26	Network A
10**000000** =	.128/26	Cannot use because it has been subnetted
10**000000** =	.128/27	Network B
10**100000** =	.160/27	
11**000000** =	.192/26	

The remaining networks are still available to be assigned to networks or subnetted further for better efficiency.

Step 4 Pick the Third Largest Network to Work With

Networks C and Network D = 12 hosts each

Determine the number of H bits needed for these networks:

$$2^H - 2 \geq 12$$

$$H = 4$$

You need 4 H bits to satisfy the requirements of Network C and Network D.

You started with a pattern of 2 N bits and 6 H bits for Network A. You have to maintain that pattern.

You now have a choice as to where to put these networks. You could go to a different /26 network, or you could go to a /27 network and try to fit them into there.

For the purposes of this example, select the other /27 network—.160/27:

101**00000** (The 1 in the third bit place is no longer bold, because it is part of the N bits.)

But you only need 4 H bits, not 5. Therefore, you are left with

101**N0000**

where

10 represents the original pattern of subnetting.

N represents the extra bit you have.

00000 represents the 5 H bits you need for Networks C and D.

Because you have this extra bit, you can create two smaller subnets from the original subnet:

101**00000**

101**10000**

Converted to decimal, these subnets are as follows:

> 101**00000** = .160

> 101**10000** = .176

These new sub-subnets will now have new subnet masks. Each sub-subnet now has 4 N bits and 4 H bits, so their new masks will be

> 11111111.11111111.11111111.11110000

or

> 255.255.255.240

or

> /28

Pick one of these new sub-subnets for Network C and one for Network D.

00**000000** =	.0/26	
01**000000** =	.64/26	Network A
10**000000** =	.128/26	Cannot use because it has been subnetted
10**000000** =	.128/27	Network B
10**100000** =	.160/27	Cannot use because it has been subnetted
101**00000**	.160/28	Network C
101**10000**	.176/28	Network D
11**000000** =	.192/26	

You have now used two of the original four subnets to satisfy the requirements of four networks. Now all you need to do is determine the network numbers for the serial links between the routers.

Step 5 Determine Network Numbers for Serial Links

All serial links between routers have the same property in that they only need two addresses in a network—one for each router interface.

Determine the number of H bits needed for these networks:

> $2^H - 2 \geq 2$

> $H = 2$

You need 2 H bits to satisfy the requirements of Networks E, F, G, and H.

You have two of the original subnets left to work with.

For the purposes of this example, select the .0/26 network:

00**000000**

But you need only 2 H bits, not 6. Therefore, you are left with

00**NNNN**00

where

00 represents the original pattern of subnetting.

NNNN represents the extra bits you have.

00 represents the 2 H bits you need for the serial links.

Because you have 4 **N** bits, you can create 16 sub-subnets from the original subnet:

00**000000** = .0/30

00**000100** = .4/30

00**001000** = .8/30

00**001100** = .12/30

00**010000** = .16/30

.

.

.

00**111000** = .56/30

00**111100** = .60/30

You need only four of them. You can hold the rest for future expansion or recombine them for a new, larger subnet:

00**010000** = .16/30

00**010100** = .20/30

00**011000** = .24/30

00**011100** = .32/30

.

.

.

00**111000** = .56/30

00**111100** = .60/30

The first four of these can be combined into the following:

00**010000** = .16/28

The rest of the /30 subnets can be combined into two /28 networks:

00**100000** = .32/28

00**110000** = .48/28

Or these two subnets can be combined into one larger /27 network

00**010000** = .32/27

Going back to the original table, you now have the following:

00**000000** =	.0/26	Cannot use because it has been subnetted
00**000000** =	.0/30	Network E
00**000100** =	.4/30	Network F
00**001000** =	.8/30	Network G
00**001100** =	.12/30	Network H
00**010000** =	.16/28	Future growth
00**100000** =	.32/27	Future growth
01**000000** =	.64/26	Network A
10**000000** =	.128/26	Cannot use because it has been subnetted
10**000000** =	.128/27	Network B
10**100000** =	160/27	Cannot use because it has been subnetted
101**00000**	160/28	Network C
101**10000**	176/28	Network D
11**000000** =	.192/26	Future growth

Looking at the plan, you can see that no number is used twice. You have now created an IP plan for the network and have made the plan as efficient as possible, wasting no addresses in the serial links and leaving room for future growth. This is the power of VLSM!

CHAPTER 3

Route Summarization

Route summarization, or supernetting, is needed to reduce the number of routes that a router advertises to its neighbor. Remember that for every route you advertise, the size of your update grows. It has been said that if there were no route summarization, the Internet backbone would have collapsed from the sheer size of its own routing tables back in 1997!

Routing updates, whether done with a distance vector or link-state protocol, grow with the number of routes you need to advertise. In simple terms, a router that needs to advertise ten routes needs ten specific lines in its update packet. The more routes you have to advertise, the bigger the packet. The bigger the packet, the more bandwidth the update takes, reducing the bandwidth available to transfer data. But with route summarization, you can advertise many routes with only one line in an update packet. This reduces the size of the update, allowing you more bandwidth for data transfer.

Also, when a new data flow enters a router, the router must do a lookup in its routing table to determine which interface the traffic must be sent out. The larger the routing tables, the longer this takes, leading to more used router CPU cycles to perform the lookup. Therefore, a second reason for route summarization is that you want to minimize the amount of time and router CPU cycles that are used to route traffic.

NOTE This example is a very simplified explanation of how routers send updates to each other. For a more in-depth description, I highly recommend you go out and read Jeff Doyle's book *Routing TCP/IP*, Volume I, 2nd edition, Cisco Press. This book has been around for many years and is considered by most to be the authority on how the different routing protocols work. If you are considering continuing on in your certification path to try and achieve the CCIE, you need to buy Doyle's book—and memorize it; it's that good.

Example for Understanding Route Summarization

Refer to Figure 3-1 to assist you as you go through the following explanation of an example of route summarization.

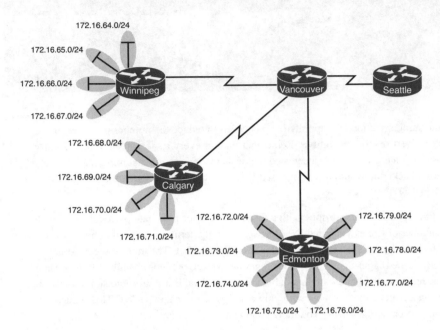

Figure 3-1 Four-City Network Without Route Summarization

As you can see from Figure 3-1, Winnipeg, Calgary, and Edmonton each have to advertise internal networks to the main router located in Vancouver. Without route summarization, Vancouver would have to advertise 16 networks to Seattle. You want to use route
summarization to reduce the burden on this upstream router.

Step 1: Summarize Winnipeg's Routes

To do this, you need to look at the routes in binary to see if there are any specific bit
patterns that you can use to your advantage. What you are looking for are common bits
on the network side of the addresses. Because all of these networks are /24 networks,
you want to see which of the first 24 bits are common to all four networks.

172.16.64.0 = *10101100.00010000.01000000*.00000000

172.16.65.0 = *10101100.00010000.01000001*.00000000

172.16.66.0 = *10101100.00010000.01000010*.00000000

172.16.67.0 = *10101100.00010000.01000011*.00000000

Common bits: *10101100.00010000.010000*xx

You see that the first 22 bits of the four networks are common. Therefore, you can summarize the four routes by using a subnet mask that reflects that the first 22 bits are common. This is a /22 mask, or 255.255.252.0. You are left with the summarized address of

172.16.64.0/22

This address, when sent to the upstream Vancouver router, will tell Vancouver: "If you have any packets that are addressed to networks that have the first 22 bits in the pattern of 10101100.00010000.010000xx.xxxxxxxx, then send them to me here in Winnipeg."

By sending one route to Vancouver with this supernetted subnet mask, you have advertised four routes in one line, instead of using four lines. Much more efficient!

Step 2: Summarize Calgary's Routes

For Calgary, you do the same thing that you did for Winnipeg—look for common bit patterns in the routes:

> 172.16.68.0 = *10101100.00010000.010001*00.00000000
>
> 172.16.69.0 = *10101100.00010000.010001*01.00000000
>
> 172.16.70.0 = *10101100.00010000.010001*10.00000000
>
> 172.16.71.0 = *10101100.00010000.010001*11.00000000
>
> Common bits: *10101100.00010000.010001*xx

Once again, the first 22 bits are common. The summarized route is therefore

> 172.16.68.0/22

Step 3: Summarize Edmonton's Routes

For Edmonton, you do the same thing that we did for Winnipeg and Calgary—look for common bit patterns in the routes:

> 172.16.72.0 = *10101100.00010000.01001*000.00000000
>
> 172.16.73.0 = *10101100.00010000.01001*001.00000000
>
> 172.16.74.0 = *10101100.00010000 01001*010.00000000
>
> 172.16.75.0 = *10101100.00010000 01001*011.00000000
>
> 172.16.76.0 = *10101100.00010000.01001*100.00000000
>
> 172.16.77.0 = *10101100.00010000.01001*101.00000000
>
> 172.16.78.0 = *10101100.00010000.01001*110.00000000
>
> 172.16.79.0 = *10101100.00010000.01001*111.00000000
>
> Common bits: *10101100.00010000.01001*xxx

For Edmonton, the first 21 bits are common. The summarized route is therefore

> 172.16.72.0/21

Figure 3-2 shows what the network looks like, with Winnipeg, Calgary, and Edmonton sending their summarized routes to Vancouver.

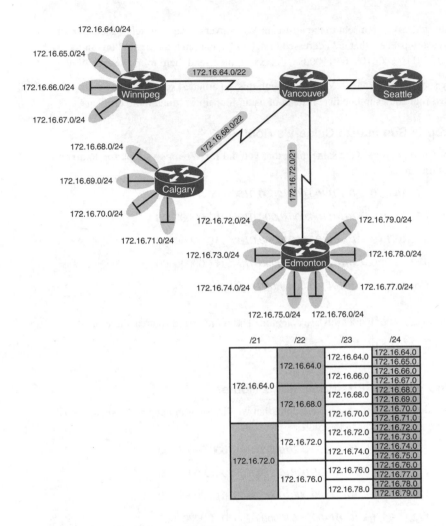

Figure 3-2   Four-City Network with Edge Cities Summarizing Routes

Step 4: Summarize Vancouver's Routes

Yes, you can summarize Vancouver's routes to Seattle. You continue in the same format as before. Take the routes that Winnipeg, Calgary, and Edmonton sent to Vancouver, and look for common bit patterns:

172.16.64.0 = *10101100.00010000.01000000.00000000*

172.16.68.0 = *10101100.00010000.01000100.00000000*

172.16.72.0 = *10101100.00010000.01001000.00000000*

Common bits: *10101100.00010000.0100*xxxx

Because there are 20 bits that are common, you can create one summary route for Vancouver to send to Seattle:

172.16.64.0/20

Vancouver has now told Seattle that in one line of a routing update, 16 different networks are being advertised. This is much more efficient than sending 16 lines in a routing update to be processed.

Figure 3-3 shows what the routing updates would look like with route summarization taking place.

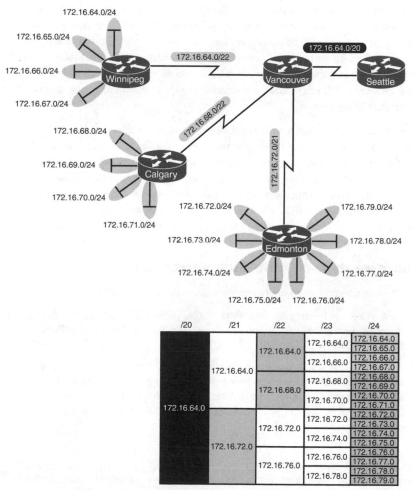

Figure 3-3   Four-City Network with Complete Route Summarization

Route Summarization and Route Flapping

Another positive aspect of route summarization has to do with route flapping. *Route flapping* is when a network, for whatever reason (such as interface hardware failure or misconfiguration), goes up and down on a router, causing that router to constantly advertise changes about that network. Route summarization can help insulate upstream neighbors from these problems.

Consider router Edmonton from Figure 3-1. Suppose that network 172.16.74.0/24 goes down. Without route summarization, Edmonton would advertise Vancouver to remove that network. Vancouver would forward that same message upstream to Calgary, Winnipeg, Seattle, and so on. Now assume the network comes back online a few seconds later. Edmonton would have to send another update informing Vancouver of the change. Each time a change needs to be advertised, the router must use CPU resources. If that route were to flap, the routers would constantly have to update their own tables, as well as advertise changes to their neighbors. In a CPU-intensive protocol such as OSPF, the constant hit on the CPU might make a noticeable change to the speed at which network traffic reaches its destination.

Route summarization enables you to avoid this problem. Even though Edmonton would still have to deal with the route constantly going up and down, no one else would notice. Edmonton advertises a single summarized route, 172.16.72.0/21, to Vancouver. Even though one of the networks is going up and down, this does not invalidate the route to the other networks that were summarized. Edmonton will deal with its own route flap, but Vancouver will be unaware of the problem downstream in Edmonton. Summarization can effectively protect or insulate other routers from route flaps.

Requirements for Route Summarization

To create route summarization, there are some necessary requirements:

- Routers need to be running a classless routing protocol, as they carry subnet mask information with them in routing updates. (Examples are RIP v2, OSPF, EIGRP, IS-IS, and BGP.)
- Addresses need to be assigned in a hierarchical fashion for the summarized address to have the same high-order bits. It does no good if Winnipeg has network 172.16.64.0 and 172.16.67.0 while 172.16.65.0 resides in Calgary and 172.16.66.0 is assigned in Edmonton. No summarization could take place from the edge routers to Vancouver.

TIP Because most networks use NAT and the ten networks internally, it is important when creating your network design that you assign network subnets in a way that they can be easily summarized. A little more planning now can save you a lot of grief later.

CHAPTER 4

Cables and Connections

This chapter provides information and commands concerning the following topics:

- Connecting a rollover cable to your router or switch
- Using a USB cable to connect to your router or switch
- Determining what your terminal settings should be
- Understanding the setup of different LAN connections
- Identifying different serial cable types
- Determining which cable to use to connect your router or switch to another device
- 568A versus 568B cables

Connecting a Rollover Cable to Your Router or Switch

Figure 4-1 shows how to connect a rollover cable from your PC to a router or switch.

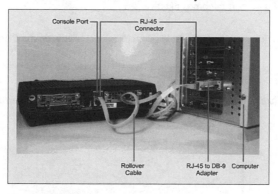

Figure 4-1   Rollover Cable Connection

Using a USB Cable to Connect to Your Router or Switch

On newer Cisco devices, a USB serial console connection is also supported. A USB cable (USB type A to 5-pin mini type B) and operating system driver are needed to establish connectivity. Figure 4-2 shows a Cisco device that can use either a mini-USB connector or a traditional RJ-45 connector.

Figure 4-2 Different Console Port Connections

NOTE Only one console port can be active at a time. If a cable is plugged into the USB port, the RJ-45 port becomes inactive.

NOTE The OS driver for the USB cable connection is available on the Cisco.com website.

Terminal Settings

Figure 4-3 illustrates the settings that you should configure to have your PC connect to a router or switch.

Figure 4-3 PC Settings to Connect to a Router or Switch

LAN Connections

Table 4-1 shows the various port types and connections between LAN devices.

TABLE 4-1   LAN Connections

Port or Connection	Port Type	Connected To	Cable
Ethernet	RJ-45	Ethernet switch	RJ-45
T1/E1 WAN	RJ-48C/CA81A	T1 or E1 network	Rollover
Console	8 pin	Computer COM port	Rollover
Console	USB	Computer USB port	USB
AUX	8 pin	Modem	RJ-45

Serial Cable Types

Figure 4-4 shows the DB-60 end of a serial cable that connects to a 2500 series router.

Figure 4-5 shows the newer smart serial end of a serial cable that connects to a smart serial port on your router. Smart serial ports are found on modular routers, such as the newest ISR2 series (x900), ISR (x800) series, or on older modular routers such as the 1700 or 2600 series.

Figure 4-6 shows examples of the male DTE and the female DCE ends that are on the other side of a serial or smart serial cable.

Most laptops available today come equipped with USB ports, not serial ports. For these laptops, you need a USB-to-serial connector, as shown in Figure 4-7.

Figure 4-4   Serial Cable (2500)

Figure 4-5   Smart Serial Cable (1700, 2600, ISR, ISR2)

Figure 4-6   V.35 DTE and DCE Cables

NOTE   CCNA focuses on *V.35 cables* for back-to-back connections between routers.

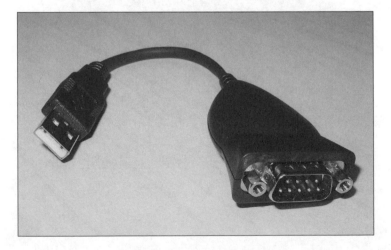

Figure 4-7   USB-to-Serial Connector for Laptops

Which Cable to Use?

Table 4-2 describes which cable should be used when wiring your devices together. It is important to ensure you have proper cabling; otherwise, you might be giving yourself problems before you even get started.

TABLE 4-2   Determining Which Cables to Use When Wiring Devices Together

If Device A Has a:	And Device B Has a:	Then Use This Cable:
Computer COM port	RJ-45 Console of router/switch	Rollover
Computer USB port	USB Console of router/switch	USB type A to 5-pin mini type B with appropriate OS drivers
Computer NIC	Switch	Straight-through
Computer NIC	Computer NIC	Crossover
Switch port	Router's Ethernet port	Straight-through
Switch port	Switch port	Crossover (check for uplink button or toggle switch to defeat this)
Router's Ethernet port	Router's Ethernet port	Crossover
Computer NIC	Router's Ethernet port	Crossover
Router's serial port	Router's serial port	Cisco serial DCE/DTE cables

Table 4-3 lists the pinouts for straight-through, crossover, and rollover cables.

TABLE 4-3   Pinouts for Different Cables

Straight-Through Cable	Crossover Cable	Rollover Cable
Pin 1 – Pin 1	Pin 1 – Pin 3	Pin 1 – Pin 8
Pin 2 – Pin 2	Pin 2 – Pin 6	Pin 2 – Pin 7
Pin 3 – Pin 3	Pin 3 – Pin 1	Pin 3 – Pin 6
Pin 4 – Pin 4	Pin 4 – Pin 4	Pin 4 – Pin 5
Pin 5 – Pin 5	Pin 5 – Pin 5	Pin 5 – Pin 4
Pin 6 – Pin 6	Pin 6 – Pin 2	Pin 6 – Pin 3
Pin 7 – Pin 7	Pin 7 – Pin 7	Pin 7 – Pin 2
Pin 8 – Pin 8	Pin 8 – Pin 8	Pin 8 – Pin 1

568A Versus 568B Cables

There are two different standards released by the EIA/TIA group about UTP wiring: 568A and 568B. Although 568B is newer and is the recommended standard, either one can be used. The difference between these two standards is pin assignments, not in the use of the different colors (see Table 4-4). The 568A standard is more compatible with voice connections and the Universal Service Order Codes (USOC) standard for telephone infrastructure in the United States. In both 568A and USOC standards, the blue and orange pairs are now on the center four pins; therefore, the colors match more closely with 568A than with the 568B standard. So, which one is preferred? Information here from the standards bodies on this matter is sketchy at best. 568B was traditionally widespread in the United States, whereas places such as Canada and Australia use a lot of 568A. However, 568A is now becoming more dominant in the United States, too.

TIP   Use 568A in new installations, and 568B if connecting to an existing 568B system.

TABLE 4-4   UTP Wiring Standards

568A Standard				568B Standard			
Pin	Color	Pair	Description	Pin	Color	Pair	Description
1	White/green	3	RecvData +	1	White/orange	2	TxData +
2	Green	3	RecvData -	2	Orange	2	TxData -
3	White/orange	2	Txdata +	3	White/green	3	RecvData +
4	Blue	1	Unused	4	Blue	1	Unused
5	White/blue	1	Unused	5	White/blue	1	Unused
6	Orange	2	TxData -	6	Green	3	RecvData -
7	White/brown	4	Unused	7	White/brown	4	Unused
8	Brown	4	Unused	8	Brown	4	Unused

TIP   Odd pin numbers are always the striped wires.

A straight-through cable is one with both ends using the same standard (A or B).
A crossover cable is one that has 568A on one end and 568B on the other end.

CHAPTER 5

The Command Line Interface

This chapter provides information and commands concerning the following topics:

- Shortcuts for entering commands
- Using the (Tab⇆) key to enter complete commands
- Console error messages
- Using the question mark for help
- **enable** command
- **exit** command
- **disable** command
- **logout** command
- Setup mode
- Keyboard help
- History commands
- **terminal** commands
- **show** commands
- Using the pipe parameter (|) with the **show** command

Shortcuts for Entering Commands

To enhance efficiency, Cisco IOS Software has some shortcuts for entering commands. Although these are great to use in the real world, when it comes time to write a vendor exam, make sure you know the full commands, not just the shortcuts.

Router>**enable** = Router>**enab** = Router>**en**	Entering a shortened form of a command is sufficient as long as there is no confusion about which command you are attempting to enter.
Router#**configure** **terminal** is the same as Router#**config t**	

Using the (Tab⇆) Key to Complete Commands

When you are entering a command, you can use the (Tab⇆) key to complete the command. Enter the first few characters of a command and press the (Tab⇆) key. If the characters are unique to the command, the rest of the command is entered in for you. This is helpful if you are unsure about the spelling of a command.

```
Router#sh (Tab⇥) = Router#show
```

Console Error Messages

You may see three types of console errors messages when working in the CLI:

- Ambiguous command
- Incomplete command
- Incorrect command

Error Message	Meaning	What to Do
% Ambiguous Command: "show con"	Not enough characters were entered to allow device to recognize the command.	Reenter the command with a question mark (?) immediately after the last character. **show con?** All possible keywords will be displayed.
% Incomplete Command	More parameters need to be entered to complete the command.	Reenter the command followed by a question mark (?). Include a space between the command and the question mark (?).
% Invalid input detected at ^ marker	The command entered has an error. The ^ marks the location of the error.	Reenter the command, correcting the error at the location of the ^. If you are unsure what the error is, reenter the command with a question mark (?) at the point of the error to display the commands or parameters available.

Using the Question Mark for Help

The following output shows you how using the question mark can help you work through a command and all its parameters.

`Router#?`	Lists all commands available in the current command mode
`Router#c?` `clear clock`	Lists all the possible choices that start with the letter c
`Router#cl?` `clear clock`	Lists all the possible choices that start with the letters cl
`Router#clock` `% Incomplete Command`	Tells you that more parameters need to be entered

`Router#clock ?` `Set`	Shows all subcommands for this command (in this case, **Set**, which sets the time and date)

`Router#clock set`
`19:50:00 14 July`
`2007 ?` Enter
	Pressing the Enter key confirms the time and date configured.

`Router#`	No error message/Incomplete command message means the command was entered successfully.

enable Command

`Router>enable` `Router#`	Moves the user from user mode to privileged mode

exit Command

`Router#exit`
Or
`Router>exit`
	Logs a user off

`Router(config-if)#exit` `Router(config)#`	Moves you back one level
`Router(config)#exit` `Router#`	Moves you back one level

disable Command

`Router#disable` `Router>`	Moves you from privileged mode back to user mode

logout Command

`Router#logout`	Performs the same function as **exit**

Setup Mode

Setup mode starts automatically if there is no startup configuration present.

`Router#setup`	Enters startup mode from the command line

NOTE   The answer inside the square brackets, [ ], is the default answer. If this is the answer you want, just press ⏎Enter.Pressing Ctrl-C at any time will end the setup process, shut down all interfaces, and take you to user mode (Router>).

NOTE   You *cannot* use setup mode to configure an entire router. It does only the basics. For example, you can only turn on RIPv1, but not Open Shortest Path First Protocol (OSPF) or Enhanced Interior Gateway Routing Protocol (EIGRP). You cannot create access control lists (ACL) here or enable Network Address Translation (NAT). You can assign an IP address to an interface, but not to a subinterface. All in all, setup mode is very limiting.

Entering setup mode is not a recommended practice. Instead, you should use the command-line interface (CLI), which is more powerful:

> Would you like to enter the initial configuration dialog? [yes]: **no**

> Would you like to enable autoinstall? [yes]: **no**

Autoinstall is a feature that tries to broadcast out all interfaces when attempting to find a configuration. If you answer **yes**, you must wait for a few minutes while it looks for a configuration to load. Very frustrating. Answer **no**.

Keyboard Help

The keystrokes in the following table are meant to help you edit the configuration. Because you'll want to perform certain tasks again and again, Cisco IOS Software provides certain keystroke combinations to help make the process more efficient.

^	Shows you where you made a mistake in entering a command

`Router#confog t`
     ^
 	
`% Invalid input`
`detected at '^'`
`marker.`
`Router#config t`
`Router(config)#`	

Ctrl-A	Moves cursor to beginning of line
Ctrl-B	Moves cursor back one word
Ctrl-B (or ←)	Moves cursor back one character
Ctrl-E	Moves cursor to end of line
Ctrl-F (or →)	Moves cursor forward one character
Ctrl-F	Moves cursor forward one word
Ctrl-⬆Shift-6	Allows the user to interrupt an IOS process such as ping or traceroute
Ctrl-Z	Moves you from any prompt back down to privileged mode
$	Indicates that the line has been scrolled to the left

| Router#**terminal no editing**

Router# | Turns off the ability to use the previous keyboard shortcuts |
| Router#**terminal editing**

Router# | Reenables enhanced editing mode (can use above keyboard shortcuts) |

History Commands

| Ctrl-P (or ↑) | Recalls commands in the history buffer in a backward sequence, beginning with the most recent command |
| Ctrl-N (or ↓) | Returns to more recent commands in the history buffer after recalling commands with the Ctrl-P key sequence |

terminal Commands

Router#**terminal no editing** Router#	Turns off the ability to use keyboard shortcuts.
Router#**terminal editing** Router#	Reenables enhanced editing mode (can use keyboard shortcuts).
Router#**terminal length** x	Sets the number of lines displayed in a **show** command to *x*, where *x* is a number between 0 and 512. The default is 24.

NOTE   The default value of the **terminal length** *x* command is 24.

NOTE   If you set the **terminal length** *x* command to zero (0), the router will not pause between screens of output.

Router#**terminal history size_** *number* See the next row for an example.	Sets the number of commands in the buffer that can be recalled by the router (maximum 256)
Router#**terminal history size 25**	Causes the router to now remember the last 25 commands in the buffer
Router#**no terminal history size 25**	Sets the history buffer back to 10 commands, which is the default

NOTE The **history size** command provides the same function as the **terminal history size** command.

Be careful when you set the size to something larger than the default. By telling the router to keep the last 256 commands in a buffer, you are taking memory away from other parts of the router. What would you rather have: a router that remembers what you last typed in or a router that routes as efficiently as possible?

show Commands

`Router#show version`	Displays information about the current Cisco IOS Software
`Router#show flash`	Displays information about flash memory
`Router#show history`	Lists all commands in the history buffer

NOTE The last line of output from the **show version** command tells you what the configuration register is set to.

Using the Pipe Parameter (|) with the show Command

By using a pipe (|) character in conjunction with a **show** command, you can filter out specific information that you are interested in.

`Router#show running-config	include hostname`	Displays configuration information that includes the specific word *hostname*
`Router#show running-config	section FastEthernet 0/1`	Displays configuration information about the section FastEthernet 0/1
`The Pipe Parameter (|) OptionsParameter`	**Description**
`begin`	Shows all output from a certain point, starting with the line that matches the filtering expression.
`Router#show running-config	begin line con 0`	Output begins with the first line that has the expression "line con 0."
`exclude`	Excludes all output lines that match the filtering expression.
`Router#show running-config	exclude interface`	Any line with the expression "interface" will not be shown as part of the output.
`include`	Includes all output lines that match the filtering expression.
`Router#show running-config	include duplex`	Any line that has the expression "duplex" will be shown as part of the output.
`section`	Shows the entire section that starts with the filtering expression.
`Router#show running-config	section interface GigabitEthernet0/0`	Displays information about interface GigabitEthernet0/0.

NOTE   You can use the pipe parameter and filters with any **show** command.

NOTE   The filtering expression has to match *exactly* with the output you want to filter. You cannot use shortened forms of the items you are trying to filter. For example, the command

```
Router#show running-config | section gig0/0
```

will not work because there is no section in the running-config called gig0/0. You must use the expression GiagbitEthernet0/0 with no spelling errors or extra spaces added in.

CHAPTER 6

Configuring a Single Cisco Router

This chapter provides information and commands concerning the following topics:

- Router modes
- Entering global configuration mode
- Configuring a router, specifically
  - Names
  - Passwords
  - Password encryption
  - Interface names
  - Moving between interfaces
  - Configuring a serial interface
  - Configuring a Fast Ethernet interface
  - Configuring a Gigabit Ethernet interface
  - Creating a message-of-the-day (MOTD) banner
  - Creating a login banner
  - Setting the clock time zone
  - Assigning a local host name to an IP address
  - The **no ip domain-lookup** command
  - The **logging synchronous** command
  - The **exec-timeout** command
  - Saving configurations
  - Erasing configurations
- **show** commands to verify the router configurations
- EXEC commands in configuration mode: the **do** command

Router Modes

`Router>`	User mode
`Router#`	Privileged mode (also known as EXEC-level mode)
`Router(config)#`	Global configuration mode
`Router(config-if)#`	Interface mode
`Router(config-subif)#`	Subinterface mode

Router(config-line)#	Line mode
Router(config-router)#	Router configuration mode

TIP   There are other modes than these. Not all commands work in all modes. Be careful. If you type in a command that you know is correct—**show running-config**, for example—and you get an error, make sure that you are in the correct mode.

Entering Global Configuration Mode

Router>	Limited viewing of configuration. You cannot make changes in this mode.
Router#	You can see the configuration and move to make changes.
Router#**configure terminal** Router(config)#	Moves to global configuration mode. This prompt indicates that you can start making changes.

Configuring a Router Name

This command works on both routers and switches.

Router(config)#**hostname Cisco**	The name can be any word you choose.
Cisco(config)#	

Configuring Passwords

These commands work on both routers and switches.

Router(config)#**enable password cisco**	Sets **enable** password
Router(config)#**enable secret class**	Sets **enable secret** password
Router(config)#**line console 0**	Enters console line mode
Router(config-line)#**password console**	Sets console line mode password to console
Router(config-line)#**login**	Enables password checking at login
Router(config)#**line vty 0 4**	Enters vty line mode for all five vty lines
Router(config-line)#**password telnet**	Sets vty password to telnet
Router(config-line)#**login**	Enables password checking at login
Router(config)#**line aux 0**	Enters auxiliary line mode
Router(config-line)#**password backdoor**	Sets auxiliary line mode password to backdoor
Router(config-line)#**login**	Enables password checking at login

CAUTION   The **enable secret** *password* is encrypted by default. The **enable** *password* is not. For this reason, recommended practice is that you *never* use the **enable** *password* command. Use only the **enable secret** *password* command in a router or switch configuration.You cannot set both **enable secret** *password* and **enable** *password* to the same password. Doing so defeats the use of encryption.

Password Encryption

Router(config)#**service password-encryption**	Applies a weak encryption to passwords
Router(config)#**enable password cisco**	Sets enable password to cisco
Router(config)#**line console 0**	Moves to console line mode
Router(config-line)#**password Cisco**	Continue setting passwords as above
	. . .
Router(config)#**no service password-encryption**	Turns off password encryption

CAUTION   If you have turned on service password encryption, used it, and then turned it off, any passwords that you have encrypted will stay encrypted. New passwords will remain unencrypted.

Interface Names

One of the biggest problems that new administrators face is the interface names on the different models of routers. With all the different Cisco devices in production networks today, some administrators are becoming confused about the names of their interfaces.

The following chart is a *sample* of some of the different interface names for various routers. This is by no means a complete list. Refer to the hardware guide of the specific router that you are working on to see the different combinations, or use the following command to see which interfaces are installed on your particular router:

router#**show ip interface brief**

Router Model	Port Location/Slot Number	Slot/Port Type	Slot Numbering Range	Example
2501	On board	Ethernet	Interface-type number	ethernet0 (e0)
	On board	Serial	Interface-type number	serial0 (s0) & s1
2514	On board	Ethernet	Interface-type number	e0 & e1
	On board	Serial	Interface-type number	s0 & s1
1721	On board	Fast Ethernet	Interface-type number	fastethernet0 (fa0)
	Slot 0	WAC (WIN interface card) (serial)	Interface-type number	s0 & s1

Router Model	Port Location/Slot Number	Slot/Port Type	Slot Numbering Range	Example
1760	On board	Fast Ethernet	Interface-type 0/port	fa0/0
	Slot 0	WIC/VIC (voice interface card)	Interface-type 0/port	s0/0 & s0/1 v0/0 & v0/1
	Slot 1	WIC/VIC	Interface-type 1/port	s1/0 & s1/1 v1/0 & v1/1
	Slot 2	VIC	Interface-type 2/port	v2/0 & v2/1
	Slot 3	VIC	Interface-type 3/port	v3/0 & v3/1
2610	On board	Ethernet	Interface-type 0/port	e0/0
	Slot 0	WIC (Serial)	Interface-type 0/port	s0/0 & s0/1
2611	On board	Ethernet	Interface-type 0/port	e0/0 & e0/1
	Slot 0	WIC (Serial)	Interface-type 0/port	s0/0 & s0/1
2620	On board	Fast Ethernet	Interface-type 0/port	fa0/0
	Slot 0	WIC (serial)	Interface-type 0/port	s0/0 & s0/1
2621	On board	Fast Ethernet	Interface-type 0/port	fa0/0 & fa0/1
	Slot 0	WIC (serial)	Interface-type 0/port	s0/0 & s0/1
1841	On board	Fast Ethernet	Interface-type 0/port	fa0/0 & fa0/1
	Slot 0	High-speed WAN interface card (HWIC)/ WIC/VWIC	Interface-type 0/slot/ port	s0/0/0 & s0/0/1
1841	Slot 1	HWIC/WIC/ VWIC	Interface-type 0/slot/ port	s0/1/0 & s0/1/1
2801	On board	Fast Ethernet	Interface-type 0/port	fa0/0 & fa0/1
	Slot 0	VIC/VWIC (voice only)	Interface-type 0/slot/ port	voice0/0/0– voice0/0/3
	Slot 1	HWIC/WIC/ VWIC	Interface-type 0/slot/ port	0/1/0–0/1/3 (single-wide HWIC) 0/1/0–0/1/7 (double-wide HWIC)
	Slot 2	WIC/VIC/ VWIC	Interface-type 0/slot/ port	0/2/0–0/2/3

Router Model	Port Location/Slot Number	Slot/Port Type	Slot Numbering Range	Example
	Slot 3	HWIC/WIC/ VWIC	Interface-type 0/slot/ port	0/3/0–0/3/3 (single-wide HWIC) 0/3/0–0/3/7 (double-wide HWIC)
2811	Built in to chassis front	USB	Interface-type port	usb0 & usb 1
	Built in to chassis rear	Fast Ethernet Gigabit Ethernet	Interface-type 0/port	fa0/0 & fa0/1 gi0/0 & gi0/1
	Slot 0	HWIC/ HWIC-D/WIC/ VWIC/VIC	Interface-type 0/slot/ port	s0/0/0 & s0/0/1 fa0/0/0 & 0/0/1
	Slot 1	HWIC/ HWIC-D/WIC/ VWIC/VIC	Interface-type 0/slot/ port	s0/1/0 & s0/1/1 fa0/1/0 & 0/1/1
	NME slot	NM/NME	Interface-type 1/port	gi1/0 & gi1/1 s1/0 & s1/1
1941 / 1941w	On board	Gigabit Ethernet	Interface-type 0/port	gi0/0 & gi0/1
	Slot 0	EHWIC	Interface-type 0/slot/ port	s0/0/0 & s0/0/1
	Slot 1	EHWIC	Interface-type 0/slot/ port	s0/1/0 & s0/1/1
	Built in to chassis back	USB	Interface-type port	usb0 & usb 1
2901 2911	On board	Gigabit Ethernet	Interface-type 0/port	gi0/0 & gi0/1 gi0/2 (2911 only)
	Slot 0	EHWIC	Interface-type 0/slot/ port	s0/0/0 & s0/0/1
	Slot 1	EHWIC	Interface-type 0/slot/ port	s0/1/0 & s0/1/1
	Slot 2	EHWIC	Interface-type 0/slot/ port	s0/2/0 & s0/2/1
	Slot 3	EHWIC	Interface-type 0/slot/ port	s0/3/0 & s0/3/1
	Built in to chassis back	USB	Interface-type port	usb0 & usb 1

Moving Between Interfaces

What happens in Column 1 is the same thing occurring in Column 3.

`Router(config)` `#interface serial 0/0/0`	Moves to serial interface configuration mode	`Router(config)` `#interface serial 0/0/0`	Moves to serial interface configuration mode
`Router(config-if)#exit`	Returns to global configuration mode	`Router(config-if)` `#interface fastethernet 0/0`	Moves directly to Fast Ethernet 0/0 configuration mode
`Router(config)` `# interface fastethernet 0/0`	Moves to Fast Ethernet interface configuration mode	`Router(config-if)#`	In Fast Ethernet 0/0 configuration mode now
`Router(config-if)#`	In Fast Ethernet 0/0 configuration mode now	`Router(config-if)#`	Prompt does not change; be *careful*

Configuring a Serial Interface

`Router(config)#interface serial 0/0/0`	Moves to serial interface 0/0/0 configuration mode
`Router(config-if)#description Link to ISP`	Optional descriptor of the link is locally significant
`Router(config-if)#ip address 192.168.10.1 255.255.255.0`	Assigns address and subnet mask to interface
`Router(config-if)#clock rate 56000`	Assigns a clock rate for the interface
`Router(config-if)#no shutdown`	Turns interface on

TIP   The **clock rate** command is used *only* on a *serial* interface that has a *DCE* cable plugged into it. There must be a clock rate set on every serial link between routers. It does not matter which router has the DCE cable plugged into it or which interface the cable is plugged into. Serial 0/0/0 on one router can be plugged into Serial 0/0/1 on another router.

Configuring a Fast Ethernet Interface

Router(config)#**interface fastethernet 0/0**	Moves to Fast Ethernet 0/0 interface configuration mode
Router(config-if)#**description Accounting LAN**	Optional descriptor of the link is locally significant
Router(config-if)#**ip address 192.168.20.1 255.255.255.0**	Assigns address and subnet mask to interface
Router(config-if)#**no shutdown**	Turns interface on

Configuring a Gigabit Ethernet Interface

Router(config)#**interface gigabitethernet 0/0**	Moves to gigabitethernet 0/0 interface configuration mode
Router(config-if)#**description Human Resources LAN**	Optional descriptor of the link is locally significant
Router(config-if)#**ip address 192.168.30.1 255.255.255.0**	Assigns an address and subnet mask to interface
Router(config-if)#**no shutdown**	Turns interface on

Creating a Message-of-the-Day Banner

Router(config)#**banner motd #** **Building Power will be interrupted** **next Tuesday evening from 8 - 10** **PM. #** Router(config)#	# is known as a *delimiting character*. The delimiting character must surround the banner message and can be any character so long as it is not a character used within the body of the message.

TIP   The MOTD banner is displayed on all terminals and is useful for sending messages that affect all users. Use the **no banner motd** command to disable the MOTD banner. The MOTD banner displays before the login prompt and the login banner, if one has been created.

Creating a Login Banner

Router(config)#**banner login** **#Authorized Personnel Only! Please** **enter your username and password.** **#** Router(config)#	# is known as a *delimiting character*. The delimiting character must surround the banner message and can be any character so long as it is not a character used within the body of the message.

TIP   The login banner displays before the username and password login prompts. Use the **no banner login** command to disable the login banner. The MOTD banner displays before the login banner.

Setting the Clock Time Zone

Router(config)#clock timezone EST -5	Sets the time zone for display purposes. Based on coordinated universal time. (Eastern standard time is 5 hours behind UTC.)

Assigning a Local Host Name to an IP Address

Router(config)#ip host london 172.16.1.3	Assigns a host name to the IP address. After this assignment, you can use the host name rather than an IP address when trying to telnet or ping to that address.
Router#ping london = Router#ping 172.16.1.3	Both commands execute the same objective: sending a ping to address 172.16.1.3.

TIP   The default port number in the **ip host** command is 23, or Telnet. If you want to telnet to a device, just enter the IP host name itself:

Router#**london** = Router#**telnet london** = Router#**telnet 172.16.1.3**

The no ip domain-lookup Command

Router(config)#no ip domain-lookup Router(config)#	Turns off trying to automatically resolve an unrecognized command to a local host name

TIP   Ever type in a command incorrectly and end up having to wait for a minute or two as the router tries to *translate* your command to a domain server of 255.255.255.255? The router is set by default to try to resolve any word that is not a command to a Domain Name System (DNS) server at address 255.255.255.255. If you are not going to set up DNS, turn off this feature to save you time as you type, especially if you are a poor typist.

The logging synchronous Command

Router(config)#line console 0	Moves to line console configuration mode
Router(config-line)#logging synchronous	Turns on synchronous logging. Information items sent to the console will not interrupt the command you are typing. The command will be moved to a new line.

TIP Ever try to type in a command and an informational line appears in the middle of what you were typing? Lose your place? Do not know where you are in the command, so you just press Enter and start all over? The **logging synchronous** command tells the router that if any informational items get displayed on the screen, your prompt and command line should be moved to a new line, so as not to confuse you. The informational line does not get inserted into the middle of the command you are trying to type. If you were to continue typing, the command would execute properly, even though it looks wrong on the screen.

The exec-timeout Command

`Router(config)#line console 0`	Moves to line console configuration mode
`Router(config-line)` `#exec-timeout 0 0`	Sets the time limit when the console automatically logs off. Set to **0 0** (minutes seconds) means the console never logs off.
`Router(config-line)#`	

TIP The command **exec-timeout 0 0** is great for a lab environment because the console never logs out. This is considered to be bad security and is dangerous in the real world. The default for the **exec-timeout** command is 10 minutes and zero (0) seconds (**exec-timeout 10 0**).

Saving Configurations

`Router#copy running-config` `startup-config`	Saves the running configuration to local NVRAM
`Router#copy running-config tftp`	Saves the running configuration remotely to a TFTP server

Erasing Configurations

`Router#erase startup-config`	Deletes the startup configuration file from NVRAM

TIP The running configuration is still in dynamic memory. Reload the router to clear the running configuration.

show Commands

`Router#show ?`	Lists all **show** commands available.
`Router#show interfaces`	Displays statistics for all interfaces.
`Router#show interface` `serial 0/0/0`	Displays statistics for a specific interface (in this case, serial 0/0/0).
`Router#show ip` `interface brief`	Displays a summary of all interfaces, including status and IP address assigned.

`Router#show controllers serial 0/0/0`	Displays statistics for interface hardware. Statistics display if the clock rate is set and if the cable is DCE, DTE, or not attached.
`Router#show clock`	Displays time set on device.
`Router#show hosts`	Displays local host-to-IP address cache. These are the names and addresses of hosts on the network to which you can connect.
`Router#show users`	Displays all users connected to device.
`Router#show history`	Displays the history of commands used at this edit level.
`Router#show flash`	Displays info about flash memory.
`Router#show version`	Displays info about loaded software version.
`Router#show arp`	Displays the Address Resolution Protocol (ARP) table.
`Router#show protocols`	Displays status of configured Layer 3 protocols.
`Router#show startup-config`	Displays the configuration saved in NVRAM.
`Router#show running-config`	Displays the configuration currently running in RAM.

EXEC Commands in Configuration Mode: The do Command

Router(config)#**do show running-config**	Executes the privileged-level **show running-config** command while in global configuration mode.
Router(config)#	The router remains in global configuration mode after the command has been executed.

TIP The **do** command is useful when you want to execute EXEC commands, such as **show**, **clear**, or **debug**, while remaining in global configuration mode or in any configuration submode. You cannot use the **do** command to execute the **configure terminal** command because it is the **configure terminal** command that changes the mode to global configuration mode.

Configuration Example: Basic Router Configuration

Figure 6-1 illustrates the network topology for the configuration that follows, which shows a basic router configuration using the commands covered in this chapter.

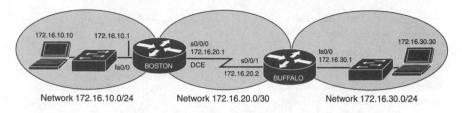

Figure 6-1 Network Topology for Basic Router Configuration

Boston Router

`Router>`**`enable`**	Enters privileged mode.
`Router#`**`clock set 18:30:00`** **`15 May 2013`**	Sets the local time on the router.
`Router#`**`configure terminal`**	Enters global configuration mode.
`Router(config)#`**`hostname Boston`**	Sets the router name to Boston.
`Boston(config)#`**`no ip`** **`domain-lookup`**	Turns off name resolution on unrecognized commands (spelling mistakes).
`Boston(config)#`**`banner motd #`** **`This is the Boston Router.`** **`Authorized Access Only`** **`#`**	Creates an MOTD banner.
`Boston(config)#`**`clock timezone`** **`EST -5`**	Sets time zone to eastern standard time (–5 from UTC).
`Boston(config)#`**`enable secret cisco`**	Enables secret password set to cisco.
`Boston(config)#`**`service`** **`password-encryption`**	Passwords will be given weak encryption.
`Boston(config)#`**`line console 0`**	Enters line console mode.
`Boston(config-line)#`**`logging`** **`synchronous`**	Commands will not be interrupted by unsolicited messages.
`Boston(config-line)#`**`password class`**	Sets the password to class.
`Boston(config-line)#`**`login`**	Enables password checking at login.
`Boston(config-line)#`**`line vty 0 4`**	Moves to virtual Telnet lines 0 through 4.
`Boston(config-line)#`**`password class`**	Sets the password to class.
`Boston(config-line)#`**`login`**	Enables password checking at login.
`Boston(config-line)#`**`line aux 0`**	Moves to line auxiliary mode.
`Boston(config-line)#`**`password class`**	Sets the password to class.
`Boston(config-line)#`**`login`**	Enables password checking at login.
`Boston(config-line)#`**`exit`**	Moves back to global configuration mode.

`Boston(config)#no service` `password-encryption`	Turns off password encryption.
`Boston(config)#interface` `fastethernet 0/0`	Moves to interface Fast Ethernet 0/0 configuration mode.
`Boston(config-if)#description` `Engineering LAN`	Sets locally significant description of the interface.
`Boston(config-if)#ip address` `172.16.10.1 255.255.255.0`	Assigns an IP address and subnet mask to the interface.
`Boston(config-if)#no shutdown`	Turns on the interface.
`Boston(config-if)#interface` `serial 0/0/0`	Moves directly to interface serial 0/0/0 configuration mode.
`Boston(config-if)#description Link` `to Buffalo Router`	Sets locally significant description of the interface.
`Boston(config-if)#ip address` `172.16.20.1 255.255.255.252`	Assigns an IP address and subnet mask to the interface.
`Boston(config-if)#clock rate 56000`	Sets a clock rate for serial transmission. The DCE cable must be plugged into this interface.
`Boston(config-if)#no shutdown`	Turns on the interface.
`Boston(config-if)#exit`	Moves back to global configuration mode.
`Boston(config)#ip host buffalo` `172.16.20.2`	Sets a local host name resolution to IP address 172.16.20.2.
`Boston(config)#exit`	Moves back to privileged mode.
`Boston#copy running-config` `startup-config`	Saves the running configuration to NVRAM.

CHAPTER 7

Static Routing

This chapter provides information and commands concerning the following topics:

- Configuring a static route on a router
- The **permanent** keyword (optional)
- Static routes and administrative distance (optional)
- Configuring a default route on a router
- Verifying static routes
- Configuration example: Static routes

Configuring a Static Route on a Router

When using the **ip route** command, you can identify where packets should be routed in two ways:

- The next-hop address
- The exit interface

Both ways are shown in the "Configuration Example: Static Routes" and the "Configuring a Default Route on a Router" sections.

`Router(config)#ip route 172.16.20.0 255.255.255.0 172.16.10.2`	172.16.20.0 = destination network. 255.255.255.0 = subnet mask. 172.16.10.2 = next-hop address. Read this to say, "To get to the destination network of 172.16.20.0, with a subnet mask of 255.255.255.0, send all packets to 172.16.10.2."
`Router(config)#ip route 172.16.20.0 255.255.255.0 serial 0/0/0`	172.16.20.0 = destination network. 255.255.255.0 = subnet mask. Serial 0/0/0 = exit interface. Read this to say, "To get to the destination network of 172.16.20.0, with a subnet mask of 255.255.255.0, send all packets out interface serial 0/0/0."

The permanent Keyword (Optional)

Without the **permanent** keyword in a static route statement, a static route will be removed if an interface goes down. A downed interface will cause the directly connected network and any associated static routes to be removed from the routing table. If the interface comes back up, the routes are returned.

Adding the **permanent** keyword to a static route statement will keep the static routes in the routing table even if the interface goes down and the directly connected networks are removed. You *cannot* get to these routes—the interface is down—but the routes remain in the table. The advantage to this is that when the interface comes back up, the static routes do not need to be reprocessed and placed back into the routing table, thus saving time and processing power.

When a static route is added or deleted, this route, along with all other static routes, is processed in one second. Before Cisco IOS Software Release 12.0, this processing time was five seconds.

The routing table processes static routes every minute to install or remove static routes according to the changing routing table.

To specify that the route will not be removed, even if the interface shuts down, enter the following command, for example:

```
Router(config)#ip route 172.16.20.0 255.255.255.0 172.16.10.2 permanent
```

Static Routes and Administrative Distance (Optional)

To specify that an administrative distance of 200 has been assigned to a given route, enter the following command, for example:

```
Router(config)#ip route 172.16.20.0 255.255.255.0 172.16.10.2 200
```

By default, a static route is assigned an administrative distance (AD) of 1. Administrative distance rates the "trustworthiness" of a route. AD is a number from 0 through 255, where 0 is absolutely trusted and 255 cannot be trusted at all. Therefore, an AD of 1 is an extremely reliable rating, with only an AD of 0 being better. An AD of 0 is assigned to a directly connected route. The following table lists the administrative distance for each type of route.

Route Type	Administrative Distance
Connected	0
Static	1
Enhanced Interior Gateway Routing Protocol (EIGRP) summary route	5
Exterior Border Gateway Protocol (eBGP)	20
EIGRP (internal)	90

Route Type	Administrative Distance
Open Shortest Path First Protocol (OSPF)	110
Intermediate System-to-Intermediate System Protocol (IS-IS)	115
RIP	120
Exterior Gateway Protocol (EGP)	140
On-Demand Routing	160
EIGRP (external)	170
Internal Border Gateway Protocol (iBGP) (external)	200
Unknown or unbelievable	255 (Will not pass traffic)

By default, a static route is always used rather than a routing protocol. By adding an AD number to your statement, however, you can effectively create a backup route to your routing protocol. If your network is using EIGRP, and you need a backup route, add a static route with an AD greater than 90. EIGRP will be used because its AD is better (lower) than the static route. If EIGRP goes down, however, the static route will be used in its place. This is known as a *floating static route*.

Configuring a Default Route on a Router

`Router(config)#ip route` `0.0.0.0 0.0.0.0 172.16.10.2`	Send all packets destined for networks not in my routing table to 172.16.10.2.
`Router(config)#ip route` `0.0.0.0 0.0.0.0 serial 0/0/0`	Send all packets destined for networks not in my routing table out my serial 0/0 interface.

NOTE   The combination of the 0.0.0.0 network address and the 0.0.0.0 mask is called a *quad-zero route*.

Verifying Static Routes

To display the contents of the IP routing table, enter the following command:

```
Router#show ip route
```

NOTE   The codes to the left of the routes in the table tell you from where the router learned the routes. A static route is described by the letter *S*. A default route is described in the routing table by S*. The asterisk (*) indicates that the last path option will be used when forwarding the packet.

Configuration Example: Static Routes

Figure 7-1 illustrates the network topology for the configuration that follows, which shows how to configure static routes using the commands covered in this chapter.

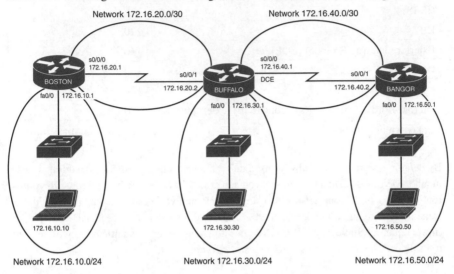

Figure 7-1 Network Topology for Static Route Configuration

NOTE The host names, passwords, and interfaces have all been configured using the commands shown in the configuration example in Chapter 6, "Configuring a Single Cisco Router."

Boston Router

`Boston>`**`enable`**	Moves to privileged mode
`Boston#`**`configure terminal`**	Moves to global configuration mode
`Boston(config)#`**`ip route`** `172.16.30.0 255.255.255.0 172.16.20.2`	Configures a static route using the next-hop address
`Boston(config)#`**`ip route`** `172.16.40.0 255.255.255.0 172.16.20.2`	Configures a static route using the next-hop address
`Boston(config)#`**`ip route`** `172.16.50.0 255.255.255.0 172.16.20.2`	Configures a static route using the next-hop address
`Boston(config)#`**`exit`**	Moves to privileged mode
`Boston#`**`copy running-config startup-config`**	Saves the configuration to NVRAM

Buffalo Router

Buffalo>**enable**	Moves to privileged mode
Buffalo#**configure terminal**	Moves to global configuration mode
Buffalo(config)#**ip route 172.16.10.0 255.255.255.0 serial 0/0/1**	Configures a static route using the exit interface
Buffalo(config)#**ip route 172.16.50.0 255.255.255.0 serial 0/0/0**	Configures a static route using the exit interface
Buffalo(config)#**exit**	Moves to privileged mode
Buffalo#**copy running-config startup-config**	Saves the configuration to NVRAM

Bangor Router

Bangor>**enable**	Moves to privileged mode
Bangor#**configure terminal**	Moves to global configuration mode
Bangor(config)#**ip route 0.0.0.0 0.0.0.0 serial 0/0/1**	Configures a static route using the default route
Bangor(config)#**exit**	Moves to privileged mode
Bangor#**copy running-config startup-config**	Saves the configuration to NVRAM

This chapter provides information and commands concerning the following topics:

- Configuring Enhanced Interior Gateway Routing Protocol (EIGRP)
- EIGRP auto-summarization
- EIGRP manual summarization
- Passive EIGRP interfaces
- Equal-cost load balancing: Maximum paths
- Unequal-cost load balancing: **variance**
- Bandwidth use
- Authentication
- Verifying EIGRP
- Troubleshooting EIGRP
- Configuration example: EIGRP

Configuring Enhanced Interior Gateway Routing Protocol (EIGRP)

`Router(config)#router eigrp 100`	Turns on the EIGRP process. 100 is the autonomous system (AS) number, which can be a number between 1 and 65,535.
	All routers in the same autonomous system must use the same autonomous system number.
`Router(config-router)#network 10.0.0.0`	Specifies which network to advertise in EIGRP.
`Router(config-if)#bandwidth x`	Sets the bandwidth of this interface to *x* kilobits to allow EIGRP to make a better metric calculation.
	NOTE This command is entered at the interface command prompt (config-if) and not in the router process prompt (config-router). The setting can differ for each interface to which it is applied.
	TIP The **bandwidth** command is used for metric calculations only. It does not change interface performance.

`Router(config-router)#eigrp` `log-neighbor-changes`	Changes with neighbors will be displayed.
`Router(config-router)#no` `network 10.0.0.0`	Removes the network from the EIGRP process.
`Router(config)#no router` `eigrp 100`	Disables routing process 100 and removes the entire EIGRP configuration from the running configuration.
`Router(config-router)#network` `10.0.0.0 0.255.255.255`	Identifies which interfaces or networks to include in EIGRP. Interfaces must be configured with addresses that fall within the wildcard mask range of the **network** statement. A network mask can also be used here.

TIP   The use of a wildcard mask or network mask is *optional*.

TIP   There is no limit to the number of network statements (that is, **network** commands) that you can configure on a router.

TIP   If you use the **network 172.16.1.0 0.0.0.255** command with a wildcard mask, in this example the command specifies that only interfaces on the 172.16.1.0/24 subnet will participate in EIGRP. However, because EIGRP automatically summarizes routes on the major network boundary by default, the full Class B network of 172.16.0.0 will be advertised.

TIP   If you do not use the optional wildcard mask, the EIGRP process assumes that all directly connected networks that are part of the overall major network will participate in the EIGRP process and that EIGRP will attempt to establish neighbor relationships from each interface that is part of that Class A, B, or C major network.

`Router(config-`
`router)#metric`
`weights tos k1 k2 k3`
`k4 k5`
	Changes the default *k* values used in metric calculation.
	These are the default values:
	tos=0, k1=1, k2=0, k3=1, k4=0, k5=0

NOTE   *tos* is a reference to the original Interior Gateway Routing Protocol (IGRP) intention to have IGRP perform type-of-service routing. Because this was never adopted into practice, the *tos* field in this command is *always* set to zero (0).

NOTE   With default settings in place, the metric of EIGRP is reduced to the slowest bandwidth plus the sum of all the delays of the exit interfaces from the local router to the -destination network.

TIP   For two routers to form a neighbor relationship in EIGRP, the *k* values *must* match.

CAUTION   Unless you are *very* familiar with what is occurring in your network, it is recommended that you *do not* change the *k* values.

EIGRP Auto-Summarization

`Router(config-router)` `#auto-summary`	Enables auto-summarization for the EIGRP process.
	NOTE The behavior of the **auto-summary** command is disabled by default of Cisco IOS Software Versions 15 and later. Earlier software generally has automatic summarization enabled by default.
`Router(config-router)` `#no auto-summary`	Turns off the auto-summarization feature.

EIGRP Manual Summarization

`Router(config)#interface` `fastethernet 0/0`	Enters interface configuration mode.

`Router(config-if)#ip`
`summary-address`
`eigrp 100 10.10.0.0`
`255.255.0.0 75`
	Enables manual summarization for EIGRP autonomous system 100 on this specific interface for the given address and mask. An administrative distance of 75 is assigned to this summary route.

	NOTE The *administrative-distance* argument is optional in this command. Without it, an administrative distance of 5 is automatically applied to the summary route.

CAUTION   EIGRP automatically summarizes networks at the classful boundary. A poorly designed network with discontiguous subnets could have problems with connectivity if the summarization feature is left on. For instance, you could have two routers advertise the same network—172.16.0.0/16—when in fact they wanted to advertise two different networks—172.16.10.0/24 and 172.16.20.0/24.

Recommended practice is that you turn off automatic summarization if necessary, use the **ip summary-address** command, and summarize manually what you need to.

Passive EIGRP Interfaces

`Router(config)#router eigrp 110`	Starts the EIGRP routing process.
`Router(config-router)#network` `10.0.0.0`	Specifies a network to advertise in the EIGRP routing process.
`Router(config-router)#passive-` `interface fastethernet 0/0`	Prevents the sending of hello packets out the Fast Ethernet 0/0 interface. No neighbor adjacency will be formed.

`Router(config-router)` `#passive-interface default`	Prevents the sending of hello packets out all interfaces.
`Router(config)#no passive-` `interface serial 0/0/1`	Enables hello packets to be sent out interface Serial 0/0/1, thereby allowing neighbor adjacencies to form

Equal-Cost Load Balancing: Maximum Paths

`Router(config)#router eigrp 100`	Creates routing process 100
`Router(config-router)#network` `10.0.0.0`	Specifies which network to advertise in EIGRP
`Router(config-router)#maximum-paths 6`	Set the maximum number of parallel routes that EIGRP will support to 6

NOTE   With the **maximum-paths** router configuration command, up to 32 equal-cost entries can be in the routing table for the same destination. The default is four.

NOTE   Setting the **maximum-path** to 1 disables load balancing.

Unequal-Cost Load Balancing: Variance

`Router(config)#router eigrp 100`	Creates routing process 100
`Router(config-router)#network` `10.0.0.0`	Specifies which network to advertise in EIGRP
`Router(config-router)#variance n`	Instructs the router to include routes with a metric less than or equal to n times the minimum metric route for that destination, where n is the number specified by the **variance** command

NOTE   If a path is not a feasible successor, it is not used in load balancing.

NOTE   EIGRP supports up to six unequal-cost paths.

Bandwidth Use

Router(config)#interface serial 0/0/0	Enters interface configuration mode.
Router(config-if) #bandwidth 256	Sets the bandwidth of this interface to 256 kilobits to allow EIGRP to make a better metric calculation.
Router(config-if)#ip bandwidth-percent eigrp 50 100	Configures the percentage of bandwidth that may be used by EIGRP on an interface. 50 is the EIGRP autonomous system number. 100 is the percentage value. 100% * 256 = 256 kbps.

NOTE   By default, EIGRP is set to use only up to 50 percent of the bandwidth of an interface to exchange routing information. Values greater than 100 percent can be configured. This configuration option might prove useful if the bandwidth is set artificially low for other reasons, such as manipulation of the routing metric or to accommodate an oversubscribed multipoint Frame Relay configuration.

NOTE   The **ip bandwidth-percent** command relies on the value set by the **-bandwidth** command.

Authentication

Router(config)#interface serial 0/0/0	Enters interface configuration mode.
Router(config-if)#ip authentication mode eigrp 100 md5	Enables Message Digest 5 algorithm (MD5) authentication in EIGRP packets over the interface.
Router(config-if)#ip authentication key-chain eigrp 100 romeo	Enables authentication of EIGRP packets. romeo is the name of the key chain.
Router(config-if)#exit	Returns to global configuration mode.
Router(config)#key chain romeo	Identifies a key chain. The name must match the name configured in interface configuration mode above.
Router(config-keychain)#key 1	Identifies the key number.
	NOTE The range of keys is from 0 to 2147483647. The key identification numbers do not need to be consecutive. At least 1 key must be defined on a key chain.
Router(config-keychain-key)#key-string shakespeare	Identifies the key string.

	NOTE The string can contain from 1 to 80 upper-case and lowercase alphanumeric characters, except that the first character cannot be a number.
`Router(config-keychain-key)#`**`accept-lifetime`** `start-time {`**`infinite`** `| end-time | ` **`duration`** `seconds}`	Optionally specifies the period during which the key can be received.
	NOTE The default start time and the earliest acceptable date is January 1, 1993. The default end time is an infinite period.
`Router(config-keychain-key)#`**`send-lifetime`** `start-time {`**`infinite`** ` | end-time | ` **`duration`** `seconds}`	Optionally specifies the period during which the key can be sent.
	NOTE The default start time and the earliest acceptable date is January 1, 1993. The default end time is an infinite period.

NOTE   For the start time and the end time to have relevance, ensure that the router knows the correct time. Recommended practice dictates that you run Network Time Protocol (NTP) or some other time-synchronization method if you intend to set lifetimes on keys.

Verifying EIGRP

`Router#`**`show ip eigrp neighbors`**	Displays the neighbor table.
`Router#`**`show ip eigrp neighbors detail`**	Displays a detailed neighbor table.
	TIP The **show ip eigrp neighbors detail** command verifies whether a neighbor is configured as a stub router.
`Router#`**`show ip eigrp interfaces`**	Shows information for each interface.
`Router#`**`show ip eigrp interfaces serial 0/0/0`**	Shows information for a specific interface.
`Router#`**`show ip eigrp interfaces 100`**	Shows information for interfaces running process 100.
`Router#`**`show ip eigrp topology`**	Displays the topology table.
	TIP The show ip eigrp topology command shows you where your feasible successors are.

Router#**show ip eigrp traffic**	Shows the number and type of packets sent and received.
Router#**show ip route**	Shows the complete routing table.
Router#**show ip route eigrp**	Shows a routing table with only EIGRP entries.
Router#**show ip protocols**	Shows the parameters and current state of the active routing protocol process.
Router#**show key-chain**	Shows authentication key information.

Troubleshooting EIGRP

Router#**debug eigrp fsm**	Displays events/actions related to EIGRP feasible successor metrics (FSM)
Router#**debug eigrp packet**	Displays events/actions related to EIGRP packets
Router#**debug eigrp neighbor**	Displays events/actions related to your EIGRP neighbors
Router#**debug ip eigrp**	Displays events/actions related to EIGRP protocol packets.
Router#**debug ip eigrp neighbor**	Displays events/actions related to your EIGRP neighbors
Router#**debug ip eigrp notifications**	Displays EIGRP event notifications

Configuration Example: EIGRP

Figure 8-1 illustrates the network topology for the configuration that follows, which shows how to configure EIGRP using the commands covered in this chapter.

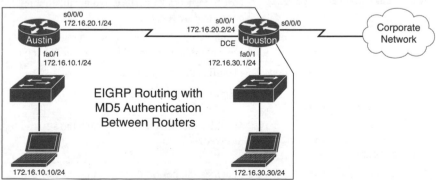

Figure 8-1 Network Topology for EIGRP Configuration

Austin Router

`Austin>enable`	Moves to privileged mode.
`Austin#configure terminal`	Moves to global configuration mode.
`Austin(config)#interface serial 0/0/0`	Enters interface configuration mode.
`Austin(config-if)#ip address 172.16.20.1 255.255.255.0`	Assigns the IP address and netmask.
`Austin(config-if)#ip authentication mode eigrp 100 md5`	Enables MD5 authentication in EIGRP packets.
`Austin(config-if)#ip authentication key-chain eigrp 100 susannah`	Enables authentication of EIGRP packets. susannah is the name of the key chain.
`Austin(config-if)#no shutdown`	Enables the interface.
`Austin(config-if)#interface fastethernet 0/1`	Enters interface configuration mode.
`Austin(config-if)#ip address 172.16.10.1 255.255.255.0`	Assigns the IP address and netmask.
`Austin(config-if)#no shutdown`	Enables the interface.
`Austin(config-if)#router eigrp 100`	Enables EIGRP routing.
`Austin(config-router)#no auto-summary`	Disables auto-summarization.
`Austin(config-router)#eigrp log-neighbor-changes`	Changes with neighbors will be displayed.
`Austin(config-router)#network 172.16.0.0`	Advertises directly connected networks (classful address only).
`Austin(config-router)#passive interface fastethernet 0/1`	Prevents the sending of hello packets out the Fast Ethernet 0/1 interface. No neighbor adjacency will be formed.
`Austin(config-router)#key chain susannah`	Identifies a key chain name, which must match the name configured in interface configuration mode.
`Austin(config-keychain)#key 1`	Identifies the key number.
`Austin(config-keychain-key)#key-string tower`	Identifies the key string.
`Austin(config-keychain-key)#accept-lifetime 06:30:00 Apr 19 2013 infinite`	Specifies the period during which the key can be received.
`Austin(config-keychain-key)#send-lifetime 06:30:00 Apr 19 2013 09:45:00 Apr 19 2013`	Specifies the period during which the key can be sent.
`Austin(config-keychain-key)#exit`	Returns to global configuration mode.

`Austin(config)#`**`exit`**	Returns to privileged mode
`Austin#`**`copy running-config startup-config`**	Saves the configuration to NVRAM.

Houston Router

`Houston>`**`enable`**	Moves to privileged mode.
`Houston#`**`configure terminal`**	Moves to global configuration mode.
`Houston(config)#`**`interface serial 0/0/1`**	Enters interface configuration mode.
`Houston(config-if)#`**`ip address 172.16.20.2 255.255.255.0`**	Assigns the IP address and netmask.
`Houston(config-if)#`**`ip authentication mode eigrp 100 md5`**	Enables MD5 authentication in EIGRP packets.
`Houston(config-if)#`**`ip authentication key-chain eigrp 100 eddie`**	Enables authentication of EIGRP packets. eddie is the name of the key chain.
`Houston(config-if)#`**`clock rate 56000`**	Sets the clock rate.
`Houston(config-if)#`**`no shutdown`**	Enables the interface.
`Houston(config-if)#`**`interface fastethernet 0/1`**	Enters interface configuration mode.
`Houston(config-if)#`**`ip address 172.16.30.1 255.255.255.0`**	Assigns the IP address and netmask.
`Houston(config-if)#`**`no shutdown`**	Enables the interface.
`Houston(config-if)#`**`router eigrp 100`**	Enables EIGRP routing.
`Houston(config-router)#`**`no auto-summary`**	Disables auto-summarization.
`Houston(config-router)#`**`eigrp log-neighbor-changes`**	Changes with neighbors will be displayed.
`Houston(config-router)#`**`network 172.16.0.0`**	Advertises directly connected networks (classful address only).
`Houston(config-router)#`**`passive interface fastethernet 0/1`**	Prevents the sending of hello packets out the Fast Ethernet 0/1 interface. No neighbor adjacency will be formed.
`Houston(config-router)#`**`key chain eddie`**	Identifies a key chain name, which must match the name configured in interface configuration mode.
`Houston(config-keychain)#`**`key 1`**	Identifies the key number.
`Houston(config-keychain-key)#`**`key-string tower`**	Identifies the key string.

Houston(config-keychain- key)#**accept-lifetime 06:30:00 Apr 19 2013 infinite**	Specifies the period during which the key can be received.
Houston(config-keychain- key)#**send-lifetime 06:30:00 Apr 19 2013 09:45:00 Apr 19 2013**	Specifies the period during which the key can be sent.
Houston(config-keychain- key)#**exit**	Returns to global configuration mode.
Houston(config)#**exit**	Returns to privileged mode.
Houston#**copy running-config startup-config**	Saves the configuration to NVRAM.

CHAPTER 9

Single-Area OSPF

This chapter provides information and commands concerning the following topics:

- Configuring OSPF
- Using wildcard masks with OSPF areas
- Loopback interfaces
- Router ID
- DR/BDR elections
- Modifying cost metrics
- Authentication: Simple
- Authentication: Using MD5 encryption
- Timers
- Propagating a default route
- Verifying OSPF configuration
- Troubleshooting OSPF
- Configuration example: Single area OSPF

Configuring OSPF

`Router(config)#router ospf 123`	Starts OSPF process 123. The process ID is any positive integer value between 1 and 65,535. The process ID *is not related to* the OSPF area. The process ID merely distinguishes one process from another within the device.
`Router(config-router)#network 172.16.10.0 0.0.0.255 area 0`	OSPF advertises interfaces, not networks. Uses the wildcard mask to determine which interfaces to advertise. Read this line to say "Any interface with an address of 172.16.10.x is to be put into area 0."
	NOTE The process ID number of one router does not have to match the process ID of any other router. Unlike Enhanced Interior Gateway Routing Protocol (EIGRP), matching this number across all routers does *not* ensure that network adjacencies will form.
`Router(config-router)#log-adjacency-changes detail`	Configures the router to send a syslog message when there is a change of state between OSPF neighbors.
	TIP Although the **log-adjacency-changes** command is on by default, only up/down events are reported unless you use the **detail** keyword.

Using Wildcard Masks with OSPF Areas

When compared to an IP address, a wildcard mask identifies which addresses get matched for placement into an area:

- A 0 (zero) in a wildcard mask means to check the corresponding bit in the address for an exact match.

- A 1 (one) in a wildcard mask means to ignore the corresponding bit in the address—can be either 1 or 0.

Example 1: 172.16.0.0 0.0.255.255

172.16.0.0 = 10101100.00010000.00000000.00000000

0.0.255.255 = 00000000.00000000.11111111.11111111

result = 10101100.00010000.*xxxxxxxx.xxxxxxxx*

172.16.*x.x* (Anything between 172.16.0.0 and 172.16.255.255 will match the example statement.)

> **TIP** An octet of all 0s means that the octet has to match exactly to the address. An octet of all 1s means that the octet can be ignored.

Example 2: 172.16.8.0 0.0.7.255

172.168.8.0 = 10101100.00010000.00001000.00000000

0.0.0.7.255 = 00000000.00000000.00000111.11111111

result = 10101100.00010000.00001*xxx.xxxxxxxx*

00001*xxx* = 00001*000* to 00001*111* = 8–15

xxxxxxxx = 00000000 to 11111111 = 0–255

Anything between 172.16.8.0 and 172.16.15.255 will match the example statement.

`Router(config-router)#network` `172.16.10.1 0.0.0.0 area 0`	Read this line to say "Any interface with an exact address of 172.16.10.1 is to be put into area 0."
`Router(config-router)#network` `172.16.10.0 0.0.255.255 area 0`	Read this line to say "Any interface with an address of 172.16.*x.x* is to be put into area 0."
`Router(config-router)#network` `0.0.0.0 255.255.255.255 area 0`	Read this line to say "Any interface with any address is to be put into area 0."

Loopback Interfaces

`Router(config)#interface` `loopback 0`	Creates a virtual interface named loopback 0, and then moves the router to interface configuration mode. The loopback interface number can be any number between 0 and 2147483647.
`Router(config-if)#ip address` `192.168.100.1 255.255.255.255`	Assigns the IP address to the interface.
	NOTE Loopback interfaces are always "up and up" and do not go down unless manually shut down. This makes loopback interfaces great for use as OSPF router IDs.

Router ID

`Router(config)#router ospf 1`	Starts OSPF process 1.
`Router(config-router)#router-id 10.1.1.1`	Sets the router ID to 10.1.1.1. If this command is used on an OSPF router process that is already active (has neighbors), the new router ID is used at the next reload or at a manual OSPF process restart.
`Router(config-router)#no router-id 10.1.1.1`	Removes the static router ID from the configuration. If this command is used on an OSPF router process that is already active (has neighbors), the old router ID behavior is used until the next reload or at a manual OSPF process restart.

NOTE The OSPF router ID is used to identify each router in the OSPF routing domain. It is a label and is expressed as an IPv4 address. The precedence used to determine the OSPF router ID is as follows:

1. The IP address set using the **router-id** command

2. The highest IP address of its loopback interfaces

3. The highest IP address of its physical interfaces

   a. This address does not have to be included in an OSPF **network** command, but it does have to be in an up/up state.

   b. If the interface used as the router ID goes down, this will trigger a recalculation of the OSPF routing table, starting with the reforming of neighbor adjacencies using the new router ID.

NOTE Even though the router ID looks like an IPv4 address, it is not routable and therefore not included in the routing table unless the OSPF process chooses an interface that has been appropriately defined by a **network** command.

DR/BDR Elections

`Router(config)#interface fastethernet 0/0`	Changes the router to interface configuration mode.
`Router(config-if)#ip ospf priority 50`	Changes the OSPF interface priority to 50.
	NOTE The assigned priority can be between 0 and 255. A priority of 0 makes the router ineligible to become a designated router (DR) or backup designated router BDR). The highest priority wins the election. A priority of 255 guarantees a tie in the election, assuming other routers are also set to 255. If all routers have the same priority, regardless of the priority number, they tie. Ties are broken by the highest router ID.

Modifying Cost Metrics

`Router(config)#interface serial 0/0/0`	Changes the router to interface configuration mode.
`Router(config-if)#bandwidth 128`	If you change the bandwidth, OSPF recalculates the cost of the link.
Or	
`Router(config-if)#ip ospf cost 1564`	Changes the cost to a value of 1564.
	NOTE The cost of a link is determined by dividing the reference bandwidth by the interface bandwidth.
	The bandwidth of the interface is a number between 1 and 10,000,000. The unit of measurement is kilobits.The cost is a number between 1 and 65,535. The cost has no unit of measurement—it is just a number.

TIP   Using the default reference bandwidth of 10^8 (or 100,000,000) means that any link that is equal to or faster than a Fast Ethernet link (100 Mbps or 100,000,000 bps) will have the same cost. This means that a router will treat a Fast Ethernet link as the same cost as a Gigabit Ethernet link. To adjust for this, you must change the OSPF cost on an interface manually or adjust the reference bandwidth to a higher value using the OSPF **auto-cost reference-bandwidth** *bandwidth* command, which is shown in the next section.

OSPF auto-cost reference-bandwidth

`Router(config)#router ospf 1`	Starts OSPF process 1.
`Router(config-router)#auto-cost reference-bandwidth 1000`	Changes the reference bandwidth that OSPF uses to calculate the cost of an interface.
	NOTE The range of the reference bandwidth is 1 to 4,294,967. The default is 100. The unit of measurement is megabits per second (Mbps).
	NOTE The value set by the **ip ospf cost** command overrides the cost resulting from the **auto-cost** command.
	TIP If you use the command **auto-cost reference-bandwidth** *bandwidth*, configure all the routers to use the same value. Failure to do so will result in routers using a different reference cost to calculate the shortest path, resulting in potential suboptimum routing paths.

Authentication: Simple

`Router(config)#router ospf 1`	Starts OSPF process 1.
`Router(config-router)#area 0 authentication`	Enables simple authentication; password will be sent in clear text.
`Router(config-router)#exit`	Returns to global configuration mode.
`Router(config)#interface fastethernet 0/0`	Moves to interface configuration mode.
`Router(config-if)#ip ospf authentication-key fred`	Sets key (password) to fred.
	NOTE The password can be any continuous string of characters that can be entered from the keyboard, up to 8 bytes in length. To be able to exchange OSPF information, all neighboring routers on the same network must have the same password.

Authentication: Using MD5 Encryption

`Router(config)#router ospf 1`	Starts OSPF process 1.
`Router(config-router)#area 0 authentication message-digest`	Enables authentication with MD5 password encryption.
`Router(config-router)#exit`	Returns to global configuration mode.
`Router(config)#interface fastethernet 0/0`	Moves to interface configuration mode.
`Router(config-if)#ip ospf message-digest-key 1 md5 fred`	1 is the *key-id*. This value must be the same as that of your neighboring router. **md5** indicates that the MD5 hash algorithm will be used. **fred** is the key (password) and must be the same as that of your neighboring router.
	NOTE If the **service password-encryption** command is not used when implementing OSPF MD5 authentication, the MD5 secret is stored as plain text in NVRAM.

Timers

`Router(config-if)#ip ospf hello-interval timer 20`	Changes the Hello Interval timer to 20 seconds.
`Router(config-if)#ip ospf dead-interval 80`	Changes the Dead Interval timer to 80 seconds.
	NOTE Hello and Dead Interval timers must match for routers to become neighbors.

Propagating a Default Route

`Router(config)#ip route 0.0.0.0 0.0.0.0 s0/0/0`	Creates a default route.
`Router(config)#router ospf 1`	Starts OSPF process 1.
`Router(config-router)#default-information originate`	Sets the default route to be propagated to all OSPF routers.
`Router(config-router)#default-information originate always`	The **always** option propagates a default "quad-zero" route even if one is not configured on this router.

	NOTE The **default-information origi-nate** command or the **default-information originate always** command is usually only to be configured on your "entrance" or "gateway" router, the router that connects your network to the outside world—the Autonomous System Boundary Router (ASBR).

Verifying OSPF Configuration

Router#**show ip protocol**	Displays parameters for all protocols running on the router
Router#**show ip route**	Displays a complete IP routing table
Router#**show ip ospf**	Displays basic information about OSPF routing processes
Router#**show ip ospf interface**	Displays OSPF info as it relates to all interfaces
Router#**show ip ospf interface fastethernet 0/0**	Displays OSPF information for interface fastethernet 0/0
Router#**show ip ospf border-routers**	Displays border and boundary router information
Router#**show ip ospf neighbor**	Lists all OSPF neighbors and their states
Router#**show ip ospf neighbor detail**	Displays a detailed list of neighbors
Router#**show ip ospf database**	Displays contents of the OSPF database
Router#**show ip ospf database nssa-external**	Displays NSSA external link states

Troubleshooting OSPF

Router#**clear ip route ***	Clears entire routing table, forcing it to rebuild
Router#**clear ip route a.b.c.d**	Clears specific route to network a.b.c.d
Router#**clear ip opsf counters**	Resets OSPF counters
Router#**clear ip ospf process**	Resets *entire* OSPF process, forcing OSPF to re-create neighbors, database, and routing table
Router#**debug ip ospf events**	Displays *all* OSPF events
Router#**debug ip ospf adja-cency**	Displays various OSPF states and DR/BDR election between adjacent routers
Router#**debug ip ospf packets**	Displays OPSF packets

Configuration Example: Single Area OSPF

Figure 9-1 illustrates the network topology for the configuration that follows, which shows how to configure Single Area OSPF using commands covered in this chapter.

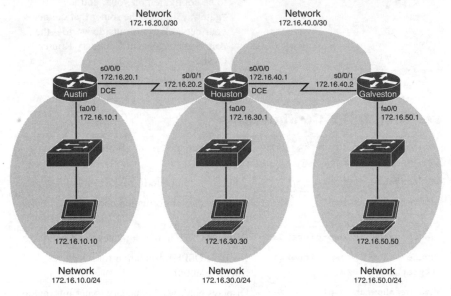

Figure 9-1   Network Topology for Single Area OSPF Configuration

Austin Router

Router>**enable**	Moves to privileged mode.
Router#**configure terminal**	Moves to global configuration mode.
Router(config)#**hostname Austin**	Sets the host name.
Austin(config)#**interface fastethernet 0/0**	Moves to interface configuration mode.
Austin(config-if)#**ip address 172.16.10.1 255.255.255.0**	Assigns an IP address and netmask.
Austin(config-if)#**no shutdown**	Enables the interface.
Austin(config-if)#**interface serial 0/0/0**	Moves to interface configuration mode.
Austin(config-if)#**ip address 172.16.20.1 255.255.255.252**	Assigns an IP address and netmask.
Austin(config-if)#**clock rate 56000**	DCE cable plugged in this side.
Austin(config-if)#**no shutdown**	Enables the interface.
Austin(config-if)#**exit**	Returns to global configuration mode.
Austin(config)#**router ospf 1**	Starts OSPF process 1.

`Austin(config-router)#network 172.16.10.0 0.0.0.255 area 0`	Any interface with an address of 172.16.10.*x* is to be put into area 0.
`Austin(config-router)#network 172.16.20.0 0.0.0.255 area 0`	Any interface with an address of 172.16.20.*x* is to be put into area 0.
`Austin(config-router)#<ctrl> z`	Returns to privileged mode.
`Austin#copy running-config startup-config`	Saves the configuration to NVRAM.

Houston Router

`Router>enable`	Moves to privileged mode.
`Router#configure terminal`	Moves to global configuration mode.
`Router(config)#hostname Houston`	Sets the host name.
`Houston(config)#interface fastethernet 0/0`	Moves to interface configuration mode.
`Houston(config-if)#ip address 172.16.30.1 255.255.255.0`	Assigns an IP address and netmask.
`Houston(config-if)#no shutdown`	Enables the interface.
`Houston(config-if)#interface serial0/0/0`	Moves to interface configuration mode.
`Houston(config-if)#ip address 172.16.40.1 255.255.255.252`	Assigns an IP address and netmask.
`Houston(config-if)#clock rate 56000`	DCE cable plugged in this side.
`Houston(config-if)#no shutdown`	Enables the interface.
`Houston(config)#interface serial 0/0/1`	Moves to interface configuration mode.
`Houston(config-if)#ip address 172.16.20.2 255.255.255.252`	Assigns an IP address and netmask.
`Houston(config-if)#no shutdown`	Enables the interface.
`Houston(config-if)#exit`	Returns to global configuration mode.
`Houston(config)#router ospf 1`	Starts OSPF process 1.
`Houston(config-router)#network 172.16.0.0 0.0.255.255 area 0`	Any interface with an address of 172.16.*x.x* is to be put into area 0. One statement will now advertise all three interfaces.
`Houston(config-router)#<ctrl> z`	Returns to privileged mode.

Houston#copy running-config startup-config	Saves the configuration to NVRAM.

Galveston Router

Router>enable	Moves to privileged mode.
Router#configure terminal	Moves to global configuration mode.
Router(config)#hostname Galveston	Sets the host name.
Galveston(config)#interface fastethernet 0/0	Moves to interface configuration mode.
Galveston(config-if)#ip address 172.16.50.1 255.255.255.0	Assigns an IP address and netmask.
Galveston(config-if)#no shutdown	Enables the interface.
Galveston(config-if)#interface serial 0/0/1	Moves to interface configuration mode.
Galveston(config-if)#ip address 172.16.40.2 255.255.255.252	Assigns an IP address and netmask.
Galveston(config-if)#no shutdown	Enables the interface.
Galveston(config-if)#exit	Returns to global configuration mode.
Galveston(config)#router ospf 1	Starts OSPF process 1.
Galveston(config-router)#network 172.16.40.2 0.0.0.0 area 0	Any interface with an exact address of 172.16.40.2 is to be put into area 0. This is the most precise way to place an exact address into the OSPF routing process.
Galveston(config-router)#network 172.16.50.1 0.0.0.0 area 0	Any interface with an exact address of 172.16.50.2 is to be put into area 0.
Galveston(config-router)#<ctrl> z	Returns to privileged mode.
Galveston#copy running-config startup-config	Saves the configuration to NVRAM.

CHAPTER 10

Multi-Area OSPF

This chapter provides information and commands concerning the following topics:

- Configuring multi-area OSPF
- Passive interfaces
- Route summarization
- Inter-area summarization
- External route summarization
- Configuration example: Multi-area OSPF

Configuring Multi-Area OSPF

`Router(config)#router ospf 1`	Starts OSPF process 1. The process ID is any positive integer value between 1 and 65,535. The process ID is *not* related to the OSPF area. The process ID merely distinguishes one process from another within the device.
`Router(config-router)#network 172.16.10.0 0.0.0.255 area 0`	Read this line to say "Any interface with an address of 172.16.10.*x* is to be put into area 0."
`Router(config-router)#network 10.10.10.1 0.0.0.0 area 51`	Read this line to say "Any interface with an exact address of 10.10.10.1 is to be put into area 51."

NOTE You can enable OSPF directly on an interface with the **ip ospf** *process ID* **area** *area number* command. Because this command is configured directly on the interface, it takes precedence over the **network area** command entered in router configuration mode.

TIP If you have problems determining which wildcard mask to use to place your interfaces into an OSPF area, use the **ip ospf** *process ID* **area** *area number* command directly on the interface.

`Router(config)#interface fastethernet 0/0`	Moves to interface configuration mode
`Router(config-if)#ip ospf 1 area 51`	Places this interface into area 1 of OSPF process 1
`Router(config-if)#interface gigabitethernet 0/0`	Moves to interface configuration mode
`Router(config-if)#ip ospf 1 area 0`	Places this interface into area 0 of OSPF process 1

TIP   If you assign interfaces to OSPF areas without first using the **router ospf** *x* command, the router creates the router process for you, and it will show up in a **show running-config** output.

NOTE   You do not need to create two separate OSPF processes to create multi-area OSPF. You have one process, and merely have two (or more) network statements that are placing different links (interfaces) into different areas.

CAUTION   Creating two separate processes of OSPF means that the router will have two sets of neighbor tables, two link-state databases, and two routing tables. They will be independent of each other and will not communicate with each other. This is a huge waste of router resources.

Passive Interfaces

`Router(config)#router ospf 1`	Starts OSPF process 1.
`Router(config-router)#network 172.16.10.0 0.0.0.255 area 0`	Read this line to say "Any interface with an address of 172.16.10.*x* is to be put into area 0."
`Router(config-router)#passive-interface fastethernet 0/0`	Disables the sending of routing updates on this interface.
`Router(config-router)#passive-interface default`	Disables the sending of routing updates out all interfaces.
`Router(config-router)#no passive-interface serial 0/0/1`	Enables routing updates to be sent out interface serial 0/0/1, thereby allowing neighbor adjacencies to form.

TIP   With OSPF running on a network, the **passive-interface** command will stop the sending or receiving of routing updates on either an interface or globally. Because of this, routers will not become neighbors. To verify whether any interface has been configured as passive, use the **show ip protocols** command.

Route Summarization

In OSPF, there are two different types of summarization:

- Interarea route summarization
- External route summarization

The sections that follow provide the commands necessary to configure both types of summarization.

Interarea Route Summarization

`Router(config)#`**`router ospf 1`**	Starts OSPF process 1.
`Router(config-router)#`**`area`** `1 range 192.168.64.0` `255.255.224.0`	Area Border Router (ABR) will consolidate routes to this summary address before injecting them into a different area.
	NOTE This command is to be configured on an ABR only.
	NOTE By default, ABRs do *not* summarize routes between areas.

External Route Summarization

`Router(config)#`**`router ospf`** `123`	Starts OSPF process 1.
`Router(config-` `router)#`**`summary-address`** `192.168.64.0 255.255.224.0`	Advertises a single route for all the redistributed routes that are covered by a specified network address and netmask.
	NOTE This command is to be configured on an Autonomous System Border Router (ASBR) only.
	NOTE By default, ASBRs do *not* summarize routes.

Configuration Example: Multi-Area OSPF

Figure 10-1 shows the network topology for the configuration that follows, which demonstrates how to configure multi-area OSPF using the commands covered in this chapter.

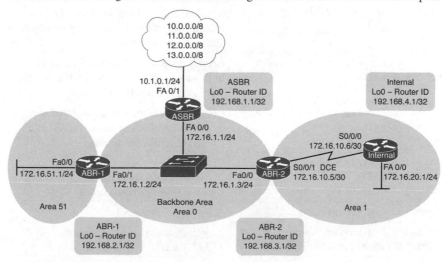

Figure 10-1   Network Topology for Multi-Area OSPF Configuration

ASBR Router

`Router>`**`enable`**	Moves to privileged mode.
`Router#`**`configure terminal`**	Moves to global configuration mode.
`Router(config)#`**`hostname ASBR`**	Sets the router host name.
`ASBR(config)#`**`interface loopback 0`**	Enters loopback interface mode.
`ASBR(config-if)#`**`ip address 192.168.1.1 255.255.255.255`**	Assigns an IP address and netmask.
`ASBR(config-if)#`**`description Router ID`**	Sets a locally significant description.
`ASBR(config-if)#`**`exit`**	Returns to global configuration mode.
`ASBR(config)#`**`interface fastethernet 0/0`**	Enters interface configuration mode.
`ASBR(config-if)#`**`ip address 172.16.1.1 255.255.255.0`**	Assigns an IP address and netmask.
`ASBR(config-if)#`**`no shutdown`**	Enables the interface.
`ASBR(config-if)#`**`interface fastethernet 0/1`**	Enters interface configuration mode.
`ASBR(config-if)#`**`ip address 10.1.0.1 255.255.255.0`**	Assigns an IP address and netmask.
`ASBR(config-if)#`**`no keepalive`**	Disables keepalive packets from being sent. This prevents the interface from going down due to no keepalive packets being received.
`ASBR(config-if)#`**`no shutdown`**	Enables the interface.
`ASBR(config-if)#`**`exit`**	Returns to global configuration mode.
`ASBR(config)#`**`ip route 0.0.0.0 0.0.0.0 10.1.0.2 fa0/1`**	Creates default route. Using both an exit interface and next-hop address on a Fast Ethernet interface prevents recursive look-ups in the routing table.
`ASBR(config)#`**`ip route 11.0.0.0 0.0.0.0 null0`**	Creates a static route to a null interface. In this example, these routes represent a simulated remote destination.
`ASBR(config)#`**`ip route 12.0.0.0 0.0.0.0 null0`**	Creates a static route to a null interface. In this example, these routes represent a simulated remote destination.
`ASBR(config)#`**`ip route 13.0.0.0 0.0.0.0 null0`**	Creates a static route to a null interface. In this example, these routes represent a simulated remote destination.
`ASBR(config)#`**`router ospf 1`**	Starts OPSF process 1.
`ASBR(config-router)#`**`network 172.16.1.0 0.0.0.255 area 0`**	Any interface with an address of 172.16.1.x is to be put into area 0.

`ASBR(config-router)#`**`default-`** **`information originate`**	Sets the default route to be propagated to all OSPF routers.
`ASBR(config-router)#`**`redistribute`** **`static`**	Redistributes static routes into the OSPF process. This turns the router into an ASBR because static routes are not part of OSPF, and the definition of an ASBR is a router that sits between OSPF and another routing process (in this case, static routing).
`ASBR(config-router)#`**`exit`**	Returns to global configuration mode.
`ASBR(config)#`**`exit`**	Returns to privileged mode.
`ASBR#`**`copy running-config`** **`startup-config`**	Saves the configuration to NVRAM.

ABR-1 Router

`Router>`**`enable`**	Moves to privileged mode.
`Router#`**`configure terminal`**	Moves to global configuration mode.
`Router(config)#`**`hostname ABR-1`**	Sets the router host name.
`ABR-1(config)#`**`interface`** **`loopback 0`**	Enters loopback interface mode.
`ABR-1(config-if)#`**`ip address`** **`192.168.2.1 255.255.255.255`**	Assigns an IP address and netmask.
`ABR-1(config-if)#`**`description`** **`Router ID`**	Sets a locally significant description.
`ABR-1(config-if)#`**`exit`**	Returns to global configuration mode.
`ABR-1(config)#`**`interface`** **`fastethernet 0/1`**	Enters interface configuration mode.
`ABR-1(config-if)#`**`ip address`** **`172.16.1.2 255.255.255.0`**	Assigns an IP address and netmask.
`ABR-1(config-if)#`**`ip ospf`** **`priority 200`**	Sets the priority for the designated router/back-up designated router (DR/BDR) election process. This router will win and become the DR.
`ABR-1(config-if)#`**`no shutdown`**	Enables the interface.
`ABR-1(config-if)#`**`exit`**	Returns to global configuration mode.
`ABR-1(config)#`**`interface`** **`fastethernet 0/0`**	Enters interface configuration mode.
`ABR-1(config-if)#`**`ip address`** **`172.16.51.1 255.255.255.0`**	Assigns an IP address and netmask.
`ABR-1(config-if)#`**`no shutdown`**	Enables the interface.
`ABR-1(config-if)#`**`exit`**	Returns to global configuration mode.
`ABR-1(config)#`**`router ospf 1`**	Starts OPSF process 1.

`ABR-1(config-router)#network` `172.16.1.0 0.0.0.255 area 0`	Any interface with an address of 172.16.1.x is to be put into area 0.
`ABR-1(config-router)#network` `172.16.51.1 0.0.0.0 area 51`	Any interface with an exact address of 172.16.51.1 is to be put into area 51.
`ABR-1(config-router)#exit`	Returns to global configuration mode.
`ABR-1(config)#exit`	Returns to privileged mode.
`ABR-1(config)#copy running-` `config startup-config`	Saves the configuration to NVRAM.

ABR-2 Router

`Router>enable`	Moves to privileged mode.
`Router#configure terminal`	Moves to global configuration mode.
`Router(config)#hostname ABR-2`	Sets the router host name.
`ABR-2(config)#interface loopback 0`	Enters loopback interface mode.
`ABR-2(config-if)#ip address` `192.168.3.1 255.255.255.255`	Assigns an IP address and netmask.
`ABR-2(config-if)#description` `Router ID`	Sets a locally significant description.
`ABR-2(config-if)#exit`	Returns to global configuration mode.
`ABR-2(config)#interface` `fastethernet 0/0`	Enters interface configuration mode.
`ABR-2(config-if)#ip address` `172.16.1.3 255.255.255.0`	Assigns an IP address and netmask.
`ABR-2(config-if)#ip ospf` `priority 100`	Sets the priority for the DR/BDR election process. This router will become the BDR to ABR-1's DR.
`ABR-2(config-if)#no shutdown`	Enables the interface.
`ABR-2(config-if)#exit`	Returns to global configuration mode.
`ABR-2(config)#interface serial` `0/0/1`	Enters interface configuration mode.
`ABR-2(config-if)#ip address` `172.16.10.5 255.255.255.252`	Assigns an IP address and netmask.
`ABR-2(config-if)#clock rate 56000`	Assigns a clock rate to the interface.
`ABR-2(config-if)#no shutdown`	Enables the interface.
`ABR-2(config-if)#exit`	Returns to global configuration mode.
`ABR-2(config)#router ospf 1`	Starts OPSF process 1.
`ABR-2(config-router)#network` `172.16.1.0 0.0.0.255 area 0`	Any interface with an address of 172.16.1.x is to be put into area 0.

`ABR-2(config-router)#`**`network`** **`172.16.10.4 0.0.0.3 area 1`**	Any interface with an address of 172.16.10.4–7 is to be put into area 1.
`ABR-2(config-router)#`**`exit`**	Returns to global configuration mode.
`ABR-2(config)#`**`exit`**	Returns to privileged mode.
`ABR-2(config)#`**`copy running-config`** **`startup-config`**	Saves the configuration to NVRAM.

Internal Router

`Router>`**`enable`**	Moves to privileged mode.
`Router#`**`configure terminal`**	Moves to global configuration mode.
`Router(config)#`**`hostname Internal`**	Sets the router host name.
`Internal(config)#`**`interface loopback 0`**	Enters loopback interface mode.
`Internal(config-if)#`**`ip address`** **`192.168.4.1 255.255.255.255`**	Assigns an IP address and netmask.
`Internal(config-if)#`**`description`** **`Router ID`**	Sets a locally significant description.
`Internal(config-if)#`**`exit`**	Returns to global configuration mode.
`Internal(config)#`**`interface`** **`fastethernet0/0`**	Enters interface configuration mode.
`Internal(config-if)#`**`ip address`** **`172.16.20.1 255.255.255.0`**	Assigns an IP address and netmask.
`Internal(config-if)#`**`no shutdown`**	Enables the interface.
`Internal(config-if)#`**`exit`**	Returns to global configuration mode.
`Internal(config)#`**`interface`** **`serial0/0/0`**	Enters interface configuration mode.
`Internal(config-if)#`**`ip address`** **`172.16.10.6 255.255.255.252`**	Assigns an IP address and netmask.
`Internal(config-if)#`**`no shutdown`**	Enables the interface.
`Internal(config-if)#`**`exit`**	Returns to global configuration mode.
`Internal(config)#`**`router ospf 1`**	Starts OPSF process 1.
`Internal(config-router)#`**`network`** **`172.16.0.0 0.0.255.255 area 1`**	Any interface with an address of 172.16.*x.x* is to be put into area 0.
`Internal(config-router)#`**`exit`**	Returns to global configuration mode.
`Internal(config)#`**`exit`**	Returns to privileged mode.
`Internal(config)#`**`copy running-config`** **`startup-config`**	Saves the configuration to NVRAM.

CHAPTER 11

Configuring a Switch

This chapter provides information and commands concerning the following topics:

- Help commands
- Command modes
- Verifying commands
- Resetting switch configuration
- Setting host names
- Setting passwords
- Setting IP addresses and default gateways
- Setting interface descriptions
- The **mdix auto** command
- Setting duplex operation
- Setting operation speed
- Managing the MAC address table
- Configuring static MAC addresses
- Switch port security
- Verifying switch port security
- Sticky MAC addresses
- Configuration example

Help Commands

switch>?	The **?** works here the same as in a router.

Command Modes

switch>**enable**	User mode, same as a router
switch#	Privileged mode
switch#**disable**	Leaves privileged mode
switch>**exit**	Leaves user mode

Verifying Commands

switch#**show version**	Displays information about software and hardware.
switch#**show flash:**	Displays information about flash memory.
switch#**show mac-address-table**	Displays the current MAC address forwarding table.
switch#**show controllers ethernet-controller**	Displays information about the Ethernet controller.
switch#**show running-config**	Displays the current configuration in DRAM.
switch#**show startup-config**	Displays the current configuration in NVRAM.
switch#**show post**	Displays whether the switch passed POST.
switch#**show vlan**	Displays the current VLAN configuration.
switch#**show interfaces**	Displays the interface configuration and status of line: up/up, up/down, admin down.
	NOTE This command is unsupported in some Cisco IOS Software releases, such as 12.2(25)FX.
switch#**show interface vlan1**	Displays setting of virtual interface VLAN 1, the default VLAN on the switch.
	NOTE This command is unsupported in some Cisco IOS Software releases, such as 12.2(25)FX.

Resetting Switch Configuration

Switch#**delete flash:vlan.dat**	Removes the VLAN database from flash memory.
Delete filename [vlan.dat]?	Press ⏎Enter.
Delete flash:vlan.dat? [confirm]	Reconfirm by pressing ⏎Enter.
Switch#**erase startup-config**	Erases the file from NVRAM.
<output omitted>	
Switch#**reload**	Restarts the switch.

Setting Host Names

Switch#**configure terminal**	Moves to global configuration mode.
Switch(config)#**hostname 2960Switch**	Creates a locally significant host name of the switch. This is the same command as the router.
2960Switch(config)#	

Setting Passwords

Setting passwords for the 2960 series switches is the same method as used for a router.

2960Switch(config)#**enable password cisco**	Sets the enable password to cisco
2960Switch(config)#**enable secret class**	Sets the encrypted secret password to class
2960Switch(config)#**line console 0**	Enters line console mode
2960Switch(config-line)#**login**	Enables password checking
2960Switch(config-line)#**password cisco**	Sets the password to cisco
2960Switch(config-line)#**exit**	Exits line console mode
2960Switch(config-line)#**line aux 0**	Enters line auxiliary mode
2960Switch(config-line)#**login**	Enables password checking
2960Switch(config-line)#**password cisco**	Sets the password to cisco
2960Switch(config-line)#**exit**	Exits line auxiliary mode
2960Switch(config-line)#**line vty 0 15**	Enters line vty mode for all 15 virtual ports
2960Switch(config-line)#**login**	Enables password checking
2960Switch(config-line)#**password cisco**	Sets the password to cisco
2960Switch(config-line)#**exit**	Exits line vty mode
2960Switch(config)#	

Setting IP Addresses and Default Gateways

2960Switch(config)#**interface vlan1**	Enters the virtual interface for VLAN 1, the default VLAN on the switch
2960Switch(config-if)#**ip address** **172.16.10.2 255.255.255.0**	Sets the IP address and netmask to allow for remote access to the switch
2960Switch(config-if)#**exit**	
2960Switch(config)#**ip default-gateway** **172.16.10.1**	Allows IP information an exit past the local network

TIP For the 2960 series switches, the IP address of the switch is just that—the IP address for the *entire* switch. That is why you set the address in VLAN 1 (the default VLAN of the switch) and not in a specific Ethernet interface. If you choose to make your management VLAN a different number, you would use these commands in that VLAN using the **interface vlan** x command, where x is the number of your management VLAN.

Setting Interface Descriptions

2960Switch(config)#**interface fastethernet 0/1**	Enters interface configuration mode.
2960Switch(config-if)#**description Finance VLAN**	Adds a description of the interface. The description is locally significant only.

TIP   The 2960 series switches have either 12 or 24 Fast Ethernet ports named fa0/1, fa0/2, ... fa0/24—there is no fastethernet 0/0.

The mdix auto Command

2960Switch(config)#**interface fastethernet 0/1**	Enters interface configuration mode
2960Switch(config-if)#**mdix auto**	Enables Auto-MDIX on the interface
2960Switch(config-if)#**no mdix auto**	Disables Auto-MDIX on the interface

TIP   When automatic medium-dependent interface crossover (Auto-MDIX) is enabled on an interface, the interface automatically detects the required cable connection type (straight-through or crossover) and configures the connection appropriately. When connecting switches without the Auto-MDIX feature, you must use straight-through cables to connect to devices such as servers, workstations, or routers and crossover cables to connect to other switches or repeaters. With Auto-MDIX enabled, you can use either type of cable to connect to other devices, and the interface automatically corrects for any incorrect cabling.

TIP   The Auto-MDIX feature is enabled by default on switches running Cisco IOS Release 12.2(18)SE or later. For releases between Cisco IOS Release 12.1(14)EA1 and 12.2(18)SE, the Auto-MDIX feature is disabled by default.

TIP   If you are working on a device where Auto-MDIX is enabled by default, the command will *not* show up when you enter **show running-config**.

CAUTION   When you enable Auto-MDIX, you must also set the interface speed and duplex to auto so that the feature operates correctly. In other words, if you use Auto-MDIX to give you the flexibility to use either type of cable to connect your switches, you lose the ability to hard-set the speed/duplex on both sides of the link.

The following table shows the different link state results from Auto-MDIX settings with correct and incorrect cabling

Local Side Auto-MDIX	Remote Side Auto-MDIX	With Correct Cabling	With Incorrect Cabling
On	On	Link up	Link up
On	Off	Link up	Link up
Off	On	Link up	Link up
Off	Off	Link up	Link down

Setting Duplex Operation

`2960Switch2960Switch(config)` `#interface fastethernet 0/1`	Moves to interface configuration mode
`2960Switch(config-if)#duplex full`	Forces full-duplex operation
`2960Switch(config-if)#duplex auto`	Enables auto-duplex config
`2960Switch(config-if)#duplex half`	Forces half-duplex operation

Setting Operation Speed

`2960Switch(config)#interface` `fastethernet 0/1`	Moves to interface configuration mode
`2960Switch(config-if)#speed 10`	Forces 10-Mbps operation
`2960Switch(config-if)#speed 100`	Forces 100-Mbps operation
`2960Switch(config-if)#speed auto`	Enables autospeed configuration

Managing the MAC Address Table

`switch#show mac address-table`	Displays current MAC address forwarding table
`switch#clear mac address-table`	Deletes all entries from current MAC address forwarding table
`switch#clear mac address-table dynamic`	Deletes only dynamic entries from table

Configuring Static MAC Addresses

`2960Switch(config)#mac address-table static aaaa.aaaa.aaaa vlan 1 interface fastethernet 0/1`	Sets a permanent address to port fastethernet 0/1 in VLAN 1
`2960Switch(config)#no mac address-table static aaaa.aaaa.aaaa vlan 1 interface fastethernet 0/1`	Removes the permanent address to port fastethernet 0/1 in VLAN 1

Switch Port Security

`Switch(config)#interface fastethernet 0/1`	Moves to interface configuration mode.
`Switch(config-if)#switchport port-security`	Enables port security on the interface.
`Switch(config-if)#switchport port-security maximum 4`	Sets a maximum limit of four MAC addresses that will be allowed on this port.
	NOTE The maximum number of secure MAC addresses that you can configure on a switch is set by the maximum number of available MAC addresses allowed in the system.
`Switch(config-if)#switchport port-security mac-address 1234.5678.90ab`	Sets a specific secure MAC address 1234.5678.90ab. You can add additional secure MAC addresses up to the maximum value configured.
`Switch(config-if)#switchport port-security violation shutdown`	Configures port security to shut down the interface if a security violation occurs.
	NOTE In shutdown mode, the port is errdisabled, a log entry is made, and manual intervention or errdisable recovery must be used to reenable the interface.
`Switch(config-if)#switchport port-security violation restrict`	Configures port security to restrict mode if a security violation occurs.
	NOTE In restrict mode, frames from a non-allowed address are dropped, and a log entry is made. The interface remains operational.
`Switch(config-if)#switchport port-security violation protect`	Configures port security to protect mode if a security violation occurs.
	NOTE In protect mode, frames from a non-allowed address are dropped, but no log entry is made. The interface remains operational.

Verifying Switch Port Security

`Switch#show port-security`	Displays security information for all interfaces
`Switch#show port-security interface fastethernet 0/5`	Displays security information for interface fastethernet 0/5
`Switch#show port-security address`	Displays MAC address table security information
`Switch#show mac address-table`	Displays the MAC address table
`Switch#clear mac address-table dynamic`	Deletes all dynamic MAC addresses

Switch#**clear mac address-table dynamic address** *aaaa.bbbb.cccc*	Deletes the specified dynamic MAC address
Switch#**clear mac address-table dynamic interface fastethernet 0/5**	Deletes all dynamic MAC addresses on interface fastethernet 0/5
Switch#**clear mac address-table dynamic vlan 10**	Deletes all dynamic MAC addresses on VLAN 10
Switch#**clear mac address-table notification**	Clears MAC notification global counters
	NOTE Beginning with Cisco IOS Software Release 12.1(11)EA1, the **clear mac address-table** command (no hyphen in mac address) replaces the **clear mac-address-table** command (with the hyphen in mac-address). The **clear mac-address-table static** command (with the hyphen in mac-address) will become obsolete in a future release.

Sticky MAC Addresses

Sticky MAC addresses are a feature of port security. Sticky MAC addresses limit switch port access to a specific MAC address that can be dynamically learned, as opposed to a network administrator manually associating a MAC address with a specific switch port. These addresses are stored in the running configuration file. If this file is saved, the sticky MAC addresses do not have to be relearned when the switch is rebooted, and thus provide a high level of switch port security.

Switch(config)#**interface fastethernet 0/5**	Moves to interface configuration mode.
Switch(config-if)#**switchport port-security mac-address sticky**	Converts all dynamic port security learned MAC addresses to sticky secure MAC addresses.
Switch(config-if)#**switchport port-security mac-address sticky vlan 10 voice**	Converts all dynamic port security learned MAC addresses to sticky secure MAC addresses on voice VLAN 10.
	NOTE The voice keyword is available only if a voice VLAN is first configured on a port and if that port is not the access VLAN.

Configuration Example

Figure 11-1 shows the network topology for the basic configuration of a 2960 series switch using commands covered in this chapter.

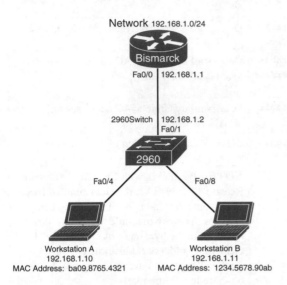

Figure 11-1 Network Topology for 2960 Series Switch Configuration

`switch>`**`enable`**	Enters privileged mode.
`switch#`**`configure terminal`**	Enters global configuration mode.
`switch(config)#`**`no ip domain-lookup`**	Turns off Domain Name System (DNS) queries so that spelling mistakes do not slow you down.
`switch(config)#`**`hostname 2960`**	Sets the host name.
`2960(config)#`**`enable secret cisco`**	Sets the encrypted secret password to cisco.
`2960(config)#`**`line console 0`**	Enters line console mode.
`2960(config-line)#`**`logging synchronous`**	Appends commands to a new line; router information will not interrupt.
`2960(config-line)#`**`login`**	User must log in to console before use.
`2960(config-line)#`**`password switch`**	Sets the password to switch.
`2960(config-line)#`**`exec-timeout 0 0`**	Console will never log out.
`2960(config-line)#`**`exit`**	Moves back to global configuration mode.
`2960(config)#`**`line aux 0`**	Moves to line auxiliary mode.
`2960(config-line)#`**`login`**	User must log in to auxiliary port before use.
`2960(config-line)#`**`password class`**	Sets the password to class.
`2960(config-line)#`**`exit`**	Moves back to global configuration mode.
`2960(config)#`**`line vty 0 15`**	Moves to configure all 16 vty ports at the same time.

`2960(config-line)#login`	User must log in to vty port before use.
`2960(config-line)#password class`	Sets the password to class.
`2960(config-line)#exit`	Moves back to global configuration mode.
`2960(config)#ip default-gateway 192.168.1.1`	Sets default gateway.
`2960(config)#interface vlan 1`	Moves to virtual interface VLAN 1 configuration mode.
`2960(config-if)#ip address 192.168.1.2 255.255.255.0`	Sets the IP address and netmask for switch.
`2960(config-if)#no shutdown`	Turns the virtual interface on.
`2960(config-if)#interface fastethernet 0/1`	Moves to interface configuration mode for fastethernet 0/1.
`2960(config-if)#description Link to Bismarck Router`	Sets a local description.
`2960(config-if)#interface fastethernet 0/4`	Moves to interface configuration mode for fastethernet 0/4.
`2960(config-if)#description Link to Workstation A`	Sets a local description.
`2960(config-if)#switchport port-security`	Activates port security.
`2960(config-if)#switchport port-security maximum 1`	Only one MAC address will be allowed in the MAC table.
`2960(config-if)#switchport port-security violation shutdown`	Port will be turned off if more than one MAC address is reported.
`2960(config-if)#interface fastethernet 0/8`	Moves to interface configuration mode for fastethernet 0/8.
`2960(config-if)#description Link to Workstation B`	Sets a local description.
`2960(config-if)#switchport port-security mac-address 1234.5678.90ab`	Sets a specific secure MAC address 1234.5678.90ab. You can add additional secure MAC addresses up to the maximum value configured.
`2960(config-if)#switchport port-security maximum 1`	Only one MAC address will be allowed in the MAC table.
`2960(config-if)#switchport port-security violation shutdown`	Port will be turned off if more than one MAC address is reported.
`2960(config-if)#exit`	Returns to global configuration mode.
`2960(config)#exit`	Returns to privileged mode.
`2960#copy running-config startup-config`	Saves the configuration to NVRAM.
`2960#`	

CHAPTER 12

VLANs

This chapter provides information and commands concerning the following topics:

- Creating static VLANs
- Using VLAN configuration mode
- Using VLAN database mode
- Assigning ports to VLANs
- Using the **range** command
- Verifying VLAN information
- Saving VLAN configurations
- Erasing VLAN configurations
- Configuration example: VLANs

Creating Static VLANs

Static VLANs occur when a switch port is manually assigned by the network administrator to belong to a VLAN. Each port is associated with a specific VLAN. By default, all ports are originally assigned to VLAN 1. You can create VLANs in two different ways:

- Using the VLAN configuration mode, which is the recommended way to create VLANs
- Using the VLAN database mode (which should not be used but is still available on some older models)

Using VLAN Configuration Mode

Switch(config)#**vlan 3**	Creates VLAN 3 and enters VLAN configuration mode for further definitions.
Switch(config-vlan)#**name Engineering**	Assigns a name to the VLAN. The length of the name can be from 1 to 32 characters.
Switch(config-vlan)#**exit**	Applies changes, increases the revision number by 1, and returns to global configuration mode.
Switch(config)#	

NOTE   This method is the only way to configure extended-range VLANs (VLAN IDs from 1006 to 4094).

NOTE   Regardless of the method used to create VLANs, the VTP revision number is increased by 1 each time a VLAN is created or changed.

Using VLAN Database Mode

CAUTION   The VLAN database mode has been deprecated and will be removed in some future Cisco IOS Software release. It is recommended to use only VLAN configuration mode.

Switch#**vlan database**	Enters VLAN database mode.
Switch(vlan)#**vlan 4 name Sales**	Creates VLAN 4 and names it Sales. The length of the name can be from 1 to 32 characters.
Switch(vlan)#**vlan 10**	Creates VLAN 10 and gives it a name of VLAN0010 as a default.
Switch(vlan)#**apply**	Applies changes to the VLAN database and increases the revision number by 1.
Switch(vlan)#**exit**	Applies changes to the VLAN database, increases the revision number by 1, *and* exits VLAN database mode.
Switch#	

NOTE   You must apply the changes to the VLAN database for the changes to take effect. You must use either the **apply** command or the **exit** command to do so. Using the Ctrl-Z command to exit out of the VLAN database does not work in this mode because it aborts all changes made to the VLAN database—you must either use **exit** or **apply** and then the **exit** command.

Assigning Ports to VLANs

Switch(config)#**interface fastethernet 0/1**	Moves to interface configuration mode
Switch(config-if)#**switchport mode access**	Sets the port to access mode
Switch(config-if)#**switchport access vlan 10**	Assigns this port to VLAN 10

NOTE   When the **switchport mode access** command is used, the port operates as a nontrunking, single VLAN interface that transmits and receives nonencapsulated frames.

TIP   An access port can belong to only one VLAN.

TIP   By default, all ports are members of VLAN 1.

Using the range Command

Switch(config)#interface range fastethernet 0/1 - 9	Enables you to set the same configuration parameters on multiple ports at the same time.
	NOTE Depending on the model of switch, there is a space before and after the hyphen in the **interface range** command. Be careful with your typing.
Switch(config-if-range)#switchport mode access	Sets ports 1–9 as access ports.
Switch(config-if-range)#switchport access vlan 10	Assigns ports 1–9 to VLAN 10.

Verifying VLAN Information

Switch#show vlan	Displays VLAN information
Switch#show vlan brief	Displays VLAN information in brief
Switch#show vlan id 2	Displays information about VLAN 2 only
Switch#show vlan name marketing	Displays information about VLAN named marketing only
Switch#show interfaces vlan x	Displays interface characteristics for the specified VLAN
Switch#show interfaces switchport	Displays VLAN information for all interfaces

Saving VLAN Configurations

The configurations of VLANs 1 through 1005 are always saved in the VLAN database. As long as the **apply** or the **exit** command is executed in VLAN database mode, changes are saved. If you are using VLAN configuration mode, the **exit** command saves the changes to the VLAN database, too.

If the VLAN database configuration is used at startup, and the startup configuration file contains extended-range VLAN configuration, this information is lost when the system boots.

If you are using VTP transparent mode, the configurations are also saved in the running configuration and can be saved to the startup configuration using the **copy running-config startup-config** command.

If the VTP mode is transparent in the startup configuration, and the VLAN database and the VTP domain name from the VLAN database matches that in the startup configuration file, the VLAN database is ignored (cleared), and the VTP and VLAN configurations in the startup configuration file are used. The VLAN database revision number remains unchanged in the VLAN database.

Erasing VLAN Configurations

`Switch#delete` `flash:vlan.dat`	Removes the entire VLAN database from flash.
	WARNING Make sure there is *no* space between the colon (:) and the characters *vlan.dat*. You can potentially erase the entire contents of the flash with this command if the syntax is not correct. Make sure you read the output from the switch. If you need to cancel, press Ctrl-C to escape back to privileged mode: (Switch#) Switch#**delete flash:vlan.dat** Delete filename [vlan.dat]? Delete flash:vlan.dat? [confirm] Switch#
`Switch(config)#interface` `fastethernet 0/5`	Moves to interface configuration mode.
`Switch(config-if)#no` `switchport access vlan 5`	Removes port from VLAN 5 and reassigns it to VLAN 1—the default VLAN.
`Switch(config-if)#exit`	Moves to global configuration mode.
`Switch(config)#no vlan 5`	Removes VLAN 5 from the VLAN database.
Or	
`Switch#vlan database`	Enters VLAN database mode.
`Switch(vlan)#no vlan 5`	Removes VLAN 5 from the VLAN database.
`Switch(vlan)#exit`	Applies changes, increases the revision number by 1, and exits VLAN database mode.

NOTE   When you delete a VLAN from a switch that is in VTP server mode, the VLAN is removed from the VLAN database for all switches in the VTP domain. When you delete a VLAN from a switch that is in VTP transparent mode, the VLAN is deleted only on that specific switch.

NOTE   You cannot delete the default VLANs for the different media types: Ethernet VLAN 1 and FDDI or Token Ring VLANs 1002 to 1005.

CAUTION   When you delete a VLAN, any ports assigned to that VLAN become inactive. They remain associated with the VLAN (and thus inactive) until you assign them to a new VLAN. Therefore, it is recommended that you reassign ports to a new VLAN or the default VLAN before you delete a VLAN from the VLAN database.

Configuration Example: VLANs

Figure 12-1 illustrates the network topology for the configuration that follows, which shows how to configure VLANs using the commands covered in this chapter.

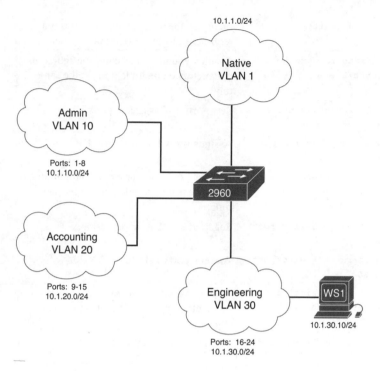

Figure 12-1   Network Topology for VLAN Configuration Example

2960 Switch

`Switch>`**`enable`**	Moves to privileged mode.
`Switch#`**`configure terminal`**	Moves to global configuration mode.
`Switch(config)#`**`hostname 2960`**	Sets the host name.
`2960(config)#`**`vlan 10`**	Creates VLAN 10 and enters VLAN configuration mode.
`2960(config-vlan)#`**`name Admin`**	Assigns a name to the VLAN.
`2960(config-vlan)#`**`exit`**	Increases the revision number by 1 and returns to global configuration mode.
`2960(config)#`**`vlan 20`**	Creates VLAN 20 and enters VLAN configuration mode.
`2960(config-vlan)#`**`name Accounting`**	Assigns a name to the VLAN.
`2960(config-vlan)#`**`vlan 30`**	Creates VLAN 30 and enters VLAN configuration mode. Note that you do not have to exit back to global configuration mode to execute this command.
`2960(config-vlan)#`**`name Engineering`**	Assigns a name to the VLAN.

`2960(config-vlan)#exit`	Increases the revision number by 1 and returns to global configuration mode.
`2960(config)#interface range fasthethernet 0/1 - 8`	Enables you to set the same configuration parameters on multiple ports at the same time.
`2960(config-if-range)#switchport mode access`	Sets ports 1–8 as access ports.
`2960(config-if-range)#switchport access vlan 10`	Assigns ports 1–8 to VLAN 10.
`2960(config-if-range)#interface range fastethernet 0/9 - 15`	Enables you to set the same configuration parameters on multiple ports at the same time.
`2960(config-if-range)#switchport mode access`	Sets ports 9–15 as access ports.
`2960(config-if-range)#switchport access vlan 20`	Assigns ports 9–15 to VLAN 20.
`2960(config-if-range)#interface range fastethernet 0/16 - 24`	Enables you to set the same configuration parameters on multiple ports at the same time.
`2960(config-if-range)#switchport mode access`	Sets ports 16–24 as access ports.
`2960(config-if-range)#switchport access vlan 30`	Assigns ports 16–24 to VLAN 30.
`2960(config-if-range)#exit`	Returns to global configuration mode.
`2960(config)#exit`	Returns to privileged mode.
`2960#copy running-config startup-config`	Saves the configuration in NVRAM.

VLAN Trunking Protocol and Inter-VLAN Communication

This chapter provides information and commands concerning the following topics:

- Dynamic Trunking Protocol (DTP)
- Setting the encapsulation type
- VLAN Trunking Protocol (VTP)
- Using global configuration mode
- Using VLAN database mode
- Verifying VTP
- Inter-VLAN communication using an external router: Router-on-a-stick
- Inter-VLAN communication on a multilayer switch through a switch virtual interface (SVI)
- Removing L2 switchport capability of a switch port
- Configuring Inter-VLAN communication
- Inter-VLAN communication tips
- Configuration example: Inter-VLAN communication

Dynamic Trunking Protocol

`Switch(config)#interface fastethernet 0/1`	Moves to interface configuration mode.
`Switch(config-if)#switchport mode dynamic desirable`	Makes the interface actively attempt to convert the link to a trunk link.
	NOTE With the **switchport mode dynamic desirable** command set, the interface becomes a trunk link if the neighboring interface is set to **trunk**, **desirable**, or **auto**.
`Switch(config-if)#switchport mode dynamic auto`	Makes the interface able to convert into a trunk link.
	NOTE With the **switchport mode dynamic auto** command set, the interface becomes a trunk link if the neighboring interface is set to **trunk** or **desirable**.
`Switch(config-if)#switchport nonegotiate`	Prevents the interface from generating DTP frames.

	NOTE Use the **switchport mode nonegotiate** command only when the interface switchport mode is **access** or **trunk**. You must manually configure the neighboring interface to establish a trunk link.
`Switch(config-if)#switchport mode trunk`	Puts the interface into permanent trunking mode and negotiates to convert the link into a trunk link.
	NOTE With the **switchport mode trunk** command set, the interface becomes a trunk link even if the neighboring interface is not a trunk link.

Dynamic Trunking Protocol (DTP)

TIP   The default mode is dependent on the platform. For the 2960, the default mode is dynamic auto.

TIP   On a 2960 switch, the default for all ports is to be an access port. However, with the default DTP mode being dynamic auto, an access port can be converted into a trunk port if that port receives DTP information from the other side of the link if that other side is set to **trunk** or **desirable**. It is therefore recommended to hard-code all access ports as access ports with the **switchport mode access** command. This way, DTP information will not inadvertently change an access port to a trunk port. Any port set with the **switchport mode access** command ignores any DTP requests to convert the link.

Setting the Encapsulation Type

Depending on the series of switch that you are using, you might have a choice as to what type of VLAN encapsulation you want to use: the Cisco proprietary Inter-Switch Link (ISL) or the IEEE Standard 802.1q (dot1q). The 2960 switch supports only dot1q trunking.

`3560Switch(config)#interface fastethernet 0/1`	Moves to interface configuration mode
`3560Switch(config-if)#switchport mode trunk`	Puts the interface into permanent trunking mode and negotiates to convert the link into a trunk link
`3560Switch(config-if)#switchport trunk encapsulation isl`	Specifies ISL encapsulation on the trunk link
`3560Switch(config-if)#switchport trunk encapsulation dot1q`	Specifies 802.1q encapsulation on the trunk link
`3560Switch(config-if)#switchport trunk encapsulation negotiate`	Specifies that the interface negotiate with the neighboring interface to become either an ISL or dot1q trunk, depending on the capabilities or configuration of the neighboring interface

TIP   With the **switchport trunk encapsulation negotiate** command set, the preferred trunking method is ISL.

CAUTION   The 2960 series switch supports only dot1q trunking.

VLAN Trunking Protocol (VTP)

VTP is a Cisco proprietary protocol that allows for VLAN configuration (addition, deletion, or renaming of VLANs) to be consistently maintained across a common administrative domain.

`Switch(config)#`**`vtp mode`** `client`	Changes the switch to VTP client mode.
`Switch(config)#`**`vtp mode`** `server`	Changes the switch to VTP server mode.
`Switch(config)#`**`vtp mode`** `transparent`	Changes the switch to VTP transparent mode.
	NOTE By default, all Catalyst switches are in server mode.
`Switch(config)#`**`no vtp mode`**	Returns the switch to the default VTP server mode.
`Switch(config)#`**`vtp domain`** *domain-name*	Configures the VTP domain name. The name can be from 1 to 32 characters long.
	NOTE All switches operating in VTP server or client mode must have the same domain name to ensure communication.
`Switch(config)#`**`vtp password`** *password*	Configures a VTP password. In Cisco IOS Software Release 12.3 and later, the password is an ASCII string from 1 to 32 characters long. If you are using a Cisco IOS Software release earlier than 12.3, the password length ranges from 8 to 64 characters long.
	NOTE To communicate with each other, all switches must have the same VTP password set.
`Switch(config)#`**`vtp v2-mode`**	Sets the VTP domain to Version 2. This command is for Cisco IOS Software Release 12.3 and later. If you are using a Cisco IOS Software release earlier than 12.3, the command is **vtp version 2**.
	NOTE VTP Versions 1 and 2 are not interoperable. All switches must use the same version. The biggest difference between Versions 1 and 2 is that Version 2 has support for Token Ring VLANs.
`Switch(config)#`**`vtp pruning`**	Enables VTP pruning.
	NOTE By default, VTP pruning is disabled. You need to enable VTP pruning on only 1 switch in VTP server mode.

NOTE   Only VLANs included in the pruning-eligible list can be pruned. VLANs 2 through 1001 are pruning eligible by default on trunk ports. Reserved VLANs and extended-range VLANs cannot be pruned. To change which eligible VLANs can be pruned, use the interface-specific **switchport trunk pruning vlan** command:

```
Switch(config-if)#switchport trunk pruning vlan remove 4, 20-30
! Removes VLANs 4 and 20-30
Switch(config-if)#switchport trunk pruning vlan except 40-50
! All VLANs are added to the pruning list except for 40-50
```

Verifying VTP

Switch#**show vtp status**	Displays general information about VTP configuration
Switch#**show vtp counters**	Displays the VTP counters for the switch

NOTE   If trunking has been established before VTP is set up, VTP information is propagated throughout the switch fabric almost immediately. However, because VTP information is advertised only every 300 seconds (5 minutes), unless a change has been made to force an update, it can take several minutes for VTP information to be propagated.

Inter-VLAN Communication Using an External Router: Router-on-a-Stick

Router(config)#**interface fastethernet 0/0**	Moves to interface configuration mode.
Router(config-if)#**duplex full**	Sets the interface to full duplex.
Router(config-if)#**no shutdown**	Enables the interface.
Router(config-if)#**interface fastethernet 0/0.1**	Creates subinterface 0/0.1 and moves to subinterface configuration mode.
Router(config-subif)#**description Management VLAN 1**	(Optional) Sets the locally significant description of the subinterface.
Router(config-subif)#**encapsulation dot1q 1 native**	Assigns VLAN 1 to this subinterface. VLAN 1 will be the native VLAN. This subinterface will use the 802.1q trunking protocol.
Router(config-subif)#**ip address 192.168.1.1 255.255.255.0**	Assigns the IP address and netmask.
Router(config-subif)#**interface fastethernet 0/0.10**	Creates subinterface 0/0.10 and moves to subinterface configuration mode.
Router(config-subif)#**description Accounting VLAN 10**	(Optional) Sets the locally significant description of the subinterface.
Router(config-subif)#**encapsulation dot1q 10**	Assigns VLAN 10 to this subinterface. This subinterface will use the 802.1q trunking protocol.
Router(config-subif)#**ip address 192.168.10.1 255.255.255.0**	Assigns the IP address and netmask.

`Router(config-subif)#exit`	Returns to interface configuration mode.
`Router(config-if)#exit`	Returns to global configuration mode.
`Router(config)#`	

NOTE The subnets of the VLANs are directly connected to the router. Routing between these subnets does not require a dynamic routing protocol. In a more complex topology, these routes need to either be advertised with whatever dynamic routing protocol is being used or be redistributed into whatever dynamic routing protocol is being used.

NOTE Routes to the subnets associated with these VLANs appear in the routing table as directly connected networks.

NOTE In production environments, VLAN 1 should not be used as the management VLAN because it poses a potential security risk; all ports are in VLAN 1 by default, and it an easy mistake to add a nonmanagement user to the management VLAN.

Inter-VLAN Communication on a Multilayer Switch Through a Switch Virtual Interface

NOTE Rather than using an external router to provide inter-VLAN communication, a multilayer switch can perform the same task through the use of a switched virtual interface (SVI).

Removing L2 Switchport Capability of a Switch Port

`3750Switch(config)#interface fastethernet 0/1`	Moves to interface configuration mode.
`3750Switch(config-if)#no switchport`	Creates a Layer 3 port on the switch.
	NOTE **The no switchport** command can be used on physical ports only on a Layer 3-capable switch.

Configuring Inter-VLAN Communication

`3560Switch(config)#interface vlan 1`	Creates a virtual interface for VLAN 1 and enters interface configuration mode
`3560Switch(config-if)#ip address 172.16.1.1 255.255.255.0`	Assigns IP address and netmask
`3560Switch(config-if)#no shutdown`	Enables the interface
`3560Switch(config)#interface vlan 10`	Creates a virtual interface for VLAN 10 and enters interface configuration mode
`3560Switch(config-if)#ip address 172.16.10.1 255.255.255.0`	Assigns an IP address and netmask
`3560Switch(config-if)#no shutdown`	Enables the interface

3560Switch(config)#**interface vlan 20**	Creates a virtual interface for VLAN 20 and enters interface configuration mode
3560Switch(config-if)#**ip address 172.16.20.1 255.255.255.0**	Assigns an IP address and netmask
3560Switch(config-if)#**no shutdown**	Enables the interface
3560Switch(config-if)#**exit**	Returns to global configuration mode
3560Switch(config)#**ip routing**	Enables routing on the switch

Inter-VLAN Communication Tips

- Although most routers support both ISL and dot1q encapsulation, some switch models only support dot1q, such as the 2960 series.

- If you need to use ISL as your trunking protocol, use the command **encapsulation isl** *x*, where *x* is the number of the VLAN to be assigned to that subinterface.

- Recommended best practice is to use the same number of the VLAN number for the subinterface number. It is easier to troubleshoot VLAN 10 on subinterface fa0/0.10 than on fa0/0.2.

- The native VLAN (usually VLAN 1) cannot be configured on a subinterface for Cisco IOS Software releases that are earlier than 12.1(3)T. Native VLAN IP addresses therefore need to be configured on the physical interface. Other VLAN traffic is configured on subinterfaces:

```
Router(config)#interface fastethernet 0/0
Router(config-if)#encapsulation dot1q 1 native
Router(config-if)#ip address 192.168.1.1 255.255.255.0
Router(config-if)#interface fastethernet 0/0.10
Router(config-subif)#encapsulation dot1q 10
Router(config-subif)#ip address 192.168.10.1 255.255.255.0
```

Configuration Example: Inter-VLAN Communication

Figure 13-1 illustrates the network topology for the configuration that follows, which shows how to configure inter-VLAN communication using commands covered in this chapter. Some commands used in this configuration are from previous chapters.

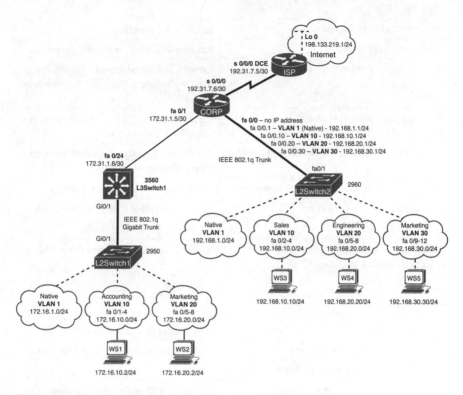

Figure 13-1 Network Topology for Inter-VLAN Communication Configuration

ISP Router

`Router>`**`enable`**	Moves to privileged mode.
`Router>#`**`configure terminal`**	Moves to global configuration mode.
`Router(config)#`**`hostname ISP`**	Sets the host name.
`ISP(config)#`**`interface loopback 0`**	Moves to interface configuration mode.
`ISP(config-if)#`**`description simulated address representing remote website`**	Sets the locally significant interface description.
`ISP(config-if)#`**`ip address 198.133.219.1 255.255.255.0`**	Assigns an IP address and netmask.
`ISP(config-if)#`**`interface serial 0/0/0`**	Moves to interface configuration mode.
`ISP(config-if)#`**`description WAN link to the Corporate Router`**	Sets the locally significant interface description.
`ISP(config-if)#`**`ip address 192.31.7.5 255.255.255.252`**	Assigns an IP address and netmask.
`ISP(config-if)#`**`clock rate 56000`**	Assigns a clock rate to the interface; DCE cable is plugged into this interface.

`ISP(config-if)#no shutdown`	Enables the interface.
`ISP(config-if)#exit`	Returns to global configuration mode.
`ISP(config-if)#router eigrp 10`	Creates Enhanced Interior Gateway Routing Protocol (EIGRP) routing process 10.
`ISP(config-router)#network 198.133.219.0`	Advertises directly connected networks (classful address only).
`ISP(config-router)#network 192.31.7.0`	Advertises directly connected networks (classful address only).
`ISP(config-router)#no auto-summary`	Disables automatic summarization.
`ISP(config-router)#exit`	Returns to global configuration mode.
`ISP(config)#exit`	Returns to privileged mode.
`ISP#copy running-config startup-config`	Saves the configuration to NVRAM.

CORP Router

`Router>enable`	Moves to privileged mode.
`Router>#configure terminal`	Moves to global configuration mode.
`Router(config)#hostname CORP`	Sets the host name.
`CORP(config)#no ip domain-lookup`	Turns off Domain Name System (DNS) resolution to avoid wait time due to DNS lookup of spelling errors.
`CORP(config)#interface serial 0/0/0`	Moves to interface configuration mode.
`CORP(config-if)#description link to ISP`	Sets the locally significant interface description.
`CORP(config-if)#ip address 192.31.7.6 255.255.255.252`	Assigns an IP address and netmask.
`CORP(config-if)#no shutdown`	Enables the interface.
`CORP(config)#interface fastethernet 0/1`	Moves to interface configuration mode.
`CORP(config-if)#description link to 3560 Switch`	Sets the locally significant interface description.
`CORP(config-if)#ip address 172.31.1.5 255.255.255.252`	Assigns an IP address and netmask.
`CORP(config-if)#no shutdown`	Enables the interface.
`CORP(config-if)#exit`	Returns to global configuration mode.
`CORP(config)#interface fastethernet 0/0`	Enters interface configuration mode.
`CORP(config-if)#duplex full`	Enables full-duplex operation to ensure trunking will take effect between here and L2Switch2.
`CORP(config-if)#no shutdown`	Enables the interface.

`CORP(config-if)#interface fastethernet 0/0.1`	Creates a virtual subinterface and moves to subinterface configuration mode.
`CORP(config-subif)#description Management VLAN 1 - Native VLAN`	Sets the locally significant interface description.
`CORP(config-subif)#encapsulation dot1q 1 native`	Assigns VLAN 1 to this subinterface. VLAN 1 will be the native VLAN. This subinterface will use the 802.1q trunking protocol.
`CORP(config-subif)#ip address 192.168.1.1 255.255.255.0`	Assigns an IP address and netmask.
`CORP(config-subif)#interface fastethernet 0/0.10`	Creates a virtual subinterface and moves to subinterface configuration mode.
`CORP(config-subif)#description Sales VLAN 10`	Sets the locally significant interface description.
`CORP(config-subif)#encapsulation dot1q 10`	Assigns VLAN 10 to this subinterface. This subinterface will use the 802.1q trunking protocol.
`CORP(config-subif)#ip address 192.168.10.1 255.255.255.0`	Assigns an IP address and netmask.
`CORP(config-subif)#interface fastethernet 0/0.20`	Creates a virtual subinterface and moves to subinterface configuration mode.
`CORP(config-subif)#description Engineering VLAN 20`	Sets the locally significant interface description.
`CORP(config-subif)#encapsulation dot1q 20`	Assigns VLAN 20 to this subinterface. This subinterface will use the 802.1q trunking protocol.
`CORP(config-subif)#ip address 192.168.20.1 255.255.255.0`	Assigns an IP address and netmask.
`CORP(config-subif)#interface fastethernet 0/0.30`	Creates a virtual subinterface and moves to subinterface configuration mode.
`CORP(config-subif)#description Marketing VLAN 30`	Sets the locally significant interface description.
`CORP(config-subif)#encapsulation dot1q 30`	Assigns VLAN 30 to this subinterface. This subinterface will use the 802.1q trunking protocol.
`CORP(config-subif)#ip add 192.168.30.1 255.255.255.0`	Assigns an IP address and netmask.
`CORP(config-subif)#exit`	Returns to interface configuration mode.
`CORP(config-if)#exit`	Returns to global configuration mode.

`CORP(config)#router eigrp 10`	Creates EIGRP routing process 10 and moves to router configuration mode.
`CORP(config-router)#network 192.168.1.0`	Advertises the 192.168.1.0 network.
`CORP(config-router)#network 192.168.10.0`	Advertises the 192.168.10.0 network.
`CORP(config-router)#network 192.168.20.0`	Advertises the 192.168.20.0 network.
`CORP(config-router)#network 192.168.30.0`	Advertises the 192.168.30.0 network.
`CORP(config-router)#network 172.31.0.0`	Advertises the 172.31.0.0 network.
`CORP(config-router)#network 192.31.7.0`	Advertises the 192.31.7.0 network.
`CORP(config-router)#no auto-summary`	Turns off automatic summarization at classful boundary.
`CORP(config-router)#exit`	Returns to global configuration mode.
`CORP(config)#exit`	Returns to privileged mode.
`CORP#copy running-config startup-config`	Saves the configuration in NVRAM.

L2Switch2 (Catalyst 2960)

`Switch>enable`	Moves to privileged mode.
`Switch#configure terminal`	Moves to global configuration mode.
`Switch(config)#hostname L2Switch2`	Sets the host name.
`L2Switch2(config)#no ip domain-lookup`	Turns off DNS resolution.
`L2Switch2(config)#vlan 10`	Creates VLAN 10 and enters VLAN-configuration mode.
`L2Switch2(config-vlan)#name Sales`	Assigns a name to the VLAN.
`L2Switch2(config-vlan)#exit`	Returns to global configuration mode.
`L2Switch2(config)#vlan 20`	Creates VLAN 20 and enters VLAN configuration mode.
`L2Switch2(config-vlan)#name Engineering`	Assigns a name to the VLAN.
`L2Switch2(config-vlan)#vlan 30`	Creates VLAN 30 and enters VLAN configuration mode. Note that you do not have to exit back to global configuration mode to execute this command.
`L2Switch2(config-vlan)#name Marketing`	Assigns a name to the VLAN.
`L2Switch2(config-vlan)#exit`	Returns to global configuration mode.

L2Switch2(config)#**interface range fastethernet 0/2 - 4**	Enables you to set the same configuration parameters on multiple ports at the same time.
L2Switch2(config-if-range)#**switchport mode access**	Sets ports 2–4 as access ports.
L2Switch2(config-if-range)#**switchport access vlan 10**	Assigns ports 2–4 to VLAN 10.
L2Switch2(config-if-range)#**interface range fastethernet 0/5 - 8**	Enables you to set the same configuration parameters on multiple ports at the same time.
L2Switch2(config-if-range)#**switchport mode access**	Sets ports 5–8 as access ports.
L2Switch2(config-if-range)#**switchport access vlan 20**	Assigns ports 5–8 to VLAN 20.
L2Switch2(config-if-range)#**interface range fastethernet 0/9 - 12**	Enables you to set the same configuration parameters on multiple ports at the same time.
L2Switch2(config-if-range)#**switchport mode access**	Sets ports 9–12 as access ports.
L2Switch2(config-if-range)#**switchport access vlan 30**	Assigns ports 9–12 to VLAN 30.
L2Switch2(config-if-range)#**exit**	Returns to global configuration mode.
L2Switch2(config)#**interface fastethernet 0/1**	Moves to interface configuration mode.
L2Switch2(config)#**description Trunk Link to CORP Router**	Sets the locally significant interface description.
L2Switch2(config-if)#**switchport mode trunk**	Puts the interface into trunking mode and negotiates to convert the link into a trunk link.
L2Switch2(config-if)#**exit**	Returns to global configuration mode.
L2Switch2(config)#**interface vlan 1**	Creates a virtual interface for VLAN 1 and enters interface configuration mode.
L2Switch2(config-if)#**ip address 192.168.1.2 255.255.255.0**	Assigns an IP address and netmask.
L2Switch2(config-if)#**no shutdown**	Enables the interface.
L2Switch2(config-if)#**exit**	Returns to global configuration mode.
L2Switch2(config)#**ip default-gateway 192.168.1.1**	Assigns a default gateway address.
L2Switch2(config)#**exit**	Returns to privileged mode.
L2Switch2#**copy running-config startup-config**	Saves the configuration in NVRAM.

L3Switch1 (Catalyst 3560)

`Switch>enable`	Moves to privileged mode
`Switch#configure terminal`	Moves to global configuration mode
`Switch(config)#hostname L3Switch1`	Sets the hostname
`L3Switch1(config)#no ip domain-lookup`	Turns off DNS queries so that spelling mistakes will not slow you down
`L3Switch1(config)#vtp mode server`	Changes the switch to VTP server mode
`L3Switch1(config)#vtp domain testdomain`	Configures the VTP domain name to testdomain
`L3Switch1(config)#vlan 10`	Creates VLAN 10 and enters VLAN configuration mode
`L3Switch1(config-vlan)#name Accounting`	Assigns a name to the VLAN
`L3Switch1(config-vlan)#exit`	Returns to global configuration mode
`L3Switch1(config)#vlan 20`	Creates VLAN 20 and enters VLAN configuration mode
`L3Switch1(config-vlan)#name Marketing`	Assigns a name to the VLAN
`L3Switch1(config-vlan)#exit`	Returns to global configuration mode
`L3Switch1(config)#interface gigabitethernet 0/1`	Moves to interface configuration mode
`L3Switch1(config-if)#switchport trunk encapsulation dot1q`	Specifies 802.1q encapsulation on the trunk link
`L3Switch1(config-if)#switchport mode trunk`	Puts the interface into trunking mode and negotiates to convert the link into a trunk link
`L3Switch1(config-if)#exit`	Returns to global configuration mode
`L3Switch1(config)#ip routing`	Enables IP routing on this device
`L3Switch1(config)#interface vlan 1`	Creates a virtual interface for VLAN 1 and enters interface configuration mode
`L3Switch1(config-if)#ip address 172.16.1.1 255.255.255.0`	Assigns an IP address and netmask
`L3Switch1(config-if)#no shutdown`	Enables the interface
`L3Switch1(config-if)#interface vlan 10`	Creates a virtual interface for VLAN 10 and enters interface configuration mode
`L3Switch1(config-if)#ip address 172.16.10.1 255.255.255.0`	Assigns an IP address and mask
`L3Switch1(config-if)#no shutdown`	Enables the interface
`L3Switch1(config-if)#interface vlan 20`	Creates a virtual interface for VLAN 20 and enters interface configuration mode

`L3Switch1(config-if)#ip address 172.16.20.1 255.255.255.0`	Assigns an IP address and mask
`L3Switch1(config-if)#no shutdown`	Enables the interface
`L3Switch1(config-if)#exit`	Returns to global configuration mode
`L3Switch1(config)#interface fastethernet 0/24`	Enters interface configuration mode
`L3Switch1(config-if)#no switchport`	Creates a Layer 3 port on the switch
`L3Switch1(config-if)#ip address 172.31.1.6 255.255.255.252`	Assigns an IP address and netmask
`L3Switch1(config-if)#exit`	Returns to global configuration mode
`L3Switch1(config)#router eigrp 10`	Creates EIGRP routing process 10 and moves to router configuration mode
`L3Switch1(config-router)#network 172.16.0.0`	Advertises the 172.16.0.0 classful network
`L3Switch1(config-router)#network 172.31.0.0`	Advertises the 172.31.0.0 classful network
`L3Switch1(config-router)#no auto-summary`	Turns off automatic summarization at classful boundary
`L3Switch1(config-router)#exit`	Applies changes and returns to global configuration mode
`L3Switch1(config)#exit`	Returns to privileged mode
`L3Switch1#copy running-config startup-config`	Saves configuration in NVRAM

L2Switch1 (Catalyst 2960)

`Switch>enable`	Moves to privileged mode
`Switch#configure terminal`	Moves to global configuration mode
`Switch(config)#hostname L2Switch1`	Sets the host name
`L2Switch1(config)#no ip domain-lookup`	Turns off DNS queries so that spelling mistakes will not slow you down
`L2Switch1(config)#vtp domain testdomain`	Configures the VTP domain name to testdomain
`L2Switch1(config)#vtp mode client`	Changes the switch to VTP client mode
`L2Switch1(config)#interface range fastethernet 0/1 - 4`	Enables you to set the same configuration parameters on multiple ports at the same time
`L2Switch1(config-if-range)#switchport mode access`	Sets ports 1–4 as access ports
`L2Switch1(config-if-range)#switchport access vlan 10`	Assigns ports 1–4 to VLAN 10

`L2Switch1(config-if-range)#`**`interface range fastethernet 0/5 - 8`**	Enables you to set the same configuration parameters on multiple ports at the same time
`L2Switch1(config-if-range)#`**`switchport mode access`**	Sets ports 5–8 as access ports
`L2Switch1(config-if-range)#`**`switchport access vlan 20`**	Assigns ports 5–8 to VLAN 20
`L2Switch1(config-if-range)#`**`exit`**	Returns to global configuration mode
`L2Switch1(config)#`**`interface gigabitethernet 0/1`**	Moves to interface configuration mode
`L2Switch1(config-if)#`**`switchport mode trunk`**	Puts the interface into trunking mode and negotiates to convert the link into a trunk link
`L2Switch1(config-if)#`**`exit`**	Returns to global configuration mode
`L2Switch1(config)#`**`interface vlan 1`**	Creates a virtual interface for VLAN 1 and enters interface configuration mode
`L2Switch1(config-if)#`**`ip address 172.16.1.2 255.255.255.0`**	Assigns an IP address and netmask
`L2Switch1(config-if)#`**`no shutdown`**	Enables the interface
`L2Switch1(config-if)#`**`exit`**	Returns to global configuration mode
`L2Switch1(config)#`**`ip default-gateway 172.16.1.1`**	Assigns the default gateway address
`L2Switch1(config)#`**`exit`**	Returns to privileged mode
`L2Switch1#`**`copy running-config startup-config`**	Saves the configuration in NVRAM

CHAPTER 14

Spanning Tree Protocol and EtherChannel

This chapter provides information and commands concerning the following topics:

- Spanning Tree Protocol
- Enabling Spanning Tree Protocol
- Configuring the root switch
- Configuring a secondary root switch
- Configuring port priority
- Configuring the path cost
- Configuring the switch priority of a VLAN
- Configuring STP timers
- Verifying STP
- Optional STP configurations
- Changing the spanning-tree mode
- Extended System ID
- Enabling Rapid Spanning Tree
- Troubleshooting Spanning Tree
- Configuration example: STP
- EtherChannel
- Interface modes in EtherChannel
- Guidelines for configuring EtherChannel
- Configuring Layer 2 EtherChannel
- Verifying EtherChannel
- Configuration example: EtherChannel

Spanning Tree Protocol

Enabling Spanning Tree Protocol

`Switch(config)#spanning-tree vlan 5`	Enables STP on VLAN 5
`Switch(config)#no spanning-tree vlan 5`	Disables STP on VLAN 5

NOTE   If more VLANs are defined in the VLAN Trunking Protocol (VTP) than there are spanning-tree instances, you can only have STP on 64 VLANs. If you have more than 128 VLANs, it is recommended that you use Multiple STP.

Configuring the Root Switch

`Switch(config)#spanning-tree vlan 5 root`	Modifies the switch priority from the default 32768 to a lower value to allow the switch to become the root switch for VLAN 5.
	NOTE If all other switches have extended system ID support, this switch resets its priority to 24576. If any other switch has a priority set to below 24576 already, this switch sets its own priority to 4096 *less* than the lowest switch priority. If by doing this the switch would have a priority of less than 1, this command fails.
`Switch(config)#spanning-tree vlan 5 root primary`	Switch recalculates timers along with priority to allow the switch to become the root switch for VLAN 5.
	TIP The root switch should be a backbone or distribution switch.
`Switch(config)#spanning-tree vlan 5 root primary diameter 7`	Configures the switch to be the root switch for VLAN 5 and sets the network diameter to 7.
	TIP The **diameter** keyword is used to define the maximum number of switches between any two end stations. The range is from 2 to 7 switches.
`Switch(config)#spanning-tree vlan 5 root primary hello-time 4`	Configures the switch to be the root switch for VLAN 5 and sets the hello-delay timer to 4 seconds.
	TIP The **hello-time** keyword sets the hello-delay timer to any amount between 1 and 10 seconds. The default time is 2 seconds.

Configuring a Secondary Root Switch

`Switch(config)#spanning-tree vlan 5 root secondary`	Switch recalculates timers along with priority to allow the switch to become the root switch for VLAN 5 should the primary root switch fail.
	NOTE If all other switches have extended system ID support, this switch resets its priority to 28672. Therefore, if the root switch fails, and all other switches are set to the default priority of 32768, this becomes the new root switch. For switches without extended system ID support, the switch priority is changed to 16384.

| Switch(config)#**spanning-tree vlan 5 root secondary diameter 7** | Configures the switch to be the secondary root switch for VLAN 5 and sets the network diameter to 7. |
| Switch(config)#**spanning-tree vlan 5 root secondary hello-time 4** | Configures the switch to be the secondary root switch for VLAN 5 and sets the hello-delay timer to 4 seconds. |

Configuring Port Priority

Switch(config)#**interface gigabitethernet 0/1**	Moves to interface configuration mode.
Switch(config-if)#**spanning-tree port-priority 64**	Configures the port priority for the interface that is an access port.
Switch(config-if)#**spanning-tree vlan 5 port-priority 64**	Configures the VLAN port priority for an interface that is a trunk port.
	NOTE Port priority is used to break a tie when 2 switches have equal priorities for determining the root switch. The number can be between 0 and 255. The default port priority is 128. The lower the number, the higher the priority.

Configuring the Path Cost

Switch(config)#**interface gigabitethernet 0/1**	Moves to interface configuration mode.
Switch(config-if)#**spanning-tree cost 100000**	Configures the cost for the interface that is an access port.
Switch(config-if)#**spanning-tree vlan 5 cost 1000000**	Configures the VLAN cost for an interface that is a trunk port.
	NOTE If a loop occurs, STP uses the path cost when trying to determine which interface to place into the forwarding state. A higher path cost means a lower speed transmission. The range of the cost keyword is 1 through 200000000. The default is based on the media speed of the interface.

Configuring the Switch Priority of a VLAN

| Switch(config)#**spanning-tree vlan 5 priority 12288** | Configures the switch priority of VLAN 5 to 12288 |

NOTE With the **priority** keyword, the range is 0 to 61440 in increments of 4096. The default is 32768. The lower the priority, the more likely the switch will be chosen as the root switch.Only the following numbers can be used as a priority value:

0	4096	8192	12288
16384	20480	24576	28672
32768	36864	40960	45056
49152	53248	57344	61440

CAUTION Cisco recommends caution when using this command. Cisco further recommends that the **spanning-tree vlan** x **root primary** or the **spanning-tree vlan** x **root secondary** command be used instead to modify the switch priority.

Configuring STP Timers

`Switch(config)#spanning-tree vlan 5 hello-time 4`	Changes the hello-delay timer to 4 seconds on VLAN 5
`Switch(config)#spanning-tree vlan 5 forward-time 20`	Changes the forward-delay timer to 20 seconds on VLAN 5
`Switch(config)#spanning-tree vlan 5 max-age 25`	Changes the maximum-aging timer to 25 seconds on VLAN 5

NOTE For the **hello-time** command, the range is 1 to 10 seconds. The default is 2 seconds.

For the **forward-time** command, the range is 4 to 30 seconds. The default is 15 seconds.

For the **max-age** command, the range is 6 to 40 seconds. The default is 20 seconds.

CAUTION Cisco recommends caution when using this command. Cisco further recommends that the **spanning-tree vlan** x **root primary** or the **spanning-tree vlan** x **root secondary** command be used instead to modify the switch timers.

Verifying STP

`Switch#show spanning-tree`	Displays STP information
`Switch#show spanning-tree active`	Displays STP information on active interfaces only
`Switch#show spanning-tree brief`	Displays a brief status of the STP
`Switch#show spanning-tree detail`	Displays a detailed summary of interface information
`Switch#show spanning-tree interface gigabitethernet 0/1`	Displays STP information for interface gigabitethernet 0/1
`Switch#show spanning-tree summary`	Displays a summary of port states

`Switch#`**`show spanning-tree summary totals`**	Displays the total lines of the STP section
`Switch#`**`show spanning-tree vlan 5`**	Displays STP information for VLAN 5

Optional STP Configurations

Although the following commands are not mandatory for STP to work, you might find these helpful to fine-tune your network.

PortFast

`Switch(config)#`**`interface fastethernet 0/10`**	Moves to interface configuration mode.
`Switch(config-if)#`**`spanning-tree portfast`**	Enables PortFast on an access port.
`Switch(config-if)#`**`spanning-tree portfast trunk`**	Enables PortFast on a trunk port.
	WARNING Use the portfast command only when connecting a single end station to an access or trunk port. Using this command on a port connected to a switch or hub could prevent spanning tree from detecting loops.
	NOTE If you enable the voice VLAN feature, PortFast is enabled automatically. If you disable voice VLAN, PortFast is still enabled.
`Switch#`**`show spanning-tree interface fastethernet 0/10 portfast`**	Displays PortFast information on interface fastethernet 0/10.

BPDU Guard

`Switch(config)#`**`spanning-tree portfast bpduguard default`**	Globally enables BPDU Guard.
`Switch(config)#`**`interface range fastethernet 0/1 - 5`**	Enters interface range configuration mode.
`Switch(config-if-range)#`**`spanning-tree portfast`**	Enables PortFast on all interfaces in the range.
	NOTE By default, BPDU Guard is disabled.
`Switch(config-if)#`**`spanning-tree bpduguard enable`**	Enables BPDU Guard on the interface.
`Switch(config-if)#`**`spanning-tree bpduguard disable`**	Disables BPDU Guard on the interface.

`Switch(config)#errdisable recovery cause bpduguard`	Allows port to reenable itself if the cause of the error is BPDU Guard by setting a recovery timer.
`Switch(config)#errdisable recovery interval 400`	Sets recovery timer to 400 seconds. The default is 300 seconds. The range is from 30 to 86400 seconds.
`Switch#show spanning-tree summary totals`	Verifies whether BPDU Guard is enabled or disabled.
`Switch#show errdisable recovery`	Displays errdisable recovery timer information.

Changing the Spanning-Tree Mode

Different types of spanning trees can be configured on a Cisco switch. The options vary according to the platform:

- **Per-VLAN Spanning Tree (PVST)**—There is one instance of spanning tree for each VLAN. This is a Cisco proprietary protocol.

- **Per-VLAN Spanning Tree Plus (PVST+)**—Also Cisco proprietary. Has added extensions to the PVST protocol.

- **Rapid PVST+**—This mode is the same as PVST+ except that it uses a rapid convergence based on the 802.1w standard.

- **Multiple Spanning Tree Protocol (MSTP)**—IEEE 802.1s. Extends the 802.1w Rapid Spanning Tree (RST) algorithm to multiple spanning trees. Multiple VLANs can map to a single instance of RST. You cannot run MSTP and PVST at the same time.

`Switch(config)#spanning-tree mode mst`	Enables MSTP. This command is available only on a switch running the EI software image.
`Switch(config)#spanning-tree mode pvst`	Enables PVST. This is the default setting.
`Switch(config)#spanning-tree mode rapid-pvst`	Enables Rapid PVST+.

Extended System ID

`Switch(config)#spanning-tree extend system-id`	Enables extended system ID, also known as MAC address reduction.
	NOTE Catalyst switches running software earlier than Cisco IOS Software Release 12.1(8) EA1 do not support the extended system ID.
`Switch#show spanning-tree summary`	Verifies extended system ID is enabled.
`Switch#show running-config`	Verifies extended system ID is enabled.

Enabling Rapid Spanning Tree

`Switch(config)#spanning-tree mode rapid-pvst`	Enables Rapid PVST+.
`Switch(config)#interface fastethernet 0/1`	Moves to interface configuration mode.
`Switch(config-if)#spanning-tree link-type point-to-point`	Sets the interface to be a point-to-point interface.
	NOTE By setting the link type to point to point, this means that if you connect this port to a remote port, and this port becomes a designated port, the switch negotiates with the remote port and transitions the local port to a forwarding state.
`Switch(config-if)#exit`	
`Switch(config)#clear spanning-tree detected-protocols`	
	NOTE The **clear spanning-tree detected-protocols** command restarts the protocol-migration process on the switch if any port is connected to a port on a legacy 802.1D switch.

Troubleshooting Spanning Tree

`Switch#debug spanning-tree all`	Displays all spanning-tree debugging events
`Switch#debug spanning-tree events`	Displays spanning-tree debugging topology events
`Switch#debug spanning-tree backbonefast`	Displays spanning-tree debugging BackboneFast events
`Switch#debug spanning-tree uplinkfast`	Displays spanning-tree debugging UplinkFast event
`Switch#debug spanning-tree mstp all`	Displays all MST debugging events
`Switch#debug spanning-tree switch state`	Displays spanning-tree port state changes
`Switch#debug spanning-tree pvst+`	Displays PVST+ events

Configuration Example: STP

Figure 14-1 illustrates the network topology for the configuration that follows, which shows how to configure STP using commands covered in this chapter.

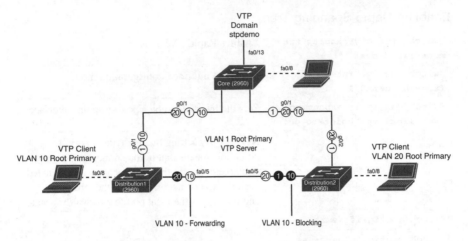

Figure 14-1   Network Topology for STP Configuration Example

Core Switch (2960)

`Switch>`**`enable`**	Moves to privileged mode.
`Switch#`**`configure terminal`**	Moves to global configuration mode.
`Switch(config)#`**`hostname Core`**	Sets the host name.
`Core(config)#`**`no ip domain-lookup`**	Turns off Dynamic Name System (DNS) queries so that spelling mistakes do not slow you down.
`Core(config)#`**`vtp mode server`**	Changes the switch to VTP server mode. This is the default mode.
`Core(config)#`**`vtp domain stpdemo`**	Configures the VTP domain name to stpdemo.
`Core(config)#`**`vlan 10`**	Creates VLAN 10 and enters VLAN configuration mode.
`Core(config-vlan)#`**`name Accounting`**	Assigns a name to the VLAN.
`Core(config-vlan)#`**`exit`**	Returns to global configuration mode.
`Core(config)#`**`vlan 20`**	Creates VLAN 20 and enters VLAN configuration mode.
`Core(config-vlan)#`**`name Marketing`**	Assigns a name to the VLAN.
`Core(config-vlan)#`**`exit`**	Returns to global configuration mode.
`Core(config)#`**`spanning-tree vlan 1 root primary`**	Configures the switch to become the root switch for VLAN 1.
`Core(config)#`**`exit`**	Returns to privileged mode.
`Core#`**`copy running-config startup-config`**	Saves the configuration to NVRAM.

Distribution 1 Switch (2960)

`Switch>`**`enable`**	Moves to privileged mode.
`Switch#`**`configure terminal`**	Moves to global configuration mode.
`Switch(config)#`**`hostname Distribution1`**	Sets the host name.
`Distribution1(config)#`**`no ip domain-lookup`**	Turns off DNS queries so that spelling mistakes do not slow you down.
`Distribution1(config)#`**`vtp domain stpdemo`**	Configures the VTP domain name to stpdemo.
`Distribution1(config)#`**`vtp mode client`**	Changes the switch to VTP client mode.
`Distribution1(config)#`**`spanning-tree vlan 10 root primary`**	Configures the switch to become the root switch of VLAN 10.
`Distribution1(config)#`**`exit`**	Returns to privileged mode.
`Distribution1#`**`copy running-config startup-config`**	Saves the configuration to NVRAM.

Distribution 2 Switch (2960)

`Switch>`**`enable`**	Moves to privileged mode.
`Switch#`**`configure terminal`**	Moves to global configuration mode.
`Switch(config)#`**`hostname Distribution2`**	Sets the host name.
`Distribution2(config)#`**`no ip domain-lookup`**	Turns off DNS queries so that spelling mistakes do not slow you down.
`Distribution2(config)#`**`vtp domain stpdemo`**	Configures the VTP domain name to stpdemo.
`Distribution2(config)#`**`vtp mode client`**	Changes the switch to VTP client mode.
`Distribution2(config)#`**`spanning-tree vlan 20 root primary`**	Configures the switch to become the root switch of VLAN 20.
`Distribution2(config)#`**`exit`**	Returns to privileged mode.
`Distribution2#`**`copy running-config startup-config`**	Saves the configuration to NVRAM.

EtherChannel

EtherChannel provides fault-tolerant, high-speed links between switches, routers, and servers. An EtherChannel consists of individual Fast Ethernet or Gigabit Ethernet links bundled into a single logical link. If a link within an EtherChannel fails, traffic previously carried over that failed link changes to the remaining links within the EtherChannel.

Interface Modes in EtherChannel

Mode	Protocol	Description
On	None	Forces the interface into an EtherChannel without PAgP or LACP. Channel only exists if connected to another interface group also in On mode.
Auto	PAgP	Places the interface into a passive negotiating state—will respond to PAgP packets but will not initiate PAgP negotiation.
Desirable	PAgP	Places the interface into an active negotiating state—will send PAgP packets to start negotiations.
Passive	LACP	Places the interface into a passive negotiating state—will respond to LACP packets but will not initiate LACP negotiation.
Active	LACP	Places the interface into an active negotiating state—will send LACP packets to start negotiations.

Guidelines for Configuring EtherChannel

- PAgP is Cisco proprietary.
- LACP is defined in 802.3ad.
- You can combine from two to eight parallel links.
- All ports must be identical:
  - Same speed and duplex
  - Cannot mix Fast Ethernet and Gigabit Ethernet
  - Cannot mix PAgP and LACP
  - Must all be VLAN trunk or nontrunk operational status

- All links must be either Layer 2 or Layer 3 in a single channel group.
- To create a channel in PAgP, sides must be set to
  - Auto-Desirable
  - Desirable-Desirable

- To create a channel in LACP, sides must be set to
  - Active-Active
  - Active-Passive

- To create a channel without using PAgP or LACP, sides must be set to On-On.
- Do *not* configure a GigaStack gigabit interface converter (GBIC) as part of an EtherChannel.

- An interface that is already configured to be a Switched Port Analyzer (SPAN) destination port will not join an EtherChannel group until SPAN is disabled.

- Do *not* configure a secure port as part of an EtherChannel.

- Interfaces with different native VLANs cannot form an EtherChannel.

- When using trunk links, ensure all trunks are in the same mode—Inter-Switch Link (ISL) or dot1q.

Configuring Layer 2 EtherChannel

`Switch(config)#interface range fastethernet 0/1 - 4`	Moves to interface range configuration mode.
`Switch(config-if-range)#channel-protocol pagp`	Specifies the PAgP protocol to be used in this channel.
`Or`	
`Switch(config-if-range)#channel-protocol lacp`	Specifies the LACP protocol to be used in this channel.
`Switch(config-if-range)#channel-group 1 mode {desirable	auto	on	passive	active }`	Creates channel group 1 and assigns interfaces 01–04 as part of it. Use whichever mode is necessary, depending on your choice of protocol.

Verifying EtherChannel

`Switch#show running-config`	Displays list of what is currently running on the device
`Switch#show running-config interface fastethernet 0/12`	Displays interface fastethernet 0/12 information
`Switch#show etherchannel`	Displays all EtherChannel information
`Switch#show etherchannel 1 port-channel`	Displays port channel information
`Switch#show etherchannel summary`	Displays a summary of EtherChannel information
`Switch#show interface port-channel 1`	Displays the general status of EtherChannel 1
`Switch#show pagp neighbor`	Shows PAgP neighbor information
`Switch#clear pagp 1 counters`	Clears PAgP channel group 1 information
`Switch#clear lacp 1 counters`	Clears LACP channel group 1 information

Configuration Example: EtherChannel

Figure 14-2 illustrates the network topology for the configuration that follows, which shows how to configure EtherChannel using commands covered in this chapter.

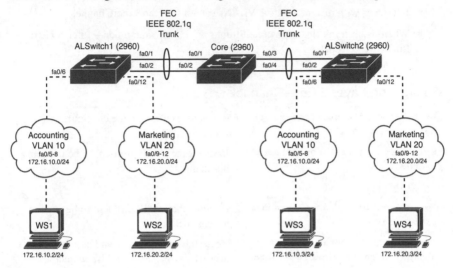

Figure 14-2 Network Topology for EtherChannel Configuration

Core (2960)

`Switch>`**`enable`**	Moves to privileged mode
`Switch#`**`configure terminal`**	Moves to global configuration mode
`Switch(config)#`**`hostname Core`**	Sets the host name
`Core(config)#`**`no ip domain-lookup`**	Turns off DNS queries so that spelling mistakes do not slow you down
`Core(config)#`**`vtp mode server`**	Changes the switch to VTP server mode
`Core(config)#`**`vtp domain testdomain`**	Configures the VTP domain name to testdomain
`Core(config)#`**`vlan 10`**	Creates VLAN 10 and enters VLAN configuration mode
`Core(config-vlan)#`**`name Accounting`**	Assigns a name to the VLAN
`Core(config-vlan)#`**`exit`**	Returns to global configuration mode
`Core(config)#`**`vlan 20`**	Creates VLAN 20 and enters VLAN configuration mode
`Core(config-vlan)#`**`name Marketing`**	Assigns a name to the VLAN
`Core(config-vlan)#`**`exit`**	Returns to global configuration mode
`Core(config)#`**`interface range fastethernet 0/1 - 4`**	Moves to interface range configuration mode

Core(config-if)#**switchport trunk encapsulation dot1q**	Specifies 802.1q encapsulation on the trunk link
Core(config-if)#**switchport mode trunk**	Puts the interface into permanent trunking mode and negotiates to convert the link into a trunk link
Core(config-if)#**exit**	Returns to global configuration mode
Core(config)#**interface range fastethernet 0/1 - 2**	Moves to interface range configuration mode
Core(config-if)#**channel-group 1 mode desirable**	Creates channel group 1 and assigns interfaces 01–02 as part of it
Core(config-if)#**exit**	Moves to global configuration mode
Core(config)#**interface range fastethernet 0/3 - 4**	Moves to interface range configuration mode
Core(config-if)#**channel-group 2 mode desirable**	Creates channel group 2 and assigns interfaces 03–04 as part of it
Core(config-if)#**exit**	Moves to global configuration mode
Core(config)#**exit**	Moves to privileged mode
Core#**copy running-config startup-config**	Saves the configuration to NVRAM

ALSwitch1 (2960)

Switch>**enable**	Moves to privileged mode
Switch#**configure terminal**	Moves to global configuration mode
Switch(config)#**hostname ALSwitch1**	Sets the host name
ALSwitch1(config)#**no ip domain-lookup**	Turns off DNS queries so that spelling mistakes do not slow you down
ALSwitch1(config)#**vtp mode client**	Changes the switch to VTP client mode
ALSwitch1(config)#**vtp domain testdomain**	Configures the VTP domain name to testdomain
ALSwitch1(config)#**interface range fastethernet 0/5 - 8**	Moves to interface range configuration mode
ALSwitch1(config-if-range)#**switchport mode access**	Sets ports 5–8 as access ports
ALSwitch1(config-if-range)#**switchport access vlan 10**	Assigns ports to VLAN 10
ALSwitch1(config-if-range)#**exit**	Moves to global configuration mode
ALSwitch1(config)#**interface range fastethernet 0/9 - 12**	Moves to interface range configuration mode
ALSwitch1(config-if-range)#**switchport mode access**	Sets ports 9–12 as access ports

`ALSwitch1(config-if-range)#`**`switchport access vlan 20`**	Assigns ports to VLAN 20
`ALSwitch1(config-if-range)#`**`exit`**	Moves to global configuration mode
`ALSwitch1(config)#`**`interface range fastethernet 0/1 - 2`**	Moves to interface range configuration mode
`ALSwitch1(config-if-range)#`**`switchport mode trunk`**	Puts the interface into permanent trunking mode and negotiates to convert the link into a trunk link
`ALSwitch1(config-if-range)#`**`channel-group 1 mode desirable`**	Creates channel group 1 and assigns interfaces 01–02 as part of it
`ALSwitch1(config-if-range)#`**`exit`**	Moves to global configuration mode
`ALSwitch1(config)#`**`exit`**	Moves to privileged mode
`ALSwitch1#`**`copy running-config startup-config`**	Saves the configuration to NVRAM

ALSwitch2 (2960)

`Switch>`**`enable`**	Moves to privileged mode
`Switch#`**`configure terminal`**	Moves to global configuration mode
`Switch(config)#`**`hostname ALSwitch2`**	Sets the host name
`ALSwitch2(config)#`**`no ip domain-lookup`**	Turns off DNS queries so that spelling mistakes do not slow you down
`ALSwitch2(config)#`**`vtp mode client`**	Changes the switch to VTP client mode
`ALSwitch2(config)#`**`vtp domain test-domain`**	Configures the VTP domain name to testdomain
`ALSwitch2(config)#`**`interface range fastethernet 0/5 - 8`**	Moves to interface range configuration mode
`ALSwitch2(config-if-range)#`**`switchport mode access`**	Sets ports 5–8 as access ports
`ALSwitch2(config-if-range)#`**`switchport access vlan 10`**	Assigns ports to VLAN 10
`ALSwitch2(config-if-range)#`**`exit`**	Moves to global configuration mode
`ALSwitch2(config)#`**`interface range fastethernet 0/9 - 12`**	Moves to interface range configuration mode
`ALSwitch2(config-if-range)#`**`switchport mode access`**	Sets ports 9–12 as access ports
`ALSwitch2(config-if-range)#`**`switchport access vlan 20`**	Assigns ports to VLAN 20
`ALSwitch2(config-if-range)#`**`exit`**	Moves to global configuration mode
`ALSwitch2(config)#`**`interface range fastethernet 0/1 - 2`**	Moves to interface range configuration mode

ALSwitch2(config-if-range)#**switchport mode trunk**	Puts the interface into permanent trunking mode and negotiates to convert the link into a trunk link
ALSwitch2(config-if-range)#**channel-group 1 mode desirable**	Creates channel group 1 and assigns interfaces 01–02 as part of it.
ALSwitch2(config-if-range)#**exit**	Moves to global configuration mode
ALSwitch2(config)#**exit**	Moves to privileged mode
ALSwitch2#**copy running-config startup-config**	Saves the configuration to NVRAM

This chapter provides information and commands concerning the following topics:

- Hot Standby Routing Protocol
    - Configuring HSRP on a router
    - Configuring HSRP on an L3 switch
    - Default HSRP configuration settings
    - Verifying HSRP
    - HSRP optimization options
    - Preempt
    - HSRP message timers
    - Interface tracking
    - Multiple HSRP groups
    - Debugging HSRP
- Virtual Router Redundancy Protocol
    - Configuring VRRP
    - Verifying VRRP
    - Debugging VRRP
- Gateway Load Balancing Protocol
    - Configuring GLBP
    - Verifying GLBP
    - Debugging GLBP
- Configuration example: HSRP on a router
- Configuration example: HSRP on an L3 switch
- Configuration Example: GLBP

Hot Standby Router Protocol

The Hot Standby Router Protocol (HSRP) provides network redundancy for IP networks, ensuring that user traffic immediately and transparently recovers from first-hop failures in network edge devices or access circuits.

Configuring HSRP on a Router

`Router(config)#interface fastethernet 0/0`	Moves to interface configuration mode.
`Router(config-if)#ip address 172.16.0.10 255.255.255.0`	Assigns an IP address and netmask.
`Router(config-if)#standby 1 ip 172.16.0.1`	Activates HSRP group 1 on the interface and creates a virtual IP address of 172.16.0.1 for use in HSRP
	NOTE The group number can be from 0 to 255. The default is 0.
`Router(config-if)#standby 1 priority 120`	Assigns a priority value of 120 to standby group 1.
	NOTE The priority value can be from 1 to 255. The default is 100. A higher priority results in that switch being elected the active switch. If the priorities of all switches in the group are equal, the switch with the *highest IP address* becomes the active switch.

Configuring HSRP on an L3 Switch

When configuring HSRP on a switch platform, the specified interface must be a Layer 3 interface:

- **Routed port:** A physical port configured as a Layer 3 port by entering the **no switchport interface** configuration command

- **SVI:** A VLAN interface created by using the **interface vlan** *vlan_id* global configuration command and by default a Layer 3 interface

- **EtherChannel port channel in Layer 3 mode:** A port-channel logical interface created by using the **interface port-channel** *port-channel-number* global configuration command and binding the Ethernet interface into the channel group

`Switch(config)#interface fastethernet 0/0`	Moves to interface configuration mode.
`Switch(config)#interface vlan 10`	Moves to interface configuration mode.
`Switch(config-if)#ip address 172.16.0.10 255.255.255.0`	Assigns an IP address and netmask.
`Switch(config-if)#standby 1 ip 172.16.0.1`	Activates HSRP group 1 on the interface and creates a virtual IP address of 172.16.0.1 for use in HSRP.
	NOTE The group number can be from 0 to 255. The default is 0.

`Switch(config-if)#`**`standby 1`** **`priority 120`**	Assigns a priority value of 120 to standby group 1.
	NOTE The priority value can be from 1 to 255. The default is 100. A higher priority results in that switch being elected the active switch. If the priorities of all switches in the group are equal, the switch with the *highest IP address* becomes the active switch.

Default HSRP Configuration Settings

Feature	Default Setting
HSRP version	Version 1.
	NOTE HSRPv1 and HSRPv2 have different packet structure. The same HSRP version must be configured on all devices of an HSRP group.
HSRP groups	None configured.
Standby group number	0.
Standby MAC address	System assigned as 0000.0c07.ac*XX*, where *XX* is the HSRP group number.
Standby priority	100.
Standby delay	0 (no delay).
Standby track interface priority	10.
Standby hello time	3 seconds.
Standby holdtime	10 seconds.

Verifying HSRP

NOTE   These commands work on both the router and the switch CLI.

`Router#`**`show running-config`**	Displays what is currently running on the router
`Router#`**`show standby`**	Displays HSRP information
`Router#`**`show standby brief`**	Displays a single-line output summary of each standby group
`Switch#`**`show standby vlan 1`**	Displays HSRP information on the VLAN 1 group

HSRP Optimization Options

Options are available that make it possible to optimize HSRP operation in the campus network. The next three sections explain three of these options: standby preempt, message timers, and interface tracking.

NOTE   These commands work on both the router and the switch CLI.

Preempt

`Router(config)#interface gigabitethernet 0/0`	Moves to interface configuration mode.
`Router(config-if)#standby 1 preempt`	This switch preempts, or takes control of, the active router if the local priority is higher than the active router.
`Router(config-if)#standby 1 preempt delay minimum 180`	Causes the local router to postpone taking over as the active router for 180 seconds since that router was last restarted.
`Router(config-if)#standby 1 preempt delay reload`	Allows for preemption to occur only after a router reloads.
`Router(config-if)#no standby 1 preempt delay reload`	Disables the preemption delay, but preemption itself is still enabled. Use **the no standby** *x* **preempt** command to eliminate preemption.
	NOTE If the **preempt** argument is not configured, the local router assumes control as the active router only if the local router receives information indicating that there is no router currently in the active state.

HSRP Message Timers

`Router(config)#interface gigabitethernet 0/0`	Moves to interface configuration mode.
`Router(config-if)#standby 1 timers 5 15`	Sets the hello timer to 5 seconds and sets the hold timer to 15 seconds.
	NOTE The hold timer is normally set to be greater than or equal to 3 times the hello timer.
	NOTE The hello timer can be from 1 to 254; the default is 3. The hold timer can be from 1 to 255; the default is 10. The default unit of time is seconds.
`Router(config-if)#standby 1 timers msec 200 msec 600`	Sets the hello timer to 200 milliseconds and sets the hold timer to 600 milliseconds.
	NOTE If the **msec** argument is used, the timers can be an integer from 15 to 999.

Interface Tracking

`Router(config)#`**`interface`** **`gigabitethernet 0/0`**	Moves to interface configuration mode.
`Router(config-if)#`**`standby`** **`1 track serial 0/0/0 25`**	HSRP will track the availability of interface Serial 0/0/0. If Serial 0/0/0 goes down, the priority of the switch in group 1 is decremented by 25.
	NOTE The default value of the **track** argument is 10.
	TIP The **track** argument does not assign a new priority if the tracked interface goes down. The **track** argument assigns a value that the priority will be decreased if the tracked interface goes down. Therefore, if you are tracking Serial 0/0/0 with a track value of 25 (**standby 1 track serial 0/0 25**) and Serial 0/0/0 goes down, the priority will be decreased by 25; assuming a default priority of 100, the new priority will now be 75.

Multiple HSRP

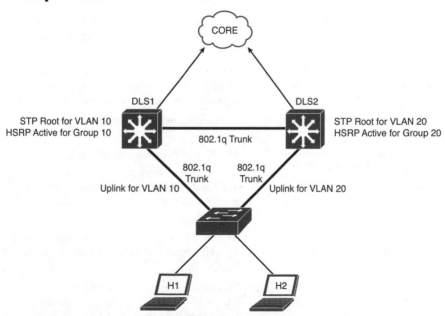

Figure 15-1   Network Topology for MHSRP Configuration Example

`DLS1(config)#spanning-tree vlan 10 root primary`	Configure spanning-tree root primary for VLAN 10.
`DLS1(config)#spanning-tree vlan 20 root secondary`	Configure spanning-tree root primary for VLAN 20.
	NOTE Load balancing can be accomplished by having one switch be the active HSRP L3 switch forwarding for half of the VLANs and the standby L3 switch for the remaining VLANs. The second HSRP L3 switch would be reversed in its active and standby VLANs. Care must be taken to ensure that spanning tree is forwarding to the active L3 switch for the correct VLANs by making that L3 switch the spanning-tree primary root for those VLANs.
`DLS1(config)#interface vlan 10`	Moves to interface configuration mode.
`DLS1(config-if)#ip address 10.1.10.2 255.255.255.0`	Assigns an IP address and netmask.
`DLS1(config-if)#standby 10 ip 10.1.10.1`	Activates HSRP group 10 on the interface and creates a virtual IP address of 10.1.10.1 for use in HSRP.
`DLS1(config-if)#standby 10 priority 110`	Assigns a priority value of 110 to standby group 10. This will be the active forwarding switch for VLAN 10.
`DLS1(config-if)#standby 10 preempt`	This switch preempts, or takes control of, VLAN 10 forwarding if the local priority is higher than the active switch VLAN 1 priority.
`DLS1(config-if)#interface vlan 20`	Moves to interface configuration mode.
`DLS1(config-if)#ip address 10.1.20.2 255.255.255.0`	Assigns an IP address and netmask.
`DLS1(config-if)#standby 20 ip 10.1.20.1`	Activates HSRP group 20 on the interface and creates a virtual IP address of 10.1.20.1 for use in HSRP.
`DLS1(config-if)#standby 20 priority 90`	Assigns a priority value of 90 to standby group 20. This switch will be the standby device for VLAN 20.
`DLS1(config-if)#standby 20 preempt`	This switch preempts, or takes control of, VLAN 20 forwarding if the local priority is higher than the active switch VLAN 20 priority.

Debugging HSRP

NOTE   These commands work on both the router and the switch CLI.

`Router#debug standby`	Displays all HSRP debugging information, including state changes and transmission/reception of HSRP packets
`Router#debug standby errors`	Displays HSRP error messages
`Router#debug standby events`	Displays HSRP event messages
`Router#debug standby events terse`	Displays all HSRP events except for hellos and advertisements
`Router#debug standby events track`	Displays all HSRP tracking events
`Router#debug standby packets`	Displays HSRP packet messages
`Router#debug standby terse`	Displays all HSRP errors, events, and packets, except for hellos and advertisements

Virtual Router Redundancy Protocol

NOTE   HSRP is Cisco proprietary. The Virtual Router Redundancy Protocol (VRRP) is an IEEE standard.

NOTE   VRRP is not supported on the Catalyst 3750-E, 3750, 3560, or 3550 platforms. VRRP is supported on the Catalyst 4500 and Catalyst 6500 platforms.

VRRP is an election protocol that dynamically assigns responsibility for one or more virtual switches to the VRRP switches on a LAN, allowing several switches on a multiaccess link to use the same virtual IP address. A VRRP switch is configured to run VRRP in conjunction with one or more other switches attached.

Configuring VRRP

`Switch(config)#interface vlan 10`	Moves to interface configuration mode.
`Switch(config-if)#ip address 172.16.100.5 255.255.255.0`	Assigns an IP address and netmask.
`Switch(config-if)#vrrp 10 ip 172.16.100.1`	Enables VRRP for group 10 on this interface with a virtual address of 172.16.100.1. The group number can be from 1 to 255.
`Switch(config-if)#vrrp 10 description Engineering Group`	Assigns a text description to the group.
`Switch(config-if)#vrrp 10 priority 110`	Sets the priority level for this VLAN. The range is from 1 to 254. The default is 100.

`Switch(config-if)#vrrp` `10 preempt`	This switch preempts, or takes over, as the virtual switch master for group 10 if it has a higher priority than the current virtual switch master.
`Switch(config-if)#vrrp` `10 preempt delay 60`	This switch preempts, but only after a delay of 60 seconds.
	NOTE The default delay period is 0 seconds.
`Switch(config-if)#vrrp` `10 timers advertise 15`	Configures the interval between successful advertisements by the virtual switch master.
	NOTE The default interval value is 1 second.
	NOTE All switches in a VRRP group must use the same timer values. If switches have different timer values set, the VRRP group will not communicate with each other.
	NOTE The range of the advertisement timer is 1 to 255 seconds. If you use the **msec** argument, you change the timer to measure in milliseconds. The range in milliseconds is 50 to 999.
`Switch(config-if)#vrrp` `10 timers learn`	Configures the switch, when acting as a virtual switch backup, to learn the advertisement interval used by the virtual switch master.
`Switch(config-if)#vrrp` `10 shutdown`	Disables VRRP on the interface, but configuration is still retained.
`Switch(config-if)#no` `vrrp 10 shutdown`	Reenables the VRRP group using the previous configuration.

Verifying VRRP

`Switch#show running-config`	Displays contents of dynamic RAM
`Switch#show vrrp`	Displays VRRP information
`Switch#show vrrp brief`	Displays a brief status of all VRRP groups
`Switch#show vrrp all`	Displays detailed information about all VRRP groups, including groups in the disabled state
`Switch#show vrrp interface` `vlan 10`	Displays information about VRRP as enabled on interface VLAN 10
`Switch#show vrrp interface` `vlan 10 brief`	Displays a brief summary about VRRP on interface VLAN 10

Debugging VRRP

Switch#**debug vrrp all**	Displays all VRRP messages
Switch#**debug vrrp error**	Displays all VRRP error messages
Switch#**debug vrrp events**	Displays all VRRP event messages
Switch#**debug vrrp packets**	Displays messages about packets sent and received
Switch#**debug vrrp state**	Displays messages about state transitions

Gateway Load Balancing Protocol

Gateway Load Balancing Protocol (GLBP) protects data traffic from a failed router or circuit, like HSRP and VRRP, while allowing packet load sharing between a group of redundant routers.

Configuring GLBP

Router(config)#**interface fastethernet 0/0**	Moves to interface configuration mode.
Router(config-if)#**ip address 172.16.100.5 255.255.255.0**	Assigns an IP address and netmask.
Router(config-if)#**glbp 10 ip 172.16.100.1**	Enables GLBP for group 10 on this interface with a virtual address of 172.16.100.1. The range of group numbers is from 0 to 1023.
Router(config-if)#**glbp 10 preempt**	Configures the switch to preempt, or take over, as the active virtual gateway (AVG) for group 10 if this switch has a higher priority than the current AVG.
Router(config-if)#**glbp 10 preempt delay minimum 60**	Configures the router to preempt, or take over, as AVG for group 10 if this router has a higher priority than the current active virtual forwarder (AVF) after a delay of 60 seconds.
Router(config-if)#**glbp 10 forwarder preempt**	Configures the router to preempt, or take over, as AVF for group 10 if this router has a higher priority than the current AVF. This command is enabled by default with a delay of 30 seconds.
Router(config-if)#**glbp 10 preempt delay minimum 60**	Configures the router to preempt, or take over, as AVF for group 10 if this router has a higher priority than the current AVF after a delay of 60 seconds.

	NOTE Members of a GLBP group elect one gateway to be the AVG for that group. Other group members provide backup for the AVG in the event that the AVG becomes unavailable. The AVG assigns a virtual MAC address to each member of the GLBP group. Each gateway assumes responsibility for forwarding packets sent to the virtual MAC address assigned to it by the AVG. These gateways are known as AVFs for their virtual MAC address. Virtual forwarder redundancy is similar to virtual gateway redundancy with an AVF. If the AVF fails, one of the secondary virtual forwarders in the listen state assumes responsibility for the virtual MAC address.
	NOTE The **glbp preempt** command uses priority to determine what happens if the AVG fails in addition to the order of ascendancy to becoming an AVG if the current AVG fails. The **glbp forwarder preempt** command uses weighting value to determine the forwarding capacity of each router in the GLBP group.
Router(config-if)#**glbp 10 priority 150**	Sets the priority level of the switch.
	NOTE The range of the **priority** argument is 1 to 255. The default priority of GLBP is 100. A higher priority number is preferred.
Router(config-if)#**glbp 10 timers 5 15**	Configures the hello timer to be set to 5 seconds and the hold timer to be 15 seconds
Router(config-if)#**glbp 10 timers msec 20200 msec 60600**	Configures the hello timer to be 20200 milliseconds and the hold timer to be 60600 milliseconds.
	NOTE The default hello timer is 3 seconds. The range of the hello timer interval is 1 to 60 seconds. If the **msec** argument is used, the timer will be measured in milliseconds, with a range of 50 to 60000.
	NOTE The default hold timer is 10 seconds. The range of the hold timer is 1 to 180 seconds. If the **msec** argument is used, the timer will be measured in milliseconds, with a range of 70 to 180000. The hello timer measures the interval between successive hello packets sent by the AVG in a GLBP group. The **hold-time** argument specifies the interval before the virtual gateway and the virtual forwarder information in the hello packet is considered invalid. It is recommended that unless you are extremely familiar with your network design and with the mechanisms of GLBP that you do not change the timers. To reset the timers back to their default values, use the **no glbp** *x* **timers** command, where *x* is the GLBP group number.

Router(config-if)#glbp 10 load-balancing host-dependent	Specifies that GLBP will load balance using the host-dependent method.
Router(config-if)#glbp 10 load-balancing weighted	Specifies that GLBP will load balance using the weighted method.
Router(config-if)#glbp 10 weighting 80	Assigns a maximum weighting value for this interface for load-balancing purposes. The value can be from 1 to 254.
Router(config-if)#glbp 10 load-balancing round-robin	Specifies that GLBP will load balance using the round-robin method

NOTE   There are three different types of load balancing in GLBP:

- **Host-dependent** uses the MAC address of a host to determine which VF MAC address the host is directed toward. This is used with stateful Network Address Translation (NAT) because NAT requires each host to be returned to the same virtual MAC address each time it sends an ARP request for the virtual IP address. It is not recommended for situations where there are a small number of end hosts (fewer than 20).

- **Weighted** allows for GLBP to place a weight on each device when calculating the amount of load sharing. For example, if there are two routers in the group, and router A has twice the forwarding capacity of router B, the weighting value should be configured to be double the amount of router B. To assign a weighting value, use the **glbp** x **weighting** y interface configuration command, where x is the GLBP group number, and y is the weighting value, a number from 1 to 254.

- **Round-robin** load balancing occurs when each VF MAC address is used sequentially in ARP replies for the virtual IP address. Round robin is suitable for any number of end hosts.

If no load balancing is used with GLBP, GLBP operates in an identical manner to HSRP, where the AVG respond to ARP requests only with its own VF MAC address, and all traffic is directed to the AVG.

Verifying GLBP

Router#show running-config	Displays contents of dynamic RAM
Router#show glbp	Displays GLBP information
Router#show glbp brief	Displays a brief status of all GLBP groups
Router#show glbp 10	Displays information about GLBP group 10
Router#show glbp vlan 10	Displays GLBP information on interface VLAN 10
Router#show glbp vlan 20 10	Displays GLBP group 10 information on interface VLAN 20

Debugging GLBP

Router#**debug condition glbp**	Displays GLBP condition messages
Router#**debug glbp errors**	Displays all GLBP error messages
Router#**debug glbp events**	Displays all GLBP event messages
Router#**debug glbp packets**	Displays messages about packets sent and received
Router#**debug glbp terse**	Displays a limited range of debugging messages

Configuration Example: GLBP

Figure 15-2 shows the network topology for the configuration that follows, which shows how to configure GLBP using commands covered in this chapter. Note that only the commands specific to GLBP are shown in this example.

NOTE   The Gateway Load Balancing Protocol (GLBP) is not supported on the Catalyst 3750-E, 3750, 3560, or 3550 platforms. GLBP is supported on the Catalyst 4500 and Catalyst 6500 platforms.

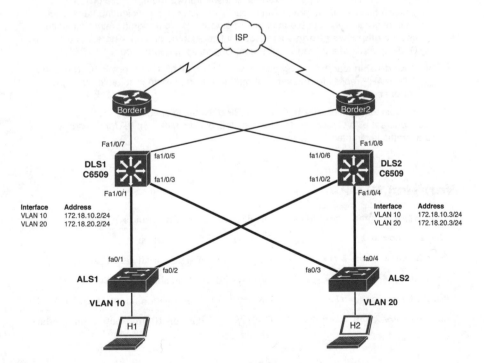

Figure 15-2   Network Topology for GLBP Configuration Example

DLS1 and DLS2 belong to GLBP groups 10 and 20. DLS1 is the AVG for GLBP group 10 and backup for GLBP group 20. DLS2 is the AVG for GLBP group 20 and backup for GLBP group 10.

DLS1 and DLS2 are responsible for the virtual IP address 172.18.10.1 on VLAN 10 and 172.18.20.1 on VLAN 20.

DLS1

`DLS1(config)#track 90 interface fastethernet 1/0/7 line-protocol`	Configures tracking object 90 to monitor the line protocol on interface fastethernet 1/0/7
`DLS1(config)#track 91 interface fastethernet 1/0/5 line-protocol`	Configures tracking object 91 to monitor the line protocol on interface fastethernet 1/0/5
`DLS1(config)#interface vlan 10`	Moves to interface configuration mode
`DLS1(config-if)#ip address 172.18.10.2 255.255.255.0`	Assigns an IP address and netmask
`DLS1(config-if)#glbp 10 ip 172.18.10.1`	Enables GLBP for group 10 on this interface with a virtual address of 172.18.10.1
`DLS1(config-if)#glbp 10 weighting 110 lower 95 upper 105`	Specifies the initial weighting value, and the upper and lower thresholds, for a GLBP gateway
`DLS1(config-if)#glbp 10 timers msec 200 msec 700`	Configures the hello timer to be 200 milliseconds and the hold timer to be 700 milliseconds
`DLS1(config-if)#glbp 10 priority 105`	Sets the priority level to 105 on the switch for VLAN 10
`DLS1(config-if)#glbp 10 preempt delay minimum 300`	Configures the switch to take over as AVG for group 10 if this switch has a higher priority than the current AVF after a delay of 300 seconds
`DLS1(config-if)#glbp 10 authentication md5 key-string xyz123`	Configures the authentication key xyz123 for GLBP packets received from the other switch in the group
`DLS1(config-if)#glbp 10 weighting track 90 decrement 10`	Configures object 90 to be tracked in group 10, and decrements the weight by 10 if the object fails
`DLS1(config-if)#glbp 10 weighting track 91 decrement 20`	Configures object 91 to be tracked in group 10, and decrements the weight by 20 if the object fails
`DLS1(config)#interface vlan 20`	Moves to interface configuration mode
`DLS1(config-if)#ip address 172.18.20.2 255.255.255.0`	Assigns an IP address and netmask

`DLS1(config-if)#glbp 20 ip` `172.18.20.1`	Enables GLBP for group 1 on this interface with a virtual address of 172.18.20.1
`DLS1(config-if)#glbp 20` `weighting 110 lower 95 upper 105`	Specifies the initial weighting value, and the upper and lower thresholds, for a GLBP gateway
`DLS1(config-if)#glbp 20 timers` `msec 200 msec 700`	Configures the hello timer to be 200 milliseconds and the hold timer to be 700 milliseconds
`DLS1(config-if)#glbp 20 prior-` `ity 100`	Sets the priority level to 100 on the switch for VLAN 20
`DLS1(config-if)#glbp 20 preempt` `delay minimum 300`	Configures the switch to take over as AVG for group 10 if this switch has a higher priority than the current AVF after a delay of 300 seconds
`DLS1(config-if)#glbp 20 authen-` `tication md5 key-string xyz123`	Configures the authentication key xyz123 for GLBP packets received from the other switch in the group
`DLS1(config-if)#glbp 20` `weighting track 90 decrement 10`	Configures object 90 to be tracked in group 20, and decrements the weight by 10 if the object fails
`DLS1(config-if)#glbp 20` `weighting track 91 decrement 10`	Configures object 91 to be tracked in group 20, and decrements the weight by 10 if the object fails

DLS2

`DLS2(config)#track 90 interface` `fastethernet 1/0/8 line-protocol`	Configures tracking object 90 to monitor the line protocol on interface fastethernet 1/0/8
`DLS2(config)#track 91 interface` `fastethernet 1/0/6 line-protocol`	Configures tracking object 91 to monitor the line protocol on interface fastethernet 1/0/6
`DLS2(config)#interface vlan 10`	Moves to interface configuration mode
`DLS2(config-if)#ip address` `172.18.10.3 255.255.255.0`	Assigns an IP address and netmask
`DLS2(config-if)#glbp 10 ip` `172.18.10.1`	Enables GLBP for group 10 on this interface with a virtual address of 172.18.10.1
`DLS2(config-if)#glbp 10` `weighting 110 lower 95 upper 105`	Specifies the initial weighting value, and the upper and lower thresholds, for a GLBP gateway
`DLS2(config-if)#glbp 10 timers` `msec 200 msec 700`	Configures the hello timer to be 200 milliseconds and the hold timer to be 700 milliseconds

`DLS2(config-if)#glbp 10 priority 100`	Sets the priority level to 100 on the switch for VLAN 10
`DLS2(config-if)#glbp 10 preempt delay minimum 300`	Configures the switch to take over as AVG for group 10 if this switch has a higher priority than the current AVF after a delay of 300 seconds
`DLS2(config-if)#glbp 10 authentication md5 key-string xyz123`	Configures the authentication key xyz123 for GLBP packets received from the other switch in the group
`DLS2(config-if)#glbp 10 weighting track 90 decrement 10`	Configures object 90 to be tracked in group 10, and decrements the weight by 10 if the object fails
`DLS2(config-if)#glbp 10 weighting track 91 decrement 20`	Configures object 91 to be tracked in group 10, and decrements the weight by 20 if the object fails
`DLS2(config)#interface vlan 20`	Moves to interface configuration mode
`DLS2(config-if)#ip address 172.18.20.3 255.255.255.0`	Assigns an IP address and netmask
`DLS2(config-if)#glbp 20 ip 172.18.20.1`	Enables GLBP for group 1 on this interface with a virtual address of 172.18.20.1
`DLS2(config-if)#glbp 20 weighting 110 lower 95 upper 105`	Specifies the initial weighting value, and the upper and lower thresholds, for a GLBP gateway
`DLS2(config-if)#glbp 20 timers msec 200 msec 700`	Configures the hello timer to be 200 milliseconds and the hold timer to be 700 milliseconds
`DLS2(config-if)#glbp 20 priority 105`	Sets the priority level to 105 on the switch for VLAN 20
`DLS2(config-if)#glbp 20 preempt delay minimum 300`	Configures the switch to take over as AVG for group 10 if this switch has a higher priority than the current AVF after a delay of 300 seconds
`DLS2(config-if)#glbp 20 authentication md5 key-string xyz123`	Configures the authentication key xyz123 for GLBP packets received from the other switch in the group
`DLS2(config-if)#glbp 20 weighting track 90 decrement 10`	Configures object 90 to be tracked in group 20, and decrements the weight by 10 if the object fails.
`DLS2(config-if)#glbp 20 weighting track 91 decrement 10`	Configures object 91 to be tracked in group 20, and decrements the weight by 10 if the object fails

This chapter provides information and commands concerning the following topics:

- Assigning IPv6 addresses to interfaces
- IPv6 and RIPng
- Configuration example: IPv6 RIP
- IPv6 tunnels: manual overlay tunnel
- Static routes in IPv6
- Floating static routes in IPv6
- Default routes in IPv6
- Verifying and troubleshooting IPv6
- IPv6 **ping**
- IPv6 **traceroute**

NOTE For an excellent overview of IPv6, I strongly recommend you read Rick Graziani's book from Cisco Press: *IPv6 Fundamentals: A Straightforward Approach to Understanding IPv6.*

Assigning IPv6 Addresses to Interfaces

Router(config)#**ipv6 unicast-routing**	Enables the forwarding of IPV6 unicast datagrams globally on the router.
Router(config)#**interface gigabitethernet 0/0**	Moves to interface configuration mode.
Router(config-if)#**ipv6 enable**	Automatically configures an IPv6 link-local address on the interface and enables IPv6 processing on the interface.
	NOTE The link-local address that the **ipv6 enable** command configures can be used only to communicate with nodes on the same link.
Router(config-if)#**ipv6 address autoconfig**	Router will configure itself with a link-local address using stateless autoconfiguration.
Router(config-if)#**ipv6 address 2001::1/64**	Configures a global IPv6 address on the interface and enables IPv6 processing on the interface.
Router(config-if)#**ipv6 address 2001:db8:0:1::/64 eui-64**	Configures a global IPv6 address with an interface identifier in the low-order 64 bits of the IPv6 address.

Router(config-if)#ipv6 address fe80::260:3eff:fe47:1530/64 link-local	Configures a specific link-local IPv6 address on the interface instead of the one that is automatically configured when IPv6 is enabled on the interface.
Router(config-if)#ipv6 unnumbered *type/number*	Specifies an unnumbered interface and enables IPv6 processing on the interface. The global IPv6 address of the interface specified by *type/number* will be used as the source address.

IPv6 and RIPng

NOTE Although RIPng is no longer part of the CCNA Certification exam objectives, it is still a valid option for setting up small networks. The following sections on RIPng are here for your information only.

Router(config)#interface serial 0/0/0	Moves to interface configuration mode.
Router(config-if)#ipv6 rip tower enable	Creates the RIPng process named tower and enables RIPng on the interface.
	NOTE Unlike RIPv1 and RIPv2, where you needed to create the RIP routing process with the **router rip** command and then use the **network** command to specify the interfaces on which to run RIP, the RIPng process is created automatically when RIPng is enabled on an interface with the **ipv6 rip** *name* **enable** command.
	TIP Be sure that you do not misspell your process name. If you do misspell the name, you will inadvertently create a second process with the misspelled name.
	NOTE Cisco IOS Software automatically creates an entry in the configuration for the RIPng routing process when it is enabled on an interface.
	NOTE The **ipv6 router rip** *process-name* command is still needed when configuring optional features of RIPng.
Router(config)#ipv6 router rip tower	Creates the RIPng process named tower if it has not already been created, and moves to router configuration mode
Router(config-router)#maximum-paths 2	Defines the maximum number of equal-cost routes that RIPng can support.
	NOTE The number of paths that can be used is a number from 1 to 64. The default is 4.

Configuration Example: IPv6 RIP

Figure 16-1 illustrates the network topology for the configuration that follows, which shows how to configure IPv6 and RIPng using the commands covered in this chapter.

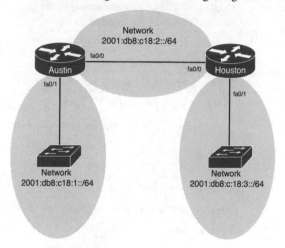

Figure 16-1 Network Topology for IPv6/RIPng Configuration Example

Austin Router

`Router>`**`enable`**	Moves to privileged mode
`Router#`**`configure terminal`**	Moves to global configuration mode
`Router(config)#`**`hostname Austin`**	Assigns a host name to the router
`Austin(config)#`**`ipv6 unicast-routing`**	Enables the forwarding of IPv6 unicast datagrams globally on the router
`Austin(config)#`**`interface fastethernet 0/0`**	Enters interface configuration mode
`Austin(config-if)#`**`ipv6 enable`**	Automatically configures an IPv6 link-local address on the interface and enables IPv6 processing on the interface
`Austin(config-if)#`**`ipv6 address 2001:db8:c18:2::/64 eui-64`**	Configures a global IPv6 address with an interface identifier in the low-order 64 bits of the IPv6 address
`Austin(config-if)#`**`ipv6 rip tower enable`**	Creates the RIPng process named tower and enables RIPng on the interface
`Austin(config-if)#`**`no shutdown`**	Activates the interface
`Austin(config-if)#`**`interface fastethernet 0/1`**	Enters interface configuration mode
`Austin(config-if)#`**`ipv6 enable`**	Automatically configures an IPv6 link-local address on the interface and enables IPv6 processing on the interface

`Austin(config-if)#ipv6 address 2001:db8:c18:1::/64 eui-64`	Configures a global IPv6 address with an interface identifier in the low-order 64 bits of the IPv6 address
`Austin(config-if)#ipv6 rip tower enable`	Creates the RIPng process named tower and enables RIPng on the interface
`Austin(config-if)#no shutdown`	Activates the interface
`Austin(config-if)#exit`	Moves to global configuration mode
`Austin(config)#exit`	Moves to privileged mode
`Austin#copy running-config startup-config`	Saves the configuration to NVRAM

Houston Router

`Router>enable`	Moves to privileged mode
`Router#configure terminal`	Moves to global configuration mode
`Router(config)#hostname Houston`	Assigns a host name to the router
`Houston(config)#ipv6 unicast-routing`	Enables the forwarding of IPv6 unicast datagrams globally on the router
`Houston(config)#interface fastethernet 0/0`	Enters interface configuration mode
`Houston(config-if)#ipv6 enable`	Automatically configures an IPv6 link-local address on the interface and enables IPv6 processing on the interface
`Houston(config-if)#ipv6 address 2001:db8:c18:2::/64 eui-64`	Configures a global IPv6 address with an interface identifier in the low-order 64 bits of the IPv6 address
`Houston(config-if)#ipv6 rip tower enable`	Creates the RIPng process named tower and enables RIPng on the interface
`Houston(config-if)#no shutdown`	Activates the interface
`Houston(config-if)#interface fastethernet 0/1`	Enters interface configuration mode
`Houston(config-if)#ipv6 enable`	Automatically configures an IPv6 link-local address on the interface and enables IPv6 processing on the interface
`Houston(config-if)#ipv6 address 2001:db8:c18:3::/64 eui-64`	Configures a global IPv6 address with an interface identifier in the low-order 64 bits of the IPv6 address
`Houston(config-if)#ipv6 rip tower enable`	Creates the RIPng process named tower and enables RIPng on the interface
`Houston(config-if)#no shutdown`	Activates the interface
`Houston(config-if)#exit`	Moves to global configuration mode

`Houston(config)#exit`	Moves to privileged mode
`Houston#copy running-config` `startup-config`	Saves the configuration to NVRAM

IPv6 Tunnels: Manual Overlay Tunnel

NOTE   Although not part of the official CCNA exam objectives, the concept of IPv6 tunnels is one that network administrators dealing with IPv6 need to be comfortable with.

Figure 16-2 illustrates the network topology for the configuration that follows, which shows how IPv6 tunnels are created.

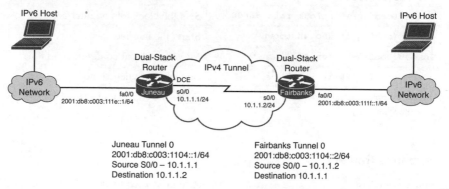

Figure 16-2   Network Topology for IPv6 Tunnel Creation

Juneau Router

`Router>enable`	Moves to privileged mode
`Router#configure terminal`	Moves to global configuration mode
`Router(config)#hostname Juneau`	Sets the host name of the router
`Juneau(config)#ipv6 unicast-routing`	Enables the forwarding of IPv6 unicast datagrams globally on the router
`Juneau(config)#interface tunnel0`	Moves to tunnel interface configuration mode
`Juneau(config-if)#ipv6 address` `2001:db8:c003:1104::1/64`	Assigns an IPv6 address to this interface
`Juneau(config-if)#tunnel source` `serial 0/0`	Specifies the source interface type and number for the tunnel interface
`Juneau(config-if)#tunnel destination` `10.1.1.2`	Specifies the destination IPv4 address for the tunnel interface

`Juneau(config-if)#tunnel mode ipv6ip`	Defines a manual IPv6 tunnel; specifically, that IPv6 is the passenger protocol and IPv4 is both the encapsulation and protocol for the IPv6 tunnel
`Juneau(config-if)#interface fastethernet 0/0`	Moves to interface configuration mode
`Juneau(config-if)#ipv6 address 2001:db8:c003:111e::1/64`	Assigns an IPv6 address to this interface
`Juneau(config-if)#no shutdown`	Activates the interface
`Juneau(config-if)#interface serial 0/0`	Moves to interface configuration mode
`Juneau(config-if)#ip address 10.1.1.1 255.255.255.252`	Assigns an IPv4 address and netmask
`Juneau(config-if)#clock rate 56000`	Sets the clock rate on interface
`Juneau(config-if)#no shutdown`	Starts the interface
`Juneau(config-if)#exit`	Moves to global configuration mode
`Juneau(config)#exit`	Moves to privileged mode
`Juneau#copy running-config startup-config`	Saves the configuration to NVRAM

Fairbanks Router

`Router>enable`	Moves to privileged mode
`Router#configure terminal`	Moves to global configuration mode
`Router(config)#hostname Fairbanks`	Sets the host name of the router
`Fairbanks(config)#interface tunnel0`	Moves to tunnel interface configuration mode
`Fairbanks(config-if)#ipv6 address 2001:db8:c003:1104::2/64`	Assigns an IPv6 address to this interface
`Fairbanks(config-if)#tunnel source serial 0/0`	Specifies the source interface type and number for the tunnel interface
`Fairbanks(config-if)#tunnel destination 10.1.1.1`	Specifies the destination IPv4 address for the tunnel interface
`Fairbanks(config-if)#tunnel mode ipv6ip`	Defines a manual IPv6 tunnel; specifically, that IPv6 is the passenger protocol and IPv4 is both the encapsulation and protocol for the IPv6 tunnel
`Fairbanks(config-if)#interface fastethernet 0/0`	Moves to interface configuration mode
`Fairbanks(config-if)#ipv6 address 2001:db8:c003:111f::1/64`	Assigns an IPv6 address to this interface
`Fairbanks(config-if)#no shutdown`	Activates the interface

`Fairbanks(config-if)#interface serial 0/0`	Moves to interface configuration mode
`Fairbanks(config-if)#ip address 10.1.1.2 255.255.255.252`	Assigns an IPv4 address and netmask
`Fairbanks(config-if)#no shutdown`	Starts the interface
`Fairbanks(config-if)#exit`	Moves to global configuration mode
`Fairbanks(config)#exit`	Moves to privileged mode
`Fairbanks#copy running-config startup-config`	Saves the configuration to NVRAM

Static Routes in IPv6

NOTE To create a static route in IPv6, you use the same format as creating a static route in IPv4.

Figure 16-3 illustrates the network topology for the configuration that follows, which shows how to configure static routes with IPv6. Note that only the static routes on the Austin router are displayed.

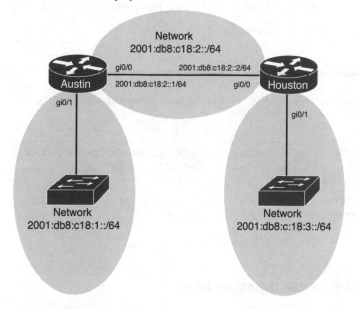

Figure 16-3 Network Topology for IPv6 Static Route Configuration

Austin(config)#**ipv6 route 2001:db8:c18:3::/64 2001:db8:c18:2::2/64**	Creates a static route configured to send all packets addressed to 2001:db8:c18:3::/64 to a next-hop address of 2001:db8:c18:2::2
Austin(config)#**ipv6 route 2001:db8:c18:3::/64 gigabitethernet 0/0**	Creates a directly attached static route configured to send packets out interface gigabitethernet 0/0
Austin(config)#**ipv6 route 2001:db8:c18:3::/64 gigabitethernet 0/0 2001:db8:c18:2::2**	Creates a fully specified static route on a broadcast interface

Floating Static Routes in IPv6

NOTE   Although not part of the CCNA exam objectives, the concept of floating static routes in IPv6 is one that network administrators dealing with IPv6 need to be comfortable with.

To create a static route with an administrative distance (AD) set to 200, as opposed to the default AD of one (1), enter the following command, for example:

Austin(config)# **ipv6 route 2001:db8:c18:3::/64 fastethernet 0/0 200**

The default ADs used in IPv4 are the same for IPv6.

Default Routes in IPv6

NOTE   To create a default route in IPv6, you use the same format as creating a default route in IPv4.

Austin(config)#**ipv6 route ::/0 2001:db8:c18:2::2/64**	Creates a default route configured to send all packets to a next-hop address of 2001:db8:c18:2::2
Austin(config)#**ipv6 route ::/0 gigabitethernet 0/0**	Creates a default route configured to send packets out interface gigabitethernet 0/0

Verifying and Troubleshooting IPv6

CAUTION   Using the **debug** command may severely affect router performance and might even cause the router to reboot. Always exercise caution when using the **debug** command. Do not leave **debug** on. Use it long enough to gather needed information, and then disable debugging with the **undebug all** command.

TIP   Send your **debug** output to a syslog server to ensure you have a copy of it in case your router is overloaded and needs to reboot.

`Router#clear ipv6 rip`	Deletes routes from the IPv6 RIP routing table and, if installed, routes in the IPv6 routing table
`Router#clear ipv6 route *`	Deletes all routes from the IPv6 routing table
	NOTE Clearing all routes from the routing table will cause high CPU utilization rates as the routing table is rebuilt.
`Router#clear ipv6 route 2001:db8:c18:3::/64`	Clears this specific route from the IPv6 routing table
`Router#clear ipv6 traffic`	Resets IPv6 traffic counters
`Router#debug ipv6 packet`	Displays debug messages for IPv6 packets
`Router#debug ipv6 rip`	Displays debug messages for IPv6 RIP routing transactions
`Router#debug ipv6 routing`	Displays debug messages for IPv6 routing table updates and route cache updates
`Router#show ipv6 interface`	Displays the status of interfaces configured for IPv6
`Router#show ipv6 interface brief`	Displays a summarized status of interfaces configured for IPv6
`Router#show ipv6 neighbors`	Displays IPv6 neighbor discovery cache information
`Router#show ipv6 protocols`	Displays the parameters and current state of the active IPv6 routing protocol processes
`Router#show ipv6 rip`	Displays information about the current IPv6 RIP process
`Router#show ipv6 route`	Displays the current IPv6 routing table
`Router#show ipv6 route summary`	Displays a summarized form of the current IPv6 routing table
`Router#show ipv6 routers`	Displays IPv6 router advertisement information received from other routers
`Router#show ipv6 static`	Displays only static IPv6 routes installed in the routing table
`Router#show ipv6 static 2001:db8:5555:0/16`	Displays only static route information about the specific address given
`Router#show ipv6 static interface serial 0/0/0`	Displays only static route information with the specified interface as the outgoing interface
`Router#show ipv6 static detail`	Displays a more detailed entry for IPv6 static routes
`Router#show ipv6 traffic`	Displays statistics about IPv6 traffic
`Router#show ipv6 tunnel`	Displays IPv6 tunnel information

IPv6 Ping

To diagnose basic network connectivity using IPv6 to the specified address, enter the following command:

```
Router#ping ipv6 2001:db8::3/64
```

The following characters can be displayed as output when using PING in IPv6.

Character	Description
!	Each exclamation point indicates receipt of a reply.
.	Each period indicates that the network server timed out while waiting for a reply.
?	Unknown error.
@	Unreachable for unknown reason.
A	Administratively unreachable. Usually means that an access control list (ACL) is blocking traffic.
B	Packet too big.
H	Host unreachable.
N	Network unreachable (beyond scope).
P	Port unreachable.
R	Parameter problem.
T	Time exceeded.
U	No route to host.

IPv6 Traceroute

To observe the path between two hosts using IPv6 to the specified address, you may use the **traceroute** command in Cisco IOS or the **tracert** Windows command:

```
Router#traceroute 2001:db8:c18:2::1
```

```
C:\Windows\system32>tracert 2001:DB8:c:18:2::1
```

This chapter provides information and commands concerning the following topics:

- Enabling OSPF for IPv6 on an interface
- Enabling an OSPF for IPv6 area range
- Enabling an IPv4 router ID for OSPFv3
- Forcing an SPF calculation

NOTE For an excellent overview of IPv6, I strongly recommend you read Rick Graziani's book from Cisco Press: *IPv6 Fundamentals: A Straightforward Approach to Understanding IPv6.*

IPv6 and OSPFv3

Working with IPv6 requires modifications to any dynamic protocol. The current version of Open Shortest Path First (OSPF), OSPFv2, was developed back in the late 1980s, when some parts of OSPF were designed to compensate for the inefficiencies of routers at that time. Now that router technology has dramatically improved, rather than modify OSPFv2 for IPv6 it was decided to create a new version of OSPF (OSPFv3), not just for IPv6, but for other newer technologies, too. This section covers using IPv6 with OSPFv3.

Enabling OSPF for IPv6 on an Interface

Router(config)#**ipv6 unicast-routing**	Enables the forwarding of IPv6 unicast datagrams globally on the router.
Router(config)#**ipv6 router ospf 1**	Creates the OSPFv3 process if it has not already been created and moves to router configuration mode.
Router(config)#**interface gigabitethernet 0/0**	Moves to interface configuration mode.

`Router(config-if)# ipv6 address` `2001:db8:0:1::/64`	Configures a global IPv6 address on the interface and enables IPv6 processing on the interface.
`Router(config-if)#ipv6 ospf 1` `area 0`	Enables OSPFv3 process 1 on the interface and places this interface into area 0.
	NOTE Just like OSPFv2 for IPv4, the process ID is locally significant and can be a positive integer from 1 to 65,535.
	NOTE The OSPFv3 process is created automatically when OSPFv3 is enabled on an interface.
	NOTE It is recommended to create the OSPFv3 process first before assigning an interface to it.
	NOTE Adding an interface to an OSPFv3 process without creating the process first will cause an error because no router ID has been created first.
	NOTE The ipv6 ospf *x* area *y* command has to be configured on each interface that will take part in OSPFv3.
`Router(config-if)#ipv6 ospf` `priority 30`	Assigns a priority number to this interface for use in the designated router (DR) election. The priority can be a number from 0 to 255. The default is 1. A router with a priority set to 0 is ineligible to become the DR or the backup DR (BDR).
`Router(config-if)#ipv6 ospf` `cost 20`	Assigns a cost value of 20 to this interface. The cost value can be an integer value from 1 to 65,535.

Enabling an OSPF for IPv6 Area Range

`Router(config)#ipv6 router` `ospf 1`	Creates the OSPFv3 process if it has not already been created and moves to router configuration mode
`Router(config-router)#area 1` `range 2001:db8::/48`	Consolidates and summarizes routes at an area boundary

Enabling an IPv4 Router ID for OSPFv3

`Router(config)#ipv6 router ospf 1`	Creates the OSPFv3 process if it has not already been created and moves to router configuration mode.
`Router(config-router)#router-id 192.168.254.255`	Creates a 32-bit router ID for this router.
	NOTE In OSPF for IPv6, it is possible that no IPv4 addresses will be configured on any interface. In this case, the user must use the router-id command to configure a router ID before the OSPF process will be started. If an IPv4 address does exist when OSPF for IPv6 is enabled on an interface, that IPv4 address is used for the router ID. If more than one IPv4 address is available, a router ID is chosen using the same rules as for OSPF Version 2.

Forcing an SPF Calculation

`Router#clear ipv6 ospf 1 process`	The OSPF database is cleared and repopulated, and then the SPF algorithm is performed.
`Router#clear ipv6 ospf 1 force-spf`	The OSPF database is not cleared; just an SPF calculation is performed.

CAUTION   As with OSPFv2, clearing the OSPFv3 database and forcing a recalculation of the Shortest Path First (SPF) algorithm is processor intensive and should be used with caution.

Verifying and Troubleshooting IPv6 and OSPFv3

`Router#debug ipv6 ospf adjacencies`	Displays debug messages about the OSPF adjacency process
`Router#show ipv6 interface brief`	Displays a summarized status of interfaces configured for IPv6
`Router#show ipv6 neighbors`	Displays IPv6 neighbor discovery cache information
`Router#show ipv6 ospf`	Displays general information about the OSPFv3 routing process
`Router#show ipv6 ospf border-routers`	Displays the internal OSPF routing table entries to an ABR or Autonomous System Boundary Router (ASBR)

`Router#show ipv6 ospf database`	Displays OSPFv3-related database information
`Router#show ipv6 ospf database database-summary`	Displays how many of each type of link-state advertisements (LSA) exist for each area in the database
`Router#show ipv6 ospf interface`	Displays OSPFv3-related interface information
`Router#show ipv6 ospf neighbor`	Displays OSPFv3-related neighbor information
`Router#show ipv6 route`	Displays the current IPv6 routing table

Configuration Example: OSPFv3

Figure 17-1 shows the network topology for the configuration that follows, which demonstrates how to configure IPv6 and OSPFv3 using the commands covered in this chapter.

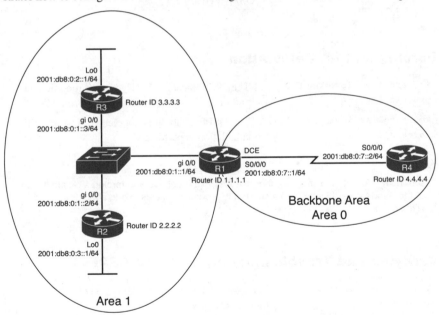

Figure 17-1   Network Topology for IPv6 and OSPFv3 Configuration

R3 Router

`Router>enable`	Moves to privileged mode
`Router#configure terminal`	Moves to global configuration mode
`Router(config)#hostname R3`	Assigns a host name to the router

`R3(config)#ipv6 unicast-routing`	Enables the forwarding of IPv6 unicast datagrams globally on the router
`R3(config)#ipv6 router ospf 1`	Creates the OSPFv3 process and moves to router configuration mode
`R3(config-router)#router-id 3.3.3.3`	Creates a 32-bit router ID for this router
`R3(config-router)#exit`	Returns to global configuration mode
`R3(config)#interface gigabitethernet 0/0`	Moves to interface configuration mode
`R3(config-if)#ipv6 address 2001:db8:0:1::3/64`	Configures a global IPv6 address on the interface and enables IPv6 processing on the interface
`R3(config-if)#ipv6 ospf 1 area 1`	Enables OSPFv3 on the interface and places this interface into area 1
`R3(config-if)#no shutdown`	Activates the interface
`R3(config-if)#interface loopback 0`	Moves to interface configuration mode
`R3(config-if)#ipv6 address 2001:db8:0:2::1/64`	Configures a global IPv6 address on the interface and enables IPv6 processing on the interface
`R3(config-if)#ipv6 ospf 1 area 1`	Enables OSPFv3 on the interface and places this interface into area 1
`R3(config-if)#exit`	Moves to global configuration mode
`R3(config)#exit`	Moves to privileged mode
`R3#copy running-config startup-config`	Saves the configuration to NVRAM

R2 Router

`Router>enable`	Moves to privileged mode
`Router#configure terminal`	Moves to global configuration mode
`Router(config)#hostname R2`	Assigns a host name to the router
`R2(config)#ipv6 unicast-routing`	Enables the forwarding of IPv6 unicast datagrams globally on the router
`R2(config)#ipv6 router ospf 1`	Creates the OSPFv3 process and moves to router configuration mode
`R2(config-router)#router-id 2.2.2.2`	Creates a 32-bit router ID for this router
`R2(config-router)#exit`	Returns to global configuration mode
`R2(config)#interface gigabitethernet 0/0`	Moves to interface configuration mode

`R2(config-if)#ipv6 address` `2001:db8:0:1::2/64`	Configures a global IPv6 addresses on the interface and enables IPv6 processing on the interface
`R2(config-if)#ipv6 ospf 1 area 1`	Enables OSPFv3 on the interface and places this interface into area 1
`R2(config-if)#no shutdown`	Starts the interface
`R2(config-if)#interface loopback 0`	Moves to interface configuration mode
`R2(config-if)#ipv6 address` `2001:db8:0:3::1/64`	Configures a global IPv6 address on the interface and enables IPv6 processing on the interface
`R2(config-if)#ipv6 ospf 1 area 1`	Enables OSPFv3 on the interface and places this interface into area 1
`R2(config-if)#no shutdown`	Starts the interface
`R2(config-if)#exit`	Moves to global configuration mode
`R2(config)#exit`	Moves to privileged mode
`R2#copy running-config startup-config`	Saves the configuration to NVRAM

R1 Router

`Router>enable`	Moves to privileged mode
`Router#configure terminal`	Moves to global configuration mode
`Router(config)#hostname R1`	Assigns a host name to the router
`R1(config)#ipv6 unicast-routing`	Enables the forwarding of IPv6 unicast datagrams globally on the router
`R1(config)#ipv6 router ospf 1`	Creates the OSPFv3 process and moves to router configuration mode
`R1(config-router)#router-id 1.1.1.1`	Creates a 32-bit router ID for this router
`R1(config-router)#exit`	Returns to global configuration mode
`R1(config)#interface` `gigabitethernet 0/0`	Moves to interface configuration mode
`R1(config-if)#ipv6 address` `2001:db8:0:1::1/64`	Configures a global IPv6 address on the interface and enables IPv6 processing on the interface
`R1(config-if)#ipv6 ospf 1 area 1`	Enables OSPFv3 on the interface and places this interface into area 1
`R1(config-if)#no shutdown`	Starts the interface
`R1(config-if)#interface serial 0/0/0`	Moves to interface configuration mode

`R1(config-if)#ipv6 address` `2001:db8:0:7::1/64`	Configures a global IPv6 address on the interface and enables IPv6 processing on the interface
`R1(config-if)#ipv6 ospf 1 area 0`	Enables OSPFv3 on the interface and places this interface into area 0
`R1(config-if)#clock rate 56000`	Assigns a clock rate to this interface
`R1(config-if)#no shutdown`	Starts the interface
`R1(config-if)#exit`	Moves to global configuration mode
`R1(config)#exit`	Moves to privileged mode
`R1#copy running-config` `startup-config`	Saves the configuration to NVRAM

R4 Router

`Router>enable`	Moves to privileged mode
`Router#configure terminal`	Moves to global configuration mode
`Router(config)#hostname R4`	Assigns a host name to the router
`R4(config)#ipv6 unicast-routing`	Enables the forwarding of IPv6 unicast datagrams globally on the router
`R4(config)#ipv6 router ospf 1`	Creates the OSPFv3 process and moves to router configuration mode
`R4(config-router)#router-id` `4.4.4.4`	Creates a 32-bit router ID for this router
`R4(config-router)#exit`	Returns to global configuration mode
`R4(config)#interface serial 0/0/0`	Moves to interface configuration mode
`R4(config-if)#ipv6 address` `2001:db8:0:7::2/64`	Configures a global IPv6 address on the interface and enables IPv6 processing on the interface
`R4(config-if)#ipv6 ospf 1 area 0`	Enables OSPFv3 on the interface and places this interface into area 0
`R4(config-if)#no shutdown`	Starts the interface
`R4(config-if)#exit`	Moves to global configuration mode
`R4(config)#exit`	Moves to privileged mode
`R4#copy running-config` `startup-config`	Saves the configuration to NVRAM

CHAPTER 18

EIGRP for IPv6

This chapter provides information and commands concerning the following topics:

- Enabling EIGRP for IPv6 on an interface
- Configuring the percentage of link bandwidth used by EIGRP
- Configuring summary addresses
- Configuring EIGRP route authentication
- Configuring EIGRP timers
- Logging EIGRP neighbor adjacency changes
- Adjusting the EIGRP for IPv6 metric weights
- Configuration example: EIGRP for IPv6

NOTE For an excellent overview of IPv6, I strongly recommend you read Rick Graziani's book from Cisco Press: *IPv6 Fundamentals: A Straightforward Approach to Understanding IPv6.*

IPv6 and EIGRP

Enabling EIGRP for IPv6 on an Interface

Router(config)#**ipv6 unicast-routing**	Enables the forwarding of IPv6 unicast datagrams globally on the router.
Router(config)#**interface serial 0/0/0**	Moves to interface configuration mode.
Router(config-if)#**ipv6 eigrp 100**	Enables IPv6 processing on an interface that has not been configured with an explicit IPv6 address
Router(config-if)#**ipv6 router eigrp 100**	Enters router configuration mode and creates an EIGRP IPv6 routing process
Router(config-router)#**eigrp router-id 10.1.1.1**	Enables the use of a fixed router ID
Router(config-router)#**no shutdown**	Brings up the EIGRP routing process

NOTE EIGRP for IPv6 starts in shutdown mode. Use the **no shutdown** command to start the process

NOTE Use the **eigrp router-id w.x.y.z** command only if an IPv4 address is not defined on the router eligible for router ID.

Configuring the Percentage of Link Bandwidth Used by EIGRP

`Router(config)#interface serial 0/0/0`	Moves to interface configuration mode
`Router(config-if)#ipv6 band-width-percent eigrp 100 75`	Configures the percentage of bandwidth (75%) that may be used by EIGRP for IPv6 on the interface

Configuring Summary Addresses

`Router(config)#interface serial 0/0/0`	Moves to interface configuration mode
`Router(config-if)#ipv6 summary-address eigrp 100 2001:0DB8:0:1::/64`	Configures a summary aggregate address for a specified interface

Configuring EIGRP Route Authentication

`Router(config)#interface serial 0/0/0`	Moves to interface configuration mode.
`Router(config-if)#ipv6 authenti-cation mode eigrp 100 md5`	Specifies the type of authentication used in EIGRP for IPv6 packets; in this case, MD5.
`Router(config-if)#ipv6 authenti-cation key-chain eigrp 100 chain1`	Enables authentication of EIGRP over IPv6 packets.
`Router(config-if)#exit`	Returns to global configuration mode.
`Router(config)#key chain chain1`	Identifies a group of authentication keys. chain1 matches the name of the key chain identified in interface configuration mode.
`Router(config-keychain)#key 1`	Identifies an authentication key on a key chain.
`Router(config-keychain-key)#key-string chain1`	Specifies the authentication string for a key.
`Router(config-keychain-key)#accept-lifetime 14:30:00 Jan 20 2010 duration 7200`	Sets the time period during which the authentication key on the key chain is received as valid.
`Router(config-keychain-key)#send-lifetime 15:00:00 Jan 20 2010 duration 36000`	Sets the time period during which an authentication key on a key chain is valid to be sent.

Configuring EIGRP Timers

`Router(config)#interface serial 0/0/0`	Moves to interface configuration mode
`Router(config-if)#ipv6 hello-interval eigrp 100 10`	Configures the hello interval for EIGRP for IPv6 process 100 to be 10 seconds
`Router(config-if)#ipv6 hold-time eigrp 100 40`	Configures the hold timer for EIGRP for IPv6 process 100 to be 40 seconds

Logging EIGRP Neighbor Adjacency Changes

`Router(config)#ipv6 router eigrp 100`	Enters router configuration mode and creates an EIGRP IPv6 routing process
`Router(config-router)#eigrp log-neighbor changes`	Enables the logging of changes in EIGRP for IPv6 neighbor adjacencies
`Router(config-router)#eigrp log-neighbor-warnings 300`	Configures the logging intervals of EIGRP neighbor warning messages to 300 seconds

Adjusting the EIGRP for IPv6 Metric Weights

`Router(config)#ipv6 router eigrp 100`	Enters router configuration mode and creates an EIGRP IPv6 routing process.
`Router(config-router)#metric weights tos k1 k2 k3 k4 k5`	Changes the default *k* values used in metric calculation. These are the default values: tos=0, k1=1, k2=0, k3=1, k4=0, k5=0

Verifying and Troubleshooting EIGRP for IPv6

`Router#clear ipv6 route *`	Deletes all routes from the IPv6 routing table. **NOTE** Clearing all routes from the routing table will cause high CPU utilization rates as the routing table is rebuilt.
`Router#clear ipv6 route 2001:db8:c18:3::/64`	Clears this specific route from the IPv6 routing table.
`Router#clear ipv6 traffic`	Resets IPv6 traffic counters.
`Router#show ipv6 eigrp topology`	Displays entries in the EIGRP IPv6 topology table.
`Router#show ipv6 eigrp neighbors`	Displays the neighbors that are discovered by EIGRP for IPv6.
`Router#show ipv6 interface brief`	Displays a summarized status of interfaces configured for IPv6.
`Router#show ipv6 neighbors`	Displays IPv6 neighbor discovery cache information.
`Router#show ipv6 protocols`	Displays the parameters and current state of the active IPv6 routing protocol processes.
`Router#show ipv6 route`	Displays the current IPv6 routing table.
`Router#show ipv6 route eigrp`	Displays the EIGRP routes in the IPv6 routing table.

Configuration Example: EIGRP for IPv6

Figure 18-1 shows the network topology for the configuration that follows, which demonstrates how to configure EIGRP for IPv6 using the commands covered in this chapter.

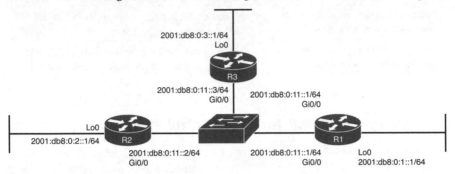

Figure 18-1 Network Topology for EIGRP for IPv6 Configuration

R3 Router

`Router>enable`	Moves to privileged mode
`Router#configure terminal`	Moves to global configuration mode
`Router(config)#hostname R3`	Assigns a host name to the router
`R3(config)#ipv6 unicast-routing`	Enables the forwarding of IPv6 unicast datagrams globally on the router
`R3(config)#ipv6 router eigrp 1`	Creates and enters EIGRP router configuration mode with the autonomous system being 1
`R3(config-router)#eigrp router-id 10.3.3.3`	Enables the use of a fixed router ID
`R3(config-router)#no shutdown`	Enables the EIGRP for the IPv6 process
`R3(config-router)#exit`	Returns to global configuration mode
`R3(config)#interface gigabitethernet 0/0`	Moves to interface configuration mode
`R3(config-if)#ipv6 address 2001:db8:0:11::3/64`	Configures a global IPv6 address on the interface and enables IPv6 processing on the interface
`R3(config-if)#ipv6 eigrp 1`	Enables EIGRP for IPv6 on the interface and places this interface into autonomous system 1
`R3(config-if)#no shutdown`	Activates the interface
`R3(config-if)#interface loopback 0`	Moves to interface configuration mode

R3(config-if)#**ipv6 address** **2001:db8:0:3::1/64**	Configures a global IPv6 address on the interface and enables IPv6 processing on the interface
R3(config-if)#**ipv6 eigrp 1**	Enables EIGRP for IPv6 on the interface and places this interface into autonomous system 1
R3(config-if)#**exit**	Moves to global configuration mode
R3(config)#**exit**	Moves to privileged mode
R3#**copy running-config startup-config**	Saves the configuration to NVRAM

R2 Router

Router>**enable**	Moves to privileged mode
Router#**configure terminal**	Moves to global configuration mode
Router(config)#**hostname R2**	Assigns a host name to the router
R2(config)#**ipv6 unicast-routing**	Enables the forwarding of IPv6 unicast datagrams globally on the router
R2(config)#**ipv6 router eigrp 1**	Creates and enters EIGRP router configuration mode with the autonomous system being 1
R2(config-router)#**eigrp router-id 10.2.2.2**	Enables the use of a fixed router ID
R2(config-router)#**no shutdown**	Enables the EIGRP for the IPv6 process
R2(config-router)#**exit**	Returns to global configuration mode
R2(config)#**interface gigabitethernet 0/0**	Moves to interface configuration mode
R2(config-if)#**ipv6 address 2001:db8:0:11::2/64**	Configures a global IPv6 addresses on the interface and enables IPv6 processing on the interface
R2(config-if)#**ipv6 eigrp 1**	Enables EIGRP for IPv6 on the interface and places this interface into autonomous system 1
R2(config-if)#**no shutdown**	Starts the interface
R2(config-if)#**interface loopback 0**	Moves to interface configuration mode
R2(config-if)#**ipv6 address 2001:db8:0:2::1/64**	Configures a global IPv6 address on the interface and enables IPv6 processing on the interface
R2(config-if)#**ipv6 eigrp 1**	Enables EIGRP for IPv6 on the interface and places this interface into autonomous system 1
R2(config-if)#**exit**	Moves to global configuration mode
R2(config)#**exit**	Moves to privileged mode
R2#**copy running-config startup-config**	Saves the configuration to NVRAM

R1 Router

`Router>enable`	Moves to privileged mode
`Router#configure terminal`	Moves to global configuration mode
`Router(config)#hostname R1`	Assigns a host name to the router
`R1(config)#ipv6 unicast-routing`	Enables the forwarding of IPv6 unicast datagrams globally on the router
`R1(config)#ipv6 unicast-routing`	Enables the forwarding of IPv6 unicast datagrams globally on the router
`R1(config)#ipv6 router eigrp 1`	Creates and enters EIGRP router configuration mode with the autonomous system being 1
`R1(config-router)#eigrp router-id 10.1.1.1`	Enables the use of a fixed router ID
`R1(config-router)#no shutdown`	Enables the EIGRP for the IPv6 process
`R1(config)#interface gigabitethernet 0/0`	Moves to interface configuration mode
`R1(config-if)#ipv6 address 2001:db8:0:11::1/64`	Configures a global IPv6 address on the interface and enables IPv6 processing on the interface
`R1(config-if)#ipv6 eigrp 1`	Enables EIGRP for IPv6 on the interface and places this interface into autonomous system 1
`R1(config-if)#no shutdown`	Starts the interface
`R1(config-if)#interface loopback 0`	Moves to interface configuration mode
`R1(config-if)#ipv6 address 2001:db8:0:1::1/64`	Configures a global IPv6 address on the interface and enables IPv6 processing on the interface
`R1(config-if)#ipv6 eigrp 1`	Enables EIGRP for IPv6 on the interface and places this interface into autonomous system 1
`R1(config-if)#exit`	Moves to global configuration mode
`R1(config)#exit`	Moves to privileged mode
`R1#copy running-config startup-config`	Saves the configuration to NVRAM

CHAPTER 19

Backing Up and Restoring Cisco IOS Software and Configurations

This chapter provides information and commands concerning the following topics:

- Boot system commands
- The Cisco IOS File System
- Viewing the Cisco IOS file System
- Commonly used URL prefixes for Cisco network devices
- Deciphering IOS image filenames
- Backing up configurations to a TFTP server
- Restoring configurations from a TFTP server
- Backing up the Cisco IOS Software to a TFTP server
- Restoring/upgrading the Cisco IOS Software from a TFTP server
- Restoring the Cisco IOS Software from ROM Monitor mode using Xmodem
- Restoring the Cisco IOS Software using the ROM Monitor environmental variables and **tftpdnld** command

Boot System Commands

Router(config)#**boot system flash** *image-name*	Loads the Cisco IOS Software with *image-name*.
Router(config)#**boot system tftp** *image-name* 172.16.10.3	Loads the Cisco IOS Software with *image-name* from a TFTP server.
Router(config)#**boot system rom**	Loads the Cisco IOS Software from ROM.
Router(config)#**exit**	
Router#**copy running-config startup-config**	Saves the running configuration to NVRAM. The router will execute commands in their order on the next reload.

TIP If you enter **boot system flash** first, that is the first place the router will go to look for the Cisco IOS Software. If you want to go to a TFTP server first, make sure that the **boot system tftp** command is the first one you enter.

TIP   If there are no **boot system** commands in the configuration, the router defaults to loading the first valid Cisco IOS image in flash memory and running it. If no valid Cisco IOS image is found in flash memory, the router attempts to boot from a network TFTP server. After six unsuccessful attempts of locating a network TFTP server, the router loads into ROMmon mode.

The Cisco IOS File System

NOTE   The Cisco IOS File System (IFS) provides a single interface to all the file systems available on a routing device, including the flash memory file system; network file systems such as TFTP, Remote Copy Protocol (RCP), and File Transfer Protocol (FTP); and any other endpoint for reading and writing data, such as NVRAM, or the running configuration.The Cisco IFS minimizes the required prompting for many commands. Instead of entering in an EXEC-level **copy** command and then having the system prompt you for more information, you can enter a single command on one line with all necessary information.

Cisco IOS Software Commands	IFS Commands
`copy tftp running-config`	`copy tftp: system:running-config`
`copy tftp startup-config`	`copy tftp: nvram:startup-config`
`show startup-config`	`more nvram:startup-config`
`erase startup-config`	`erase nvram:`
`copy running-config startup-config`	`copy system:running-config nvram:startup-config`
`copy running-config tftp`	`copy system:running-config tftp:`
`show running-config`	`more system:running-config`

Viewing the Cisco IOS File System

`Router#show file systems`	Displays all the available files systems on the device

NOTE   The Cisco IOS File System uses a URL convention to specify files on network devices and the network. Many of the most commonly used URL prefixes are also available in the Cisco IOS File System.

Commonly Used URL Prefixes for Cisco Network Devices

flash:	Flash memory. Available on all platforms. An alias for the flash: prefix is slot0.
ftp:	FTP network server.
http:	HTTP network server.

nvram:	NVRAM.
rcp:	RCP network server.
system:	Contains system memory, including the current running configuration.
tftp:	TFTP network server.
usbflash0, usbflash1	USB flash.

Deciphering IOS Image Filenames

Although it looks long and complex, there is a reason that Cisco names its IOS images they way that they do. It is important to understand the meaning behind an IOS image name so that you can correctly choose which file to work with.

There are different parts to the image filename, as follows:

c2900-universalk9-mz.SPA.152-4.M1.bin

c2900	The platform on which the image runs. In this case, it is a Cisco 2900 router.
universal	Specifies the feature set. Universal on a 2900 would include IP Base, Security, Unified Communication, and Data feature sets. Each router is activated for IP Base; the others need software activation.
	NOTE k9 in an image name means that strong encryption, such as 3DES/AES, is included.
mz	Indicates where the image runs and if it is compressed. m means the file runs from RAM. z means the file is compressed.
SPA	This software is digitally signed. There are two file extensions possible: SPA or SSA. The first character S stands for digitally signed software. The second character P in SPA means that this release is meant for production. A second character S in SSA means it is a special image and has limited use or special conditions. The third character A indicates the key version used to digitally sign the image.
152-4.M1	The version number of the software. In this case, we have major release 15, minor release 2, new feature release 4. M means Extended Maintenance Release, and 1 is the Maintenance Rebuild Number.
.bin	This is the file extension. .bin shows that this file is a binary executable file.

NOTE   The Cisco IOS naming conventions, meanings, content, and other details are subject to change.

Backing Up Configurations to a TFTP Server

`Denver#copy running-config` `startup-config`	Saves the running configuration from DRAM to NVRAM (locally).
`Denver#copy running-config tftp`	Copies the running configuration to the remote TFTP server.
`Address or name of remote` `host[ ]? 192.168.119.20`	The IP address of the TFTP server.
`Destination Filename [Denver-` `confg]?`(↵Enter)	The name to use for the file saved on the TFTP server.
`!!!!!!!!!!!!!!!`	Each bang symbol (!) = 1 datagram of data.
`624 bytes copied in 7.05 secs`	
`Denver#`	File has been transferred successfully.

NOTE   You can also use the preceding sequence for a **copy startup-config tftp** command sequence.

Restoring Configurations from a TFTP Server

`Denver#copy tftp running-config`	Copies the configuration file from the TFTP server to DRAM.
`Address or name of remote host[ ]?` `192.168.119.20`	The IP address of the TFTP server.
`Source filename [ ]?Denver-confg`	Enter the name of the file you want to retrieve.
`Destination filename [running-config]?` (↵Enter)	
`Accessing tftp://192.168.119.20/Denver-` `confg...`	

`Loading Denver-confg from`
`192.168.119.02 (via Gigabit Ethernet`
`0/0):`	

`!!!!!!!!!!!!!!`	
`[OK-624 bytes]`	
`624 bytes copied in 9.45 secs`	
`Denver#`	File has been transferred successfully.

NOTE   You can also use the preceding sequence for a **copy tftp startup-config** command sequence.

Backing Up the Cisco IOS Software to a TFTP Server

Denver#**copy flash0: tftp:**	
Source filename [ ]? **c2900-universalk9-mz. SPA.152-4.M1.bin**	Name of the Cisco IOS Software image.
Address or name of remote host [ ]? **192.168.119.20**	The address of the TFTP server.
Destination filename [**c2900-universalk9- mz.SPA.152-4.M1.bin**]? ⏎Enter	The destination filename is the same as the source filename, so just press ⏎Enter.
!! !!	
8906589 bytes copied in 263.68 seconds	
Denver#	

Restoring/Upgrading the Cisco IOS Software from a TFTP Server

Denver#**copy tftp: flash:**	
Address or name of remote host [ ]? **192.168.119.20**	
Source filename [ ]? **c2900-universalk9- mz.SPA.152-4.M1.bin**	
Destination filename [**c2900-universalk9- mz.SPA.152-4.M1.bin**]? ⏎Enter	
Accessing tftp://192.168.119.20/ **c2900-universalk9-mz.SPA.152-4.M1.bin**	
Erase flash: before copying? [confirm] ⏎Enter	If flash memory is full, erase it first.
Erasing the flash file system will remove all files	
Continue? [confirm] ⏎Enter	Press Ctrl-C if you want to cancel.
Erasing device eeeeeeeeeeeeeeeeeee... erased	Each *e* represents data being erased.
Loading **c2900-universalk9-mz.SPA.152-4. M1.bin** from **192.168.119.20**	
(via) GigabitEthernet 0/0): !!!!!!!!!!!!!! !!! !!!!!!!!!!!!!!!!!!!!!!!!!!!!!!!!!!!!!!	Each bang symbol (!) = 1 data-gram of data.
Verifying Check sum .... OK	

[OK - 8906589 Bytes]	
8906589 bytes copied in 277.45 secs	
Denver#	Success.

Restoring the Cisco IOS Software from ROM Monitor Mode Using Xmodem

The output that follows was taken from a 1720 router. Some of this output might vary from yours, depending on the router model that you are using.

`rommon 1 >`**`confreg`**	Shows the configuration summary. Step through the questions, answering defaults until you can change the console baud rate. Change it to **115200**; it makes transfer go faster.

`Configuration Summary`
 	
`enabled are:`
 	
`load rom after netboot fails`
 	
`console baud: 9600`
 	
`boot: image specified by the boot system commands`
 	
`or default to: cisco2-c1700`	

`do you wish to change the configuration? y/n`
`[n]: `**`y`**
`enable "diagnostic mode"? y/n [n]: `**`n`**
`enable "use net in IP bcast address"? y/n`
`[n]: `**`n`**
`disable "load rom after netboot fails"? y/n`
`[n]: `**`n`**
`enable "use all zero broadcast"? y/n [n]: `**`n`**
`enable "break/abort has effect"? y/n [n]: `**`n`**
`enable "ignore system config info"? y/n`
`[n]: `**`n`**
`change console baud rate? y/n [n]: `**`y`**
`enter rate: 0=9600, 1=4800, 2=1200, 3=2400`
`4=19200, 5=38400, 6=57600, 7=115200 [0]: `**`7`**
`change the boot characteristics? y/n [n]: `**`n`**
	Prompts begin to ask a series of questions that allow you to change the configuration register. Answer **n** to all questions except the one that asks you to change the console baud rate. For the enter rate, choose **7** because that is the number that represents a baud rate of 115200.

`Configuration Summary`
 	
`enabled are:`
 	
`load rom after netboot fails`
 	
`console baud: 115200`
 	
`boot: image specified by the boot system`
`commands`
 	
`or default to: cisco2-c1700`
 	
`do you wish to change the configuration? y/n`
`[n]: `**`n`**
 	
`rommon2>`
	After the summary is shown again, choose **n** to not change the configuration and go to the rommon> prompt again.

`rommon 2>`**`reset`**	Reloads the router at the new com speed. Change the HyperTerminal setting to **115200** to match the router's new console setting.
`Rommon 1>`**`xmodem c1700-js-l_121-3.bin`**	Asking to transfer this image using Xmodem.
`...<output cut>...`	
`Do you wish to continue? y/n [n ]:`**`y`**	Choose **y** to continue.
	In HyperTerminal, go to Transfer, then Send File (see Figure 16-1). Locate the Cisco IOS Software file on the hard drive and click Send (see Figure 16-2).
`Router will reload when transfer is` `completed.`	
`Reset baud rate on router.`	
`Router(config)#`**`line con 0`**	
`Router(config-line)#`**`speed 9600`**	
`Router(config-line)#`**`exit`**	HyperTerminal will stop responding. Reconnect to the router using 9600 baud, 8-N-1.

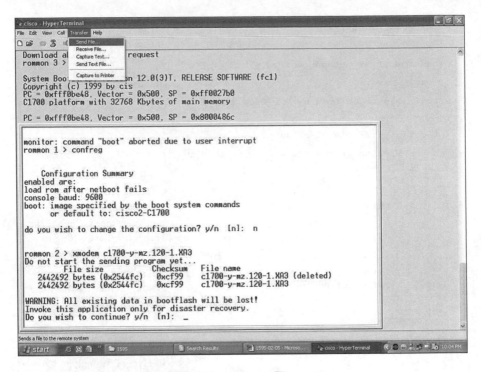

Figure 19-1 Finding the Cisco IOS Software Image File

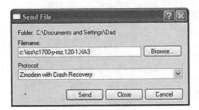

Figure 19-2 Sending the Cisco IOS Software Image File to the Router

Restoring the Cisco IOS Software Using the ROM Monitor Environmental Variables and tftpdnld Command

rommon 1>IP_ ADDRESS=192.168.100.1	Indicates the IP address for this unit.
rommon 2>IP_SUBNET_ MASK=255.255.255.0	Indicates the subnet mask for this unit.
rommon 3>DEFAULT_ GATEWAY=192.168.100.1	Indicates the default gateway for this unit.

rommon 4>**TFTP_** **SERVER=192.168.100.2**	Indicates the IP address of the TFTP server.
rommon 5>**TFTP_FILE=** **c2600-js-l_121-3.bin**	Indicates the filename to fetch from the TFTP server.
rommon 6>**tftpdnld**	Starts the process.
...<output cut>...	
Do you wish to continue? y/n: [n]:**y**	
...<output cut>...	
Rommon 7>**i**	Resets the router. The *i* stands for initialize.

NOTE Commands and environmental variables are case sensitive, so be sure that you have not accidentally added spaces between variables and answers.

CHAPTER 20

Password-Recovery Procedures and the Configuration Register

This chapter provides information and commands concerning the following topics:

- The configuration register
  - A visual representation
  - What the bits mean
  - The boot field
  - Console terminal baud rate settings
  - Changing the console line speed: CLI
  - Changing the console line speed: ROM Monitor mode
- Password-recovery procedures for Cisco routers
- Password-recovery procedures for 2960 series switches

The Configuration Register

router#**show version**	The last line of output tells you what the configuration register is set to.
router#**configure terminal**	Moves to global configuration mode.
router(config)#**config-register 0x2142**	Changes the configuration register to 2142.

A Visual Representation

The configuration register is a 16-bit field stored in NVRAM. The bits are numbered from 15 to 0 looking at the bit stream from left to right. Bits are split up into groups of 4, and each group is represented by a hexadecimal digit.

15 14 13 12 11 10 9 8 7 6 5 4 3 2 1 0	Bit places
0 0 1 0 0 0 0 1 0 1 0 0 0 0 1 0	Register bits
2 1 4 2	Bits represented in hex

What the Bits Mean

Bit Number	Hexadecimal	Meaning
00–03	0x0000–0x000F	Boot field.
06	0x0040	Ignore NVRAM contents.

Bit Number	Hexadecimal	Meaning
07	0x0080	OEM bit enabled.
08	0x0100	Break disabled.
09	0x0200	Causes system to use secondary bootstrap (typically not used).
10	0x0400	IP broadcast with all 0s.
5, 11, 12	0x0020, 0x0800, 0x1000	Console line speed.
13	0x2000	Boots default ROM software if network boot fails.
14	0x4000	IP broadcasts do not have net numbers.
15	0x8000	Enables diagnostic messages and ignores NVRAM contents.

The Boot Field

NOTE Even though there are 16 possible combinations in the boot field, only 3 are used.

Boot Field	Meaning
00	Stays at the ROM Monitor on a reload or power cycle
01	Boots the first image in flash memory as a system image
02–F	Enables default booting from flash memory Enables **boot system** commands that override default booting from flash memory

TIP Because the default boot field has 14 different ways to represent it, a configuration register setting of 0x2102 is the same as 0x2109, or 0x210F. The **boot system** command is described in Chapter 19, "Backing Up and Restoring Cisco IOS Software and Configurations."

Console Terminal Baud Rate Settings

Baud	Bit 5	Bit 12	Bit 11
115200	1	1	1
57600	1	1	0
38400	1	0	1
19200	1	0	0
9600	0	0	0
4800	0	0	1
2400	0	1	1
1200	0	1	0

Changing the Console Line Speed: CLI

router#**configure terminal**	
router(config)#**line console 0**	Enters console line mode
router(config-line)#**speed 19200**	Changes speed to 19200 baud

TIP   Cisco IOS Software does not allow you to change the console speed bits directly with the **config-register** command.

Changing the Console Line Speed: ROM Monitor Mode

rommon1>**confreg**	Shows configuration summary. Step through the questions, answering with the defaults until you can change the console baud rate.
Configuration Summary enabled are: load rom after netboot fails console baud: 9600 boot: image specified by the boot system commands or default to: *x* (name of system image)	
do you wish to change the configuration? y/n [n]: **y** enable "diagnostic mode"? y/n [n]: **n** enable "use net in IP bcast address"? y/n [n]: **n** disable "load rom after netboot fails"? y/n [n]: **n** enable "use all zero broadcast"? y/n [n]: **n** enable "break/abort has effect"? y/n [n]: **n** enable "ignore system config info"? y/n [n]: **n** change console baud rate? y/n [n]: **y** enter rate: 0=9600, 1=4800, 2=1200, 3=2400 4=19200, 5=38400, 6=57600, 7=115200 [0]: **7**	
Configuration Summary enabled are: load rom after netboot fails console baud: 115200 boot: image specified by the boot system commands or default to: *x* (name of system image)	
change the boot characteristics? y/n [n]: **n**	After the summary is shown again, choose **n** to not change the configuration and go to the rommon>prompt again.
rommon2>	

TIP Make sure that after you change the console baud rate, you change your terminal program to match the same rate!

Password-Recovery Procedures for Cisco Routers

Step	2500 Series Commands	1700/2600/ISR/ISR2 Series Commands
Step 1: Boot the router and interrupt the boot sequence as soon as text appears on the screen. The Break sequence differs depending on the terminal program you are using. In HyperTerminal and PuTTY, the command is Ctrl-Break. In TeraTerm, the command is Alt-B. Make sure you know the correct sequence.	Press Ctrl - Break >	Press Ctrl - Break rommon 1>
Step 2: Change the configuration register to ignore contents of NVRAM.	>o/r 0x2142 >	rommon 1>confreg 0x2142 rommon 2>
Step 3: Reload the router.	>i	rommon 2>reset
Step 4: Enter privileged EXEC mode. (Do not enter setup mode.)	Router>enable Router#	Router>enable Router#
Step 5: Copy the startup configuration into the running configuration.	Router#copy startup-config running-config ...<output cut>... Denver#	Router#copy startup-config running-config ...<output cut>... Denver#
Step 6: Change the password.	Denver#configure terminal Denver(config)#enable secret *newpassword* Denver(config)#	Denver#configure terminal Denver(config)#enable secret *newpassword* Denver(config)#
Step 7: Reset the configuration register back to its default value.	Denver(config)#config-register 0x2102 Denver(config)#	Denver(config)#config-register 0x2102 Denver(config)#
Step 8: Save the configuration.	Denver(config)#exit Denver#copy running-config startup-config Denver#	Denver(config)#exit Denver#copy running-config startup-config Denver#

Step	2500 Series Commands	1700/2600/ISR/ISR2 Series Commands
Step 9: Verify the configuration register.	`Denver#`**`show version`**	`Denver#`**`show version`**
	`...<output cut>...`	`...<output cut>...`
	`Configuration register is 0x2142 (will be 0x2102 at next reload)`	`Configuration register is 0x2142 (will be 0x2102 at next reload)`
	`Denver#`	`Denver#`
Step 10: Reload the router.	`Denver#`**`reload`**	`Denver#`**`reload`**

Password Recovery for 2960 Series Switches

Unplug the power supply from the back of the switch.	
Press and hold the Mode button on the front of the switch.	
Plug the switch back in.	
Release the Mode button when the SYST LED blinks amber and then turns solid green. When you release the Mode button, the SYST LED blinks green.	
Issue the following commands:	
`switch: `**`flash_init`**	Initializes the flash memory.
`switch: `**`load_helper`**	
`switch: `**`dir flash:`**	Do not forget the colon. This displays which files are in flash memory.
`switch: `**`rename flash:config.text flash:config.old`**	You are renaming the configuration file. The config.text file contains the password.
`switch: `**`boot`**	Boots the switch.
When asked whether you want to enter the configuration dialog, enter **n** to exit out to the switch prompt.	Takes you to user mode.
`switch>`**`enable`**	Enters privileged mode.
`switch#`**`rename flash:config.old flash:config.text`**	Renames the configuration file back to the original name.
`Destination filename [config.text]`	Press (⏎Enter).
`switch#`**`copy flash:config.text system:running-config`**	Copies the configuration file into memory.

`768 bytes copied in 0.624 seconds`	
`2960Switch#`	The configuration file is now reloaded. Notice the new prompt.
`2960Switch#`**`configure terminal`**	Enters global configuration mode.
`2960Switch(config)#`	
`Proceed to change the passwords as needed`	
`2960Switch(config)#`**`exit`**	
`2960Switch#`**`copy running-config startup-config`**	Saves the configuration into NVRAM with new passwords.

CHAPTER 21

Cisco Discovery Protocol (CDP)

This chapter provides information and commands concerning the following topic:

- Cisco Discovery Protocol (CDP)

Cisco Discovery Protocol

Router#**show cdp**	Displays global CDP information (such as timers)
Router#**show cdp neighbors**	Displays information about neighbors
Router#**show cdp neighbors detail**	Displays more detail about the neighbor device
Router#**show cdp entry word**	Displays information about the device named word
Router#**show cdp entry ***	Displays information about all devices
Router#**show cdp interface**	Displays information about interfaces that have CDP running
Router#**show cdp interface** x	Displays information about specific interface x running CDP
Router#**show cdp traffic**	Displays traffic information—packets in/out/version
Router(config)#**cdp holdtime** x	Changes the length of time to keep CDP packets
Router(config)#**cdp timer** x	Changes how often CDP updates are sent
Router(config)#**cdp run**	Enables CDP globally (on by default)
Router(config)#**no cdp run**	Turns off CDP globally
Router(config-if)#**cdp enable**	Enables CDP on a specific interface
Router(config-if)#**no cdp enable**	Turns off CDP on a specific interface
Router#**clear cdp counters**	Resets traffic counters to 0
Router#**clear cdp table**	Deletes the CDP table
Router#**debug cdp adjacency**	Monitors CDP neighbor information
Router#**debug cdp events**	Monitors all CDP events
Router#**debug cdp ip**	Monitors CDP events specifically for IP
Router#**debug cdp packets**	Monitors CDP packet-related information

CAUTION   Although CDP is necessary for some management applications, CDP should still be disabled in some instances.

Disable CDP globally if

- CDP is not required at all.
- The device is located in an insecure environment.

Use the command **no cdp run** to disable CDP globally:

```
RouterOrSwitch(config)#no cdp run
```

Disable CDP on any interface if

- Management is not being performed.
- The switch interface is a nontrunk interface.
- The interface is connected to a nontrusted network.

Use the interface configuration command **no cdp enable** to disable CDP on a specific interface:

```
RouterOrSwitch(config)#interface fastethernet 0/1

RouterOrSwitch(config-if)#no cdp enable
```

CHAPTER 22

Remote Connectivity Using Telnet or SSH

This chapter provides information and commands concerning the following topics:

- Configuring a device to accept a remote Telnet connection
- Using Telnet to remotely connect to other devices
- Verifying Telnet
- Configuring the Secure Shell protocol (SSH)
- Verifying SSH

Configuring a Device to Accept a Remote Telnet Connection

> **NOTE**   The ability to telnet into a Cisco device is part of every Cisco IOS. You only need to assign passwords to allow a remote connection into a device.

`Router(config)#line vty 0 4`	Enters vty line mode for 5 vty lines numbered 0 through 4.
	NOTE An ISR2 router has 5 vty lines numbered 0 through 4. A 2960/3560 switch has 16 vty lines numbered 0 through 15. Make sure that you assign a password to all vty lines of your devices.
`Router(config-line)#password letmein`	Sets vty password to letmein.
`Router(config-line)#login`	Enables password checking at login.

> **NOTE**   A device must have two passwords for a remote user to be able to make changes to the configuration:
>
> - Line vty password
> - **enable** or **enable secret** password
>
> Without the **enable** or **enable secret** password, a remote user will only be able to get to user mode, not to privileged EXEC mode. Remember that without an **enable** or **enable secret** password set, a user logged in through the console will still access privileged EXEC mode. But a remote user needs one of these passwords to gain access. This is extra security.

Using Telnet to Remotely Connect to Other Devices

The following five commands all achieve the same result: the attempt to connect remotely to the router named Paris at IP address 172.16.20.1.

`Denver>`**`telnet paris`**	Enter if **ip host** command was used previously to create a mapping of an IP address to the word *paris*. **NOTE** The **ip host** command is covered in Chapter 6, "Configuring a Single Cisco Router," in the "Assigning a Local Hostname to an IP Address" section.
`Denver>`**`telnet 172.16.20.1`**	
`Denver>`**`paris`**	Enter if **ip host** command is using a default port number.
`Denver>`**`connect paris`**	
`Denver>`**`172.16.20.1`**	

Any of the preceding commands lead to the following configuration sequence:

`Paris>`	As long as vty password is set. See the Caution following this table.
`Paris>`**`exit`**	Terminates the Telnet session and returns you to the Denver prompt.
`Denver>`	
OR	
`Paris>`**`logout`**	Terminates the Telnet session and returns you to the Denver prompt.
`Denver>`	
`Paris>` Ctrl-⇧Shift-⑥, `release, then press` ⓧ	Suspends the Telnet session but does not terminate it, and returns you to the Denver prompt.
`Denver>`	
`Denver>`**`[Enter]`**	Resumes the connection to Paris.
`Paris>`	
`Denver>`**`resume`**	Resumes the connection to Paris.
`Paris>`	
`Denver>`**`disconnect paris`**	Terminates the session to Paris.
`Denver>`	

Verifying Telnet

Denver#**show sessions**	Displays connections you opened to other sites.
Denver#**show users**	Displays who is connected remotely to you.
Denver#**clear line** *x*	Disconnects the remote user connected to you on line *x*. The line number is listed in the output gained from the **show users** command.
Denver(config)#**line vty 0 4**	Moves to line configuration mode for vty lines 0–4.
Denver(config-line) **session-limit** *x*	Limits the number of simultaneous sessions per vty line to *x* number.

CAUTION   The following configuration creates a big security hole. Never use it in a live production environment. Use it in the lab only!

Denver(config)#**line vty 0 4**	Moves you to line configuration mode for vty lines 0–4.
Denver(config-line)#**no password**	The remote user is not challenged when telnetting to this device.
Denver(config-line)#**no login**	The remote user moves straight to user mode.

NOTE   A device must have two passwords for a remote user to be able to make changes to the configuration:

- Line vty password (or have it explicitly turned off; see the preceding Caution)
- **Enable** or **enable secret** password

Without the **enable** or **enable secret** password, a remote user will only be able to get to user mode, not to privileged mode. This is extra security.

Configuring the Secure Shell Protocol (SSH)

CAUTION   SSH Version 1 implementations have known security issues. It is recommended to use SSH Version 2 whenever possible.

NOTE   The device name cannot be the default *switch* (on a switch) or *router* (on a router). Use the **hostname** command to configure a new host name of the device

The Cisco implementation of SSH requires Cisco IOS Software to support Rivest-Shamir-Adleman (RSA) authentication and minimum Data Encryption Standard (DES) encryption—a cryptographic software image.

`Denver(config)#username Roland password tower`	Creates a locally significant username/password combination. These are the credentials needed to be entered when connecting to the router with SSH client software.
`Denver(config)#ip domain-name test.lab`	Creates a host domain for the router.
`Denver(config)#crypto key generate rsa`	Enables the SSH server for local and remote authentication on the router and generates an RSA key pair.
`Denver(config)#ip ssh version 2`	Enables SSH Version 2 on the device.

NOTE To work, SSH requires a local username database, a local IP domain, and an RSA key to be generated.

`Denver(config)#line vty 0 4`	Move to vty configuration mode for all 5 vty lines of the router.
`Denver(config-line)#login local`	Enables password checking on a per-user basis. Username and password will be checked against the data entered with the **username** global configuration command.
`Denver(config-line)#transport input ssh`	Limits remote connectivity to SSH connections only; disables Telnet.

Verifying SSH

`Denver#show ip ssh`	Verifies that SSH is enabled
`Denver#show ssh`	Checks the SSH connection to the device

CHAPTER 23

Verifying End-to-End Connectivity

This chapter provides information and commands concerning the following topics:

- ICMP redirect messages
- The **ping** command
- Examples of using the **ping** and the extended **ping** commands
- The **traceroute** command

ICMP Redirect Messages

Router(config-if)#**no ip redirects**	Disables ICMP redirects from this specific interface
Router(config-if)#**ip redirects**	Reenables ICMP redirects from this specific interface

The ping Command

Router#**ping** *w.x.y.z*	Checks for Layer 3 connectivity with device at IPv4 address *w.x.y.z*
Router#**ping aaaa:aaaa:a aaa:aaaa:aaaa:aaaa:aaaa :aaaa**	Checks for Layer 3 connectivity with device at IPv6 address aaaa:aaaa:aaaa:aaaa:aaaa:aaaa:aaaa:aaaa
Router#**ping**	Enters extended ping mode, which provides more options

The following table describes the possible ping output characters.

Character	Meaning
!	Successful receipt of a reply.
.	Device timed out while waiting for a reply.
U	A destination unreachable error protocol data unit (PDU) was received.
Q	Source quench (destination too busy).
M	Could not fragment.
?	Unknown packet type.
&	Packet lifetime exceeded.

Examples of Using the ping and the Extended ping Commands

Router#**ping** 172.16.20.1	Performs a basic Layer 3 test to IPv4 address 172.16.20.1.
Router#**ping paris**	Same as above but through the IP host name.
Router#**ping** 2001:**db8:D1A5:C900::2**	Checks for Layer 3 connectivity with device at IPv6 address 2001:db8:D1A5:C900::2.
Router#**ping**	Enters extended ping mode; can now change parameters of ping test.
Protocol [ip]: ⏎Return	Press ⏎Return to use ping for IP.
Target IP address: **172.16.20.1**	Enter the target IP address.
Repeat count [5]: **100**	Enter the number of echo requests you want to send. The default is 5.
Datagram size [100]: ⏎Return	Enter the size of datagrams being sent. The default is 100.
Timeout in Seconds [2]: ⏎Return	Enter the timeout delay between sending echo requests.
Extended commands [n]: **yes**	Allows you to configure extended commands.
Source address or interface: **10.0.10.1**	Allows you to explicitly set where the pings are originating from.
Type of Service [0]	Allows you to set the TOS field in the IP header.
Set DF bit in IP header [no]	Allows you to set the DF bit in the IP header.
Validate reply data? [no]	Allows you to set whether you want validation.
Data Pattern [0xABCD]	Allows you to change the data pattern in the data field of the ICMP echo request packet.

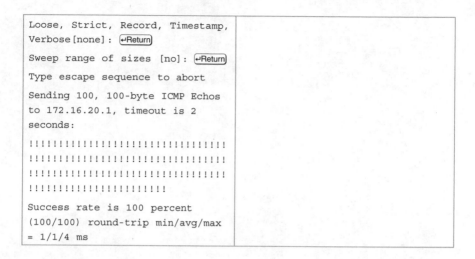

```
Loose, Strict, Record, Timestamp,
Verbose [none] : (↵Return)

Sweep range of sizes [no] : (↵Return)

Type escape sequence to abort

Sending 100, 100-byte ICMP Echos
to 172.16.20.1, timeout is 2
seconds:

!!!!!!!!!!!!!!!!!!!!!!!!!!!!!!!!!!!
!!!!!!!!!!!!!!!!!!!!!!!!!!!!!!!!!!!
!!!!!!!!!!!!!!!!!!!!!!!!!!!!!!!!!!!
!!!!!!!!!!!!!!!!!!!!!!!!!!

Success rate is 100 percent
(100/100) round-trip min/avg/max
= 1/1/4 ms
```

The traceroute Command

The **traceroute** command (or **tracert** in Windows) is a utility that allows observation of the path between two hosts.

Router#**traceroute** 172.16.20.1	Discovers the route taken to travel to the IPv4 destination of 172.16.20.1
Router#**traceroute** paris	Command with IP host name rather than IP address
Router#**traceroute** 2001:db8:D1A5:C900::2	Discovers the route taken to travel to the IPv6 destination of 2001:db8:D1A5:C900::2
Router#**trace** 172.16.20.1	Common shortcut spelling of the **traceroute** command

NOTE In Windows operating systems, the command to allow observation between two hosts is **tracert**:

C:\Windows\system32>**tracert 172.16.20.1**

CHAPTER 24

Configuring Network Management Protocols

This chapter provides information and commands concerning the following topics:

- Configuring SNMP
- Configuring syslog
- Syslog message format
- Severity levels
- Syslog message example
- Configuring NetFlow
- Verifying NetFlow

Configuring SNMP

Router(config)#snmp-server community academy ro	Sets a read-only (ro) community string called academy
Router(config)#snmp-server community academy rw	Sets a read-write (rw) community string called academy
Router(config)#snmp-server location 2nd Floor IDF	Defines an SNMP string that describes the physical location of the SNMP server
Router(config)#snmp-server contact Scott Empson 555-5243	Defines an SNMP string that describes the sysContact information

NOTE A community string is like a password. In the case of the first command, the community string grants you access to SNMP.

Configuring Syslog

Router(config)#**logging on**	Enables logging to all supported destinations.
Router(config)#**logging 192.168.10.53**	Logging messages will be sent to a syslog server host at address 192.168.10.53.
Router(config)#**logging sysadmin**	Logging messages will be sent to a syslog server host named sysadmin.
Router(config)#**logging trap x**	Sets the syslog server logging level to value x, where x is a number between 0 and 7 or a word defining the level. The table that follows provides more details.
Router(config)#**service sequence-numbers**	Stamps syslog messages with a sequence number.
Router(config)#**service timestamps log datetime**	Syslog messages will now have a time stamp included.

Syslog Message Format

NOTE The general format of syslog messages generated on Cisco IOS Software is as follows:

```
seq no:timestamp: %facility-severity-MNEMONIC:description
```

Item in Syslog Message	Definition
seq no	Sequence number. Stamped only if the **service sequence-numbers** global configuration command is configured.
timestamp	Date and time of the message. Appears only if the **service timestamps log datetime** global configuration command is configured.
facility	The facility to which the message refers: SNMP, SYS, and so on.
severity	Single-digit code from 0 to 7 that defines the severity of the message. See the Syslog Severity Levels Table for descriptions of the levels.
MNEMONIC	String of text that uniquely defines the message.
description	String of text that contains detailed information about the event being reported.

Syslog Severity Levels

There are eight levels of severity in logging messages, as follows:

0	Emergencies	System is unusable
1	Alerts	Immediate action needed
2	Critical	Critical conditions
3	Errors	Error conditions
4	Warnings	Warning conditions
5	Notifications	Normal but significant conditions
6	Informational	Informational messages (default level)
7	Debugging	Debugging messages

Setting a level means you will get that level and everything numerically below it. Level 6 means you will receive messages for levels 0 through 6.

Syslog Message Example

The easiest syslog message to use as an example is the one that shows up every time you exit from global configuration back to privileged EXEC mode. You have just finished entering a command and you want to save your work, but after you type in **exit** you see something like this:

(Your output will differ depending on whether you have sequence numbers or time/date stamps configured.)

```
Router(config)#exit
Router#
*Feb 18:22:45:20.878: %SYS-5-CONFIG_I: Configured from console by
    console
Router#
```

So, what does this all mean?

- No sequence number is part of this message.
- The message occurred at Feb 18, at 22:45:20.878 (or 10:45 PM, and 20.878 seconds).
- It is a SYS Message, and it is level 5 notification.
- It is a CONFIG message, and specifically we are being told that the configuration occurred from the console.

Configuring NetFlow

NetFlow is an application for collecting IP traffic information. It is used for network accounting and security auditing.

> **CAUTION** NetFlow consumes additional memory. If you have limited memory, you might want to preset the size of the NetFlow cache to contain a smaller number of entries. The default cache size depends on the platform of the device.

`Router(config)#interface gigabitethernet 0/0`	Moves to interface configuration mode.
`Router(config-if)#ip flow ingress`	Enables NetFlow on the interface. Captures traffic that is being received by the interface.
`Router(config-if)#ip flow egress`	Enables NetFlow on the interface. Captures traffic that is being transmitted by the interface.
`Router(config-if)#exit`	Returns to global configuration mode.
`Router(config)#ip flow-export destination ip_address udp_port`	Defines the IP address of the workstation to which you want to send the NetFlow information and the UDP port on which the workstation is listening for the information.
`Router(config)#ip flow-export version x`	Specifies the version format that the export packets used.

> **NOTE** NetFlow exports data in UDP in one of five formats: 1, 5, 7, 8, 9. Version 9 is the most versatile, but is not backward compatible with Versions 5 or 8.

Verifying NetFlow

`Router#show ip interface gigabitethernet 0/0`	Displays information about the interface, including NetFlow, as being either ingress or egress enabled.
`Router#show ip flow export`	Verifies status and statistics for NetFlow accounting data export.
`Router#show ip cache flow`	Displays a summary of NetFlow statistics on a Cisco IOS router.

> **NOTE** The **show ip cache flow** command is useful for seeing which protocols use the highest volume of traffic, and between which hosts this traffic flows.

CHAPTER 25

Basic Troubleshooting

This chapter provides information and commands concerning the following topics:

- Viewing the routing table
- Clearing the routing table
- Determining the gateway of last resort
- Determining the last routing update
- OSI Layer 3 testing
- OSI Layer 7 testing
- Interpreting the **show interface** command
- Clearing interface counters
- Using CDP to troubleshoot
- The **traceroute** command
- The **show controllers** command
- **debug** commands
- Using time stamps
- Operating system IP verification commands
- The **ip http server** command
- The **netstat** command
- The **arp** command

Viewing the Routing Table

Router#**show ip route**	Displays the entire routing table
Router#**show ip route** *protocol*	Displays a table about a specific protocol (for example, RIP or IGRP)
Router#**show ip route** *w.x.y.z*	Displays information about route *w.x.y.z*
Router#**show ip route connected**	Displays a table of connected routes
Router#**show ip route static**	Displays a table of static routes
Router#**show ip route summary**	Displays a summary of all routes

Clearing the Routing Table

Router#**clear ip route ***	Clears entire routing table, forcing it to rebuild
Router#**clear ip route a.b.c.d**	Clears specific route to network a.b.c.d

Determining the Gateway of Last Resort

Router(config)#**ip default-network** *w.x.y.z*	Sets network *w.x.y.z* to be the default route. All routes not in the routing table will be sent to this network.
Router(config)#**ip route 0.0.0.0 0.0.0.0 172.16.20.1**	Specifies that all routes not in the routing table will be sent to 172.16.20.1.

NOTE   The **ip default-network** command is for use with the deprecated Cisco propri-etary Interior Gateway Routing Protocol (IGRP). Although you can use it with Enhanced Interior Gateway Routing Protocol (EIGRP) or RIP, it is not recommended. Use the **ip route 0.0.0.0 0.0.0.0** command instead.

Routers that use the **ip default-network** command must have either a specific route to that network or a **0.0.0.0 /0** default route.

Determining the Last Routing Update

Router#**show ip route**	Displays the entire routing table
Router#**show ip route** *w.x.y.z*	Displays information about route *w.x.y.z*
Router#**show ip protocols**	Displays the IP routing protocol parameters and statistics

OSI Layer 3 Testing

Router#**ping** *w.x.y.z*	Checks for Layer 3 connectivity with the device at IPv4 address *w.x.y.z*
Router#**ping** *aaaa:aaaa: aaaa:aaaa:aaaa:aaaa:aaa a:aaaa*	Checks for Layer 3 connectivity with device at IPv6 address *aaaa:aaaa:aaaa:aaaa:aaaa:aaaa:aaaa:aaaa*
Router#**ping**	Enters extended ping mode, which provides more options

NOTE   See Chapter 23, "Verifying End-to-End Connectivity" for all applicable **ping** commands.

OSI Layer 7 Testing

NOTE   See Chapter 22, "Remote Connectivity Using Telnet or SSH," for all applicable Telnet and SSH commands.

Router#**debug telnet**	Displays the Telnet negotiation process

Interpreting the show interface Command

Router#**show interface serial 0/0/0**	Displays the status and stats of the interface.
Serial 0/0/0 is *up*, line protocol is *up*	The first part refers to the physical status. The second part refers to the logical status.
...<output cut>...	
Possible output results:	
Serial 0/0/0 is *up*, line protocol is *up*	The interface is up and working.
Serial 0/0/0 is *up*, line protocol is *down*	Keepalive or connection problem (no clock rate, bad encapsulation).
Serial 0/0/0 is *down*, line protocol is *down*	Interface problem, or other end has not been configured.
Serial 0/0/0 is administratively *down*, line protocol is *down*	Interface is disabled—shut down.

Clearing Interface Counters

Router#**clear counters**	Resets all interface counters to 0
Router#**clear counters** *interface type/ slot*	Resets specific interface counters to 0

Using CDP to Troubleshoot

NOTE   See Chapter 21, "Cisco Discovery Protocol (CDP)," for all applicable CDP commands.

The traceroute Command

Router#**traceroute** *w.x.y.z*	Displays all routes used to reach the destination of *w.x.y.z*

NOTE   See Chapter 23 for all applicable **traceroute** commands.

The show controllers Command

Router#**show controllers serial 0/0/0**	Displays the type of cable plugged into the serial interface (DCE or DTE) and what the clock rate is, if it was set

debug Commands

Router#**debug all**	Turns on all possible debugging.
Router#**u all** (short form of undebug all)	Turns off all possible debugging.
Router#**show debug**	Lists what debug commands are on.
Router#**terminal monitor**	Debug output will now be seen through a Telnet session (default is to only send output on the console screen).

CAUTION   Turning all possible debugging on is extremely CPU intensive and will probably cause your router to crash. Use *extreme caution* if you try this on a production device. Instead, be selective about which **debug** commands you turn on.

Do not leave debugging turned on. After you have gathered the necessary information from debugging, turn all debugging off. If you want to turn off only one specific **debug** command and leave others on, issue the **no debug** *x* command, where *x* is the specific **debug** command you want to disable.

Using Time Stamps

Router(config)#**service timestamps**	Adds a time stamp to all system logging messages
Router(config)#**service timestamps debug**	Adds a time stamp to all debugging messages
Router(config)#**service timestamps debug uptime**	Adds a time stamp along with the total uptime of the router to all debugging messages
Router(config)#**service timestamps debug datetime localtime**	Adds a time stamp displaying the local time and the date to all debugging messages
Router(config)#**no service timestamps**	Disables all time stamps

TIP   Make sure you have the date and time set with the **clock** command at privileged mode so that the time stamps are more meaningful.

Operating System IP Verification Commands

The following are commands that you should use to verify what your IP settings are. Different operating systems have different commands.

- **ipconfig** (Windows 8/7/Vista/2000/XP):

  Click **Start > Run > Command > ipconfig** or **ipconfig/all**.

- **winipcfg** (Windows 95/98/Me):

  Click **Start > Run > winipcfg**.

- **ifconfig** (Mac/Linux):

  `#ifconfig`

The ip http server Command

`Router(config)#`**`ip http server`**	Enables the HTTP server, including the Cisco web browser user interface
`Router(config-if)#`**`no ip http server`**	Disables the HTTP server

> **CAUTION**   The HTTP server was introduced in Cisco IOS Software Release 11.0 to extend router management to the web. You have limited management capabilities to your router through a web browser if the **ip http server** command is turned on.
>
> Do not turn on the **ip http server** command unless you plan to use the browser interface for the router. Having it on creates a potential security hole because another port is open.

The netstat Command

`C\>`**`netstat`**	Used in Windows and UNIX/Linux to display TCP/IP connection and protocol information; used at the command prompt in Windows

The arp Command

The **arp** Windows command displays and modifies entries in the ARP cache that are used to store IP addresses and their resolved Ethernet (MAC) addresses.

`C:\Windows\systems32>`**`arp -a`**	Displays the entire ARP cache
`C:\Windows\system32>`**`arp -d`**	Clears the ARP cache, forcing the machine to repopulate with updated information

CHAPTER 26

Cisco IOS Licensing

This chapter provides information and commands concerning the following topics:

- Cisco licensing earlier than IOS 15.0
- Cisco licensing for the ISR G2 platforms: IOS 15.0 and later
- Verifying licenses
- Cisco License Manager
- Installing a permanent license
- Installing an evaluation license
- Backing up a license
- Uninstalling a license

Cisco Licensing Earlier Than IOS 15.0

Before IOS Version 15.0, the software image was selected based on the required needs of the customer.

There are eight different images that satisfy different requirements in different service areas, see Figure 26-1.

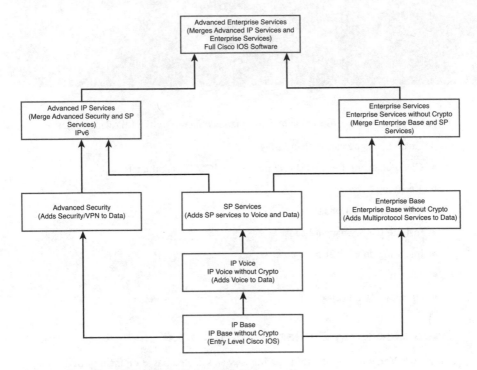

Figure 26-1   Cisco IOS Images Before IOS 15.0

Software Image/Package	Features
IP Base/IP Base without Crypto	IP Data. This is the entry-level Cisco IOS Software image.
IP Voice/IP Voice without Crypto	Adds Voice to Data: VoIP, VoFR, IP telephony.
Advanced Security	Adds Security to Data: Security and VPN features, including Cisco IOS Firewall, IDS/IPS, IPsec, 3DES, and VPN.
SP Services	Adds SP Services to Voice and Data: SSH/SSL, ATM, VoATM, MPLS.
Enterprise Base	Adds Multiprotocol Services to Data: AT, IPX, limited IBM support.
Enterprise Services	Merges Enterprise Base and SP Services. Adds full IBM support.
Advanced IP Services	Merges Advanced Security and SP Services. Adds IPv6.
Advanced Enterprise Services	Merges Advanced IP Services and Enterprise Services. Full Cisco IOS Software.

Cisco Licensing for the ISR G2 Platforms: IOS 15.0 and Later

Beginning with the ISR G2 platform (1900, 2900, and 3900 series), the router now ships with a single universal IOS image and corresponding feature set packages as shown in Figure 26-2.

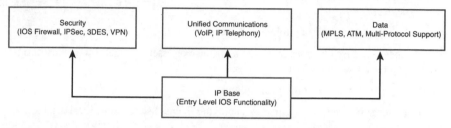

Figure 26-2 IOS Licensing for ISR G2 Platforms: IOS 15.0 and Later

Routers come with IP Base installed, and additional feature pack licenses can be installed as an addition to expand the feature set of the device.

Software Image/Package	Features
IP Base (ipbasek9)	Entry-level IOS functionality
Data (datak9)	Adds MPLS, ATM, multiprotocol support to IP Base
Unified Communication (uck9)	Adds VoIP and IP telephony to IP Base
Security (securityk9)	Adds IOS Firewall, IPS, IPsec, 3DES, and VPN to IP Base

NOTE The IP Base License is the prerequisite for installing any or all of the Data, Unified Communications, or Security Package Licenses

Verifying Licenses

Router#**show license**	Displays information about all Cisco IOS Software licenses
Router#**show license feature**	Views the technology package licenses and features licenses supported on this router

Cisco License Manager

If you work in a large environment with a lot of Cisco routers, you might want to implement the Cisco License Manager in your workplace. This software can help you manage all your software licenses, including the following:

- Discovering your network
- Inventories license features
- Given a product authorization key (PAK), securely obtains device licenses from the Cisco.com license server
- Securely deploys licenses to activate the software features on your managed devices
- Enhances security using role-based access control
- Integrates Cisco licenses into existing license or asset management applications (if you have these installed)
- Provides detailed reporting capabilities
- Reduces failure recovery time by deploying licenses stores in its local database
- Automatically retrieves and deploys licenses for a given device

NOTE   Cisco License Manager is a free software tool available at Cisco.com.

Installing a Permanent License

NOTE   If you purchase a router and identify and purchase a permanent license at the time of ordering, Cisco will preinstall the appropriate license for you. You use the following commands if you want to update your router with new technology packages after purchase.

NOTE   To install a permanent license, you must have purchased that license from Cisco, and your license file must be stored on the flash of your router.

NOTE   Permanent licenses are perpetual; no end date is associated with them. After you have installed the license onto your router, the license never expires.

Router#`license install` `stored-location-url`	Installs a license file stored in the location identified by the *stored-location-url*
Router#`reload`	Reloads the router

NOTE   A reload is not required if an evaluation license is already active on the router. A reload is required only to activate a technology package license when the evaluation license for that technology package is not active.

Router#`show version`	Verifies that the new license has been installed

NOTE   Perform the **show version** command after a reboot to confirm that your license has been installed.

Installing an Evaluation License

NOTE   Evaluation licenses are temporary licenses, allowing you to evaluate a feature set on new hardware. These temporary licenses are limited to a specific usage period of 60 days. The 60-day limit may be extended through the Cisco Technical Assistance Center (TAC) under certain circumstances.

NOTE   Depending on the hardware on your router, some evaluation licenses might not be available on your router; the UC Technology Package License is not available to install on any of the 1900 series devices, for example.

`Router(config)#license boot module` `module-name technology-package package-name`	Enables the evaluation license
`Router(config)#exit`	Returns to privileged EXEC mode
`Router#reload`	Reloads the router to allow activation of the software package

NOTE   Use the **?** to determine the *module-name* of your device. It should look like **c1900** or **c2900** or **c3900** depending on the platform.

NOTE   Use the **?** to determine which *package-names* are supported on your router.

`Router#show license`	Verifies that the new license has been installed

Backing Up a License

`Router#license save` `file-sys://lic-location`	Saves a copy of all licenses in a device. The location can be a directory or a URL that points to a file system.
`Router#license save` `flash:all_licenses.lic`	Saves a copy of all licenses to the flash memory of the device under the name all_licenses.lic.

NOTE   Use the **?** to see the storage locations supported by your device.

NOTE   Saved licenses are restored by using the **license install** command.

Uninstalling a License

To uninstall an active permanent license from an ISR G2 router, you must perform two tasks: Disable the technology package, and then clear the license.

NOTE Built-in licenses cannot be uninstalled. Only licenses that have been added by using the **license install** command can be removed.

Router(config)#**license boot module** *module-name* **technology-package** *package-name* **disable**	Disables the active license.
Router(config)#**exit**	Returns to privileged EXEC mode.
Router#**reload**	Reloads the router to make the software package inactive.
Router#**show version**	Verifies that the technology package has been disabled.
Router#**license clear** *feature-name*	Clears the technology package license from license storage.
Router#**configure terminal**	Moves to global configuration mode.
Router(config)#**no license boot module** *module-name* **technology-package** *package-name* disable	Clears the **license boot module** *module-name* **technology-package** *package-name* **disable** command that was used for disabling the active license.
Router(config)#**exit**	Returns to privileged EXEC mode.
Router#**reload**	Reloads the router. This is required to make the software package inactive.
Router#**show version**	Verifies that the license has been cleared.

CHAPTER 27

Network Address Translation

This chapter provides information and commands concerning the following topics:

- Private IP addresses: RFC 1918
- Configuring dynamic NAT: One private to one public address translation
- Configuring Port Address Translation (PAT): Many private to one public address translation
- Configuring static NAT: One private to one permanent public address translation
- Verifying NAT and PAT configurations
- Troubleshooting NAT and PAT configurations
- Configuration example: PAT
- Private IP Addresses: RFC 1918

The following table lists the address ranges as specified in RFC 1918 that can be used by anyone as internal private addresses. These will be your "inside-the-LAN" addresses that will have to be translated into public addresses that can be routed across the Internet. Any network is allowed to use these addresses; however, these addresses are not allowed to be routed onto the public Internet.

Private Addresses		
Class	RFC 1918 Internal Address Range	CIDR Prefix
A	10.0.0.0–10.255.255.255	10.0.0.0/8
B	172.16.0.0–172.31.255.255	172.16.0.0/12
C	192.168.0.0–192.168.255.255	192.168.0.0/16

Configuring Dynamic NAT: One Private to One Public Address Translation

NOTE For a complete configuration of NAT/PAT with a diagram for visual assistance, see the sample configuration at the end of this chapter.

Step 1: Define a static route on the remote router stating where the public addresses should be routed.	`ISP(config)#ip route 64.64.64.64 255.255.255.128 s0/0/0`	Informs the ISP router where to send packets with addresses destined for 64.64.64.64 255.255.255.128.
Step 2: Define a pool of usable public IP addresses on your router that will perform NAT.		The private address will receive the first available public address in the pool.
	`Corp(config)#ip nat pool scott 64.64.64.70 64.64.64.126 netmask 255.255.255.128`	Defines the following: The name of the pool is scott. (The name of the pool can be anything.) The start of the pool is 64.64.64.70. The end of the pool is 64.64.64.126. The subnet mask is 255.255.255.128.
Step 3: Create an access control list (ACL) that will identify which private IP addresses will be translated.	`Corp(config)#access-list 1 permit 172.16.10.0 0.0.0.255`	
Step 4: Link the ACL to the pool of addresses (create the translation).	`Corp(config)#ip nat inside source list 1 pool scott`	Defines the following: The source of the private addresses is from ACL 1. The pool of available public addresses is named scott.
Step 5: Define which interfaces are inside (contain the private addresses).	`Router(config)#interface gigabitethernet 0/0`	Moves to interface configuration mode.
	`Router(config-if)#ip nat inside`	You can have more than one inside interface on a router. Addresses from each inside interface are then allowed to be translated into a public address.
Step 6: Define the outside interface (the interface leading to the public network).	`Router(config-if)#exit`	Returns to global configuration mode.
	`Router(config)#interface serial 0/0/0`	Moves to interface configuration mode
	`Router(config-if)#ip nat outside`	Defines which interface is the outside interface for NAT

Configuring PAT: Many Private to One Public Address Translation

All private addresses use a single public IP address and numerous port numbers for translation. This is also known as *overloading* or *overload translations*.

Step 1: Define a static route on the remote router stating where public addresses should be routed.	`ISP(config)#ip` `route 64.64.64.64` `255.255.255.128 s0/0/0`	Informs the Internet service provider (ISP) where to send packets with addresses destined for 64.64.64.64 255.255.255.128.
Step 2: Define a pool of usable public IP addresses on your router that will perform NAT (optional).		Use this step if you have many private addresses to translate. A single public IP address can handle thousands of private addresses. Without using a pool of addresses, you can translate all private addresses into the IP address of the exit interface (the serial link to the ISP, for example).
	`Corp(config)#ip nat` `pool scott 64.64.64.70` `64.64.64.70 netmask` `255.255.255.128`	Defines the following: The name of the pool is scott. (The name of the pool can be anything.) The start of the pool is 64.64.64.70. The end of the pool is 64.64.64.70. The subnet mask is 255.255.255.128.
Step 3: Create an ACL that will identify which private IP addresses will be translated.	`Corp(config)#access-list` `1 permit 172.16.10.0` `0.0.0.255`	
Step 4 (Option 1): Link the ACL to the outside public interface (create the translation).	`Corp(config)#ip nat` `inside source list 1` `interface serial 0/0/0` `overload`	The source of the private addresses is from ACL 1. The public address to be translated into is the one assigned to serial 0/0/0. The **overload** keyword states that port numbers will be used to handle many translations.

Step 4 (Option 2): Link the ACL to the pool of addresses (create the translation).		If using the pool created in Step 1 . . .

	`Corp(config)#ip nat`
	`inside source list 1`
	`pool scott overload`
		The source of the private addresses is from ACL 1.
		
		The pool of the available addresses is named scott.
		
		The **overload** keyword states that port numbers will be used to handle many translations.

Step 5: Define which interfaces are inside (contain the private addresses).	`Corp(config)#interface` `gigabitethernet 0/0`	Moves to interface configuration mode.
	`Corp(config-if)#ip nat` `inside`	You can have more than one inside interface on a router.
Step 6: Define the outside interface (the interface leading to the public network).	`Corp(config-if)#exit`	Returns to global configuration mode.
	`Corp(config)#interface` `serial 0/0/0`	Moves to interface configuration mode.
	`Corp(config-if)#ip nat` `outside`	Defines which interface is the outside interface for NAT.

NOTE You can have an IP NAT pool of more than one address, if needed. The syntax for this is as follows:

```
Corp(config)#ip nat pool scott 64.64.64.70 64.64.64.75 netmask
255.255.255.128
```

You would then have a pool of 5 addresses (and all of their ports) available for translation.

NOTE The theoretical maximum number of translations between internal addresses and a single outside address using PAT is 65,536. Port numbers are encoded in a 16-bit field, so $2^{16} = 65,536$.

Configuring Static NAT: One Private to One Permanent Public Address Translation

Step 1: Define a static route on the remote router stating where the public addresses should be routed.	`ISP(config)#ip`
	`route 64.64.64.64`
	`255.255.255.128 s0/0`
		Informs the ISP where to send packets with addresses destined for 64.64.64.64 255.255.255.128.

Step 2: Create a static mapping on your router that will perform NAT.	`Corp(config)#ip nat inside source static 172.16.10.5 64.64.64.65`	Permanently translates the inside address of 172.16.10.5 to a public address of 64.64.64.65. Use the command for each of the private IP addresses you want to statically map to a public address.
Step 3: Define which interfaces are inside (contain the private addresses).	`Corp(config)#interface gigabitethernet 0/0`	Moves to interface configuration mode.
	`Corp(config-if)#ip nat inside`	You can have more than one inside interface on a router.
Step 4: Define the outside interface (the interface leading to the public network).	`Corp(config-if)#interface serial 0/0/0`	Moves to interface configuration mode.
	`Corp(config-if)#ip nat outside`	Defines which interface is the outside interface for NAT.

CAUTION   Make sure that you have in your router configurations a way for packets to travel back to your NAT router. Include a static route on the ISP router advertising your NAT pool and how to travel back to your internal network.

Without this in place, a packet can leave your network with a public address, but it will not be able to return if your ISP router does not know where the pool of public addresses exists in the network. You should be advertising the pool of public addresses, not your private addresses.

Verifying NAT and PAT Configurations

`Router#show access-list`	Displays access lists
`Router#show ip nat translations`	Displays the translation table
`Router#show ip nat statistics`	Displays NAT statistics
`Router#clear ip nat translations inside a.b.c.d outside e.f.g.h`	Clears a specific translation from the table before it times out
`Router#clear ip nat translations*`	Clears the entire translation table before entries time out

NOTE   The default time for a translation entry in a NAT table is 24 hours.

Troubleshooting NAT and PAT Configurations

`Router#debug ip nat`	Displays information about every packet that is translated. Be careful with this command. The router's CPU might not be able to handle this amount of output and might therefore hang the system.
`Router#debug ip nat detailed`	Displays greater detail about packets being translated.

Configuration Example: PAT

Figure 27-1 shows the network topology for the PAT configuration that follows using the commands covered in this chapter.

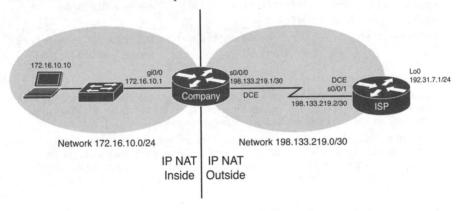

Figure 27-1   Port Address Translation Configuration

ISP Router

`router>enable`	Moves to privileged mode.
`router#configure terminal`	Moves to global configuration mode.
`router(config)#hostname ISP`	Sets the host name.
`ISP(config)#no ip domain-lookup`	Turns off Domain Name System (DNS) resolution to avoid wait time due to DNS lookup of spelling errors.
`ISP(config)#enable secret cisco`	Sets the encrypted password to cisco.
`ISP(config)#line console 0`	Moves to line console mode.
`ISP(config-line)#login`	User must log in to be able to access the console port.
`ISP(config-line)#password class`	Sets the console line password to class.

`ISP(config-line)#logging synchronous`	Commands will be appended to a new line.
`ISP(config-line)#exit`	Returns to global configuration mode.
`ISP(config)#interface serial 0/0/1`	Moves to interface configuration mode.
`ISP(config-if)#ip address 198.133.219.2 255.255.255.252`	Assigns an IP address and netmask.
`ISP(config-if)#clock rate 56000`	Assigns the clock rate to the DCE cable on this side of the link.
`ISP(config-if)#no shutdown`	Enables the interface.
`ISP(config-if)#interface loopback 0`	Creates loopback interface 0 and moves to interface configuration mode.
`ISP(config-if)#ip address 192.31.7.1255.255.255.255`	Assigns an IP address and netmask.
`ISP(config-if)#exit`	Returns to global configuration mode.
`ISP(config)#exit`	Returns to privileged mode.
`ISP#copy running-config startup-config`	Saves the configuration to NVRAM.

Company Router

`router>enable`	Moves to privileged mode.
`router#configure terminal`	Moves to global configuration mode.
`router(config)#hostname Company`	Sets the host name.
`Company(config)#no ip domain-lookup`	Turns off DNS resolution to avoid wait time due to DNS lookup of spelling errors.
`Company(config)#enable secret cisco`	Sets the secret password to cisco.
`Company(config)#line console 0`	Moves to line console mode.
`Company(config-line)#login`	User must log in to be able to access the console port.
`Company(config-line)#password class`	Sets the console line password to class.
`Company(config-line)#logging synchronous`	Commands will be appended to a new line.
`Company(config-line)#exit`	Returns to global configuration mode.
`Company(config)#interface gigabitethernet 0/0`	Moves to interface configuration mode.
`Company(config-if)#ip address 172.16.10.1 255.255.255.0`	Assigns an IP address and netmask.
`Company(config-if)#no shutdown`	Enables the interface.

`Company(config-if)#`**`interface serial 0/0/0`**	Moves to interface configuration mode.
`Company(config-if)#`**`ip address 198.133.219.1 255.255.255.252`**	Assigns an IP address and netmask.
`Company(config-if)#`**`no shutdown`**	Enables the interface.
`Company(config-if)#`**`exit`**	Returns to global configuration mode.
`Company(config)#`**`ip route 0.0.0.0 0.0.0.0 198.133.219.2`**	Sends all packets not defined in the routing table to the ISP router.
`Company(config)#`**`access-list 1 permit 172.16.10.0 0.0.0.255`**	Defines which addresses are permitted through; these addresses are those that will be allowed to be translated with NAT.
`Company(config)#`**`ip nat inside source list 1 interface serial 0/0/0 overload`**	Creates NAT by combining list 1 with the interface serial 0/0/0. Overloading will take place.
`Company(config)#`**`interface gigabitethernet 0/0`**	Moves to interface configuration mode.
`Company(config-if)#`**`ip nat inside`**	Location of private inside addresses.
`Company(config-if)#`**`interface serial 0/0/0`**	Moves to interface configuration mode.
`Company(config-if)#`**`ip nat outside`**	Location of public outside addresses.
`Company(config-if)#`⧌Ctrl⧍-⧌Z⧍	Returns to privileged mode.
`Company#`**`copy running-config startup-config`**	Saves the configuration to NVRAM.

CHAPTER 28

Dynamic Host Configuration Protocol (DHCP)

This chapter provides information and commands concerning the following topics:

- Configuring a DHCP server on an IOS router
- Verifying and troubleshooting DHCP configuration
- Configuring a DHCP helper address
- DHCP client on a Cisco IOS Software Ethernet interface
- Configuration example: DHCP

Configuring a DHCP Server on an IOS Router

`Router(config)#ip dhcp pool internal`	Creates a DHCP pool named internal. The name can be anything of your choosing.
`Router(dhcp-config)#network 172.16.10.0 255.255.255.0`	Defines the range of addresses to be leased.
`Router(dhcp-config)#default-router 172.16.10.1`	Defines the address of the default router for the client.
`Router(dhcp-config)#dns-server 172.16.10.10`	Defines the address of the Domain Name System (DNS) server for the client
`Router(dhcp-config)#netbios-name-server 172.16.10.10`	Defines the address of the NetBIOS server for the client.
`Router(dhcp-config)#domain-name fakedomainname.com`	Defines the domain name for the client.
`Router(dhcp-config)# lease 14 12 23`	Defines the lease time to be 14 days, 12 hours, 23 minutes.
`Router(dhcp-config)#lease infinite`	Sets the lease time to infinity; the default time is 1 day.
`Router(dhcp-config)#exit`	Returns to global configuration mode.
`Router(config)#ip dhcp excluded-address 172.16.10.1 172.16.10.9`	Specifies the range of addresses not to be leased out to clients.
`Router(config)#service dhcp`	Enables the DHCP service and relay features on a Cisco IOS router.
`Router(config)#no service dhcp`	Turns the DHCP service off. DHCP service is on by default in Cisco IOS Software.

Verifying and Troubleshooting DHCP Configuration

`Router#show ip dhcp binding`	Displays a list of all bindings created
`Router#show ip dhcp binding` `w.x.y.z`	Displays the bindings for a specific DHCP client with an IP address of *w.x.y.z*
`Router#clear ip dhcp binding` `a.b.c.d`	Clears an automatic address binding from the DHCP server database
`Router#clear ip dhcp binding *`	Clears all automatic DHCP bindings
`Router#show ip dhcp conflict`	Displays a list of all address conflicts recorded by the DHCP server
`Router#clear ip dhcp conflict` `a.b.c.d`	Clears address conflict from the database
`Router#clear ip dhcp conflict *`	Clears conflicts for all addresses
`Router#show ip dhcp database`	Displays recent activity on the DHCP database
`Router#show ip dhcp server` `statistics`	Displays a list of the number of messages sent and received by the DHCP server
`Router#clear ip dhcp server` `statistics`	Resets all DHCP server counters to 0
`Router#debug ip dhcp server` `{events	packets	linkage |` `class}`	Displays the DHCP process of addresses being leased and returned

Configuring a DHCP Helper Address

`Router(config)#interface` `gigabitethernet 0/0`	Moves to interface configuration mode.
`Router(config-if)#ip` `helper-address 172.16.20.2`	DHCP broadcasts will be forwarded as a unicast to this specific address rather than be dropped by the router.

NOTE   The **ip helper-address** command will forward broadcast packets as a unicast to eight different UDP ports by default:

- TFTP (port 69)
- DNS (port 53)
- Time service (port 37)
- NetBIOS name server (port 137)
- NetBIOS datagram server (port 138)
- Boot Protocol (BOOTP) client and server datagrams (ports 67 and 68)
- TACACS service (port 49)

If you want to close some of these ports, use the **no ip forward-protocol udp** x command at the global configuration prompt, where x is the port number you want to close. The following command stops the forwarding of broadcasts to port 49:

```
Router(config)#no ip forward-protocol udp 49
```

If you want to open other UDP ports, use the **ip forward-helper udp** x command, where x is the port number you want to open:

```
Router(config)#ip forward-protocol udp 517
```

DHCP Client on a Cisco IOS Software Ethernet Interface

Router(config)#interface gigabitethernet 0/0	Moves to interface configuration mode
Router(config-if)#ip address dhcp	Specifies that the interface acquire an IP address through DHCP

Configuration Example: DHCP

Figure 28-1 illustrates the network topology for the configuration that follows, which shows how to configure DHCP services on a Cisco IOS router using the commands covered in this chapter.

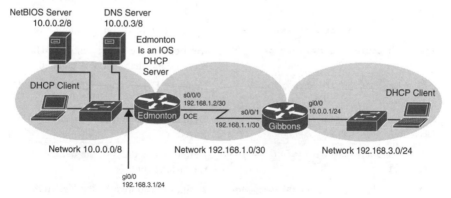

Figure 28-1   Network Topology for DHCP Configuration

Edmonton Router

router>enable	Moves to privileged mode
router#configure terminal	Moves to global configuration mode
router(config)#hostname Edmonton	Sets the host name
Edmonton(config)#interface gigabitethernet 0/0	Moves to interface configuration mode

`Edmonton(config-if)#description LAN Interface`	Sets the local description of the interface
`Edmonton(config-if)#ip address 10.0.0.1 255.0.0.0`	Assigns an IP address and netmask
`Edmonton(config-if)#no shutdown`	Enables the interface
`Edmonton(config-if)#interface serial 0/0/0`	Moves to interface configuration mode
`Edmonton(config-if)#description Link to Gibbons Router`	Sets the local description of the interface
`Edmonton(config-if)#ip address 192.168.1.2 255.255.255.252`	Assigns an IP address and netmask
`Edmonton(config-if)#clock rate 56000`	Assigns the clock rate to the DCE cable on this side of link
`Edmonton(config-if)#no shutdown`	Enables the interface
`Edmonton(config-if)#exit`	Returns to global configuration mode
`Edmonton(config)#router eigrp 10`	Enables the EIGRP routing process for autonomous system 10
`Edmonton(config-router)#network 10.0.0.0`	Advertises the 10.0.0.0 network
`Edmonton(config-router)#network 192.168.1.0`	Advertises the 192.168.1.0 network
`Edmonton(config-router)#exit`	Returns to global configuration mode
`Edmonton(config)#service dhcp`	Verifies that the router can use DHCP services and that DHCP is enabled
`Edmonton(config)#ip dhcp pool 10network`	Creates a DHCP pool called 10network
`Edmonton(dhcp-config)#network 10.0.0.0 255.0.0.0`	Defines the range of addresses to be leased
`Edmonton(dhcp-config)#default-router 10.0.0.1`	Defines the address of the default router for clients
`Edmonton(dhcp-config)#netbios-name-server 10.0.0.2`	Defines the address of the NetBIOS server for clients
`Edmonton(dhcp-config)#dns-server 10.0.0.3`	Defines the address of the DNS server for clients
`Edmonton(dhcp-config)#domain-name fakedomainname.com`	Defines the domain name for clients
`Edmonton(dhcp-config)#lease 12 14 30`	Sets the lease time to be 12 days, 14 hours, 30 minutes
`Edmonton(dhcp-config)#exit`	Returns to global configuration mode
`Edmonton(config)#ip dhcp excluded-address 10.0.0.1 10.0.0.5`	Specifies the range of addresses not to be leased out to clients

Edmonton(config)#**ip dhcp pool 192.168.3network**	Creates a DHCP pool called the 192.168.3network
Edmonton(dhcp-config)#**network 192.168.3.0 255.255.255.0**	Defines the range of addresses to be leased
Edmonton(dhcp-config)#**default-router 192.168.3.1**	Defines the address of the default router for clients
Edmonton(dhcp-config)#**netbios-name-server 10.0.0.2**	Defines the address of the NetBIOS server for clients
Edmonton(dhcp-config)#**dns-server 10.0.0.3**	Defines the address of the DNS server for clients
Edmonton(dhcp-config)#**domain-name fakedomainname.com**	Defines the domain name for clients
Edmonton(dhcp-config)#**lease 12 14 30**	Sets the lease time to be 12 days, 14 hours, 30 minutes
Edmonton(dhcp-config)#**exit**	Returns to global configuration mode
Edmonton(config)#**exit**	Returns to privileged mode
Edmonton#**copy running-config startup-config**	Saves the configuration to NVRAM

Gibbons Router

router>**enable**	Moves to privileged mode.
router#**configure terminal**	Moves to global configuration mode.
router(config)#**hostname Gibbons**	Sets the host name.
Gibbons(config)#**interface gigabitethernet 0/0**	Moves to interface configuration mode.
Gibbons(config-if)#**description LAN Interface**	Sets the local description of the interface.
Gibbons(config-if)#**ip address 192.168.3.1 255.255.255.0**	Assigns an IP address and netmask.
Gibbons(config-if)#**ip helper-address 192.168.1.2**	DHCP broadcasts will be forwarded as a unicast to this address rather than be dropped.
Gibbons(config-if)#**no shutdown**	Enables the interface.
Gibbons(config-if)#**interface serial 0/0/1**	Moves to interface configuration mode.
Gibbons(config-if)#**description Link to Edmonton Router**	Sets the local description of the interface.
Gibbons(config-if)#**ip address 192.168.1.1 255.255.255.252**	Assigns an IP address and netmask.
Gibbons(config-if)#**no shutdown**	Enables the interface.

Gibbons(config-if)#**exit**	Returns to global configuration mode.
Gibbons(config)#**router eigrp 10**	Enables the EIGRP routing process for autonomous system 10.
Gibbons(config-router)#**network 192.168.3.0**	Advertises the 192.168.3.0 network.
Gibbons(config-router)#**network 192.168.1.0**	Advertises the 192.168.1.0 network.
Gibbons(config-router)#**exit**	Returns to global configuration mode.
Gibbons(config)#**exit**	Returns to privileged mode.
Gibbons#**copy running-config startup-config**	Saves the configuration to NVRAM.

Configuring Serial Encapsulation: HDLC and PPP

This chapter provides information and commands concerning the following topics:

- Configuring HDLC encapsulation on a serial line
- Configuring Point-to-Point Protocol (PPP) on a serial line (mandatory commands)
- Configuring Point-to-Point Protocol (PPP) on a serial line (optional commands), including those commands concerning the following
  - Compression
  - Link quality
  - Multilink
  - Authentication
- Verifying and troubleshooting a serial link/PPP encapsulation
- Configuration example: PPP with CHAP authentication

Configuring HDLC Encapsulation on a Serial Line

Router#**configure terminal**	Moves to global configuration mode
Router(config)#**interface serial 0/0/0**	Moves to interface configuration mode
Router(config-if)#**encapsulation hdlc**	Sets the encapsulation mode for this interface to HDLC

NOTE HDLC is the default encapsulation for synchronous serial links on Cisco routers. You would only use the **encapsulation hdlc** command to return the link to its default state.

CAUTION Although HDLC is an open standard protocol, Cisco has modified HDLC as part of their implementation. This allowed for multiprotocol support before PPP was specified. Therefore you should only use HDLC between Cisco devices. If you are connecting to a non-Cisco device, use synchronous PPP.

Configuring Point-to-Point Protocol (PPP) on a Serial Line (Mandatory Commands)

Router#**configure terminal**	Moves to global configuration mode
Router(config)#**interface serial 0/0/0**	Moves to interface configuration mode
Router(config-if)#**encapsulation ppp**	Changes encapsulation from default HDLC to PPP

NOTE   You must execute the **encapsulation ppp** command on both sides of the serial link for the link to become active.

Configuring PPP on a Serial Line (Optional Commands): Compression

Router(config-if)#**compress predictor**	Enables the predictor compression algorithm
Router(config-if)#**compress stac**	Enables the stac compression algorithm

Configuring PPP on a Serial Line (Optional Commands): Link Quality

Router(config-if)#**ppp quality** *x*	Ensures the link has a quality of *x* percent. Otherwise, the link will shut down.

NOTE   In PPP, the Link Control Protocol allows for an optional link-quality determination phase. In this phase, the link is tested to determine whether the link quality is sufficient to bring up any Layer 3 protocols. If you use the command **ppp quality** *x*, where *x* is equal to a certain percent, you must meet that percentage of quality on the link. If the link does not meet that percentage level, the link cannot be created and will shut down.

Configuring PPP on a Serial Line (Optional Commands): Multilink

Router(config-if)#**ppp multilink**	Enables load balancing across multiple links

Configuring PPP on a Serial Line (Optional Commands): Authentication

Router(config)#**username routerb password cisco**	Sets a username of **routerb** and a password of cisco for authentication from the other side of the PPP serial link. This is used by the local router to authenticate the PPP peer.
Router(config)#**interface serial 0/0/0**	Moves to interface configuration mode.
Router(config-if)#**ppp authentication pap**	Turns on Password Authentication Protocol (PAP) authentication only.
Router(config-if)#**ppp authentication chap**	Turns on Challenge Handshake Authentication Protocol (CHAP) authentication only.
Router(config-if)#**ppp authentication pap chap**	Defines that the link will use PAP authentication, but will try CHAP if PAP fails or is rejected by other side.
Router(config-if)#**ppp authentication chap pap**	Defines that the link will use CHAP authentication, but will try PAP if CHAP fails or is rejected by other side.

TIP   When setting authentication, make sure that your usernames match the name of the router on the other side of the link, and that the passwords on each router match the other. Usernames and passwords are case sensitive. Consider the following example:

Edmonton(config)#**username Calgary password cisco**	Calgary(config)#**username Edmonton password cisco**
Edmonton(config)#**interface serial 0/0/0**	Calgary(config)#**interface serial 0/0/0**
Edmonton(config-if)#**encapsulation ppp**	Calgary(config-if)#**encapsulation ppp**
Edmonton(config-if)#**ppp authentication chap**	Calgary(config-if)#**ppp authentication chap**

NOTE   Because PAP does not encrypt its password as it is sent across the link, recommended practice is that you use CHAP as your authentication method.

Verifying and Troubleshooting a Serial Link/PPP Encapsulation

Router#**show interfaces serial** *x/x/x*	Lists information for serial interface *x/x/x*
Router#**show controllers serial** *x/x/x*	Tells you what type of cable (DCE/DTE) is plugged into your interface and whether a clock rate has been set
Router#**debug serial interface**	Displays whether serial keepalive counters are incrementing
Router#**debug ppp**	Displays any traffic related to PPP
Router#**debug ppp packet**	Displays PPP packets that are being sent and received
Router#**debug ppp negotiation**	Displays PPP packets related to the negotiation of the PPP link
Router#**debug ppp error**	Displays PPP error packets
Router#**debug ppp authentication**	Displays PPP packets related to the authentication of the PPP link
Router#**debug ppp compression**	Displays PPP packets related to the compression of packets across the link

TIP   With frequent lab use, serial cable pins often get bent, which might prevent the router from seeing the cable. The output from the command **show controllers interface serial** *x/x/x* shows no cable even though a cable is physically present.

Configuration Example: PPP with CHAP Authentication

Figure 29-1 illustrates the network topology for the configuration that follows, which shows how to configure PPP using the commands covered in this chapter.

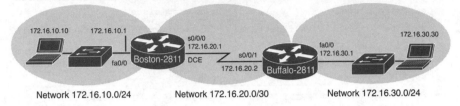

Network 172.16.10.0/24   Network 172.16.20.0/30   Network 172.16.30.0/24

Figure 29-1   Network Topology for PPP Configuration

NOTE   The host name, password, and interfaces have all been configured as per the configuration example in Chapter 6, "Configuring a Single Cisco Router."

Boston Router

Boston>**enable**	Moves to privileged mode
Boston#**configure terminal**	Moves to global configuration mode
Boston(config)#**username Buffalo password academy**	Sets the local username and password for PPP authentication of the PPP peer
Boston(config-if)#**interface serial 0/0/0**	Moves to interface configuration mode
Boston(config-if)#**description Link to Buffalo Router**	Defines the locally significant link description
Boston(config-if)#**ip address 172.16.20.1 255.255.255.252**	Assigns an IP address and netmask
Boston(config-if)#**clock rate 56000**	Sets the clock rate to the data communications equipment (DCE) side of link
Boston(config-if) #**encapsulation ppp**	Turns on PPP encapsulation
Boston(config-if)#**ppp authentication chap**	Turns on CHAP authentication
Boston(config-if)#**no shutdown**	Turns on the interface
Boston(config-if)#**exit**	Returns to global configuration mode
Boston(config)#**exit**	Returns to privileged mode
Boston#**copy running-config startup-config**	Saves the configuration to NVRAM

Buffalo Router

`Buffalo>enable`	Moves to privileged mode
`Buffalo#configure terminal`	Moves to global configuration mode
`Buffalo(config)#username Boston password academy`	Sets the username and password for PPP authentication
`Buffalo(config-if)#interface serial 0/0/1`	Moves to interface configuration mode
`Buffalo(config-if)#description Link to Boston Router`	Defines the locally significant link description
`Buffalo(config-if)#ip address 172.16.20.2 255.255.255.252`	Assigns an IP address and netmask
`Buffalo(config-if) #encapsulation ppp`	Turns on PPP encapsulation
`Buffalo(config-if)#ppp authentication chap`	Turns on CHAP authentication
`Buffalo(config-if)#no shutdown`	Turns on the interface
`Buffalo(config-if)# <Ctrl> <Z>`	Exits back to privileged mode
`Buffalo#copy running-config startup-config`	Saves the configuration to NVRAM

CHAPTER 30

Establishing WAN Connectivity Using Frame Relay

This chapter provides information and commands concerning the following topics:

- Configuring Frame Relay
  - Setting the Frame Relay encapsulation type
  - Setting the Frame Relay encapsulation LMI type
  - Setting the Frame Relay DLCI number
  - Configuring a Frame Relay **map** statement
  - Configuring a description of the interface (optional)
  - Configuring Frame Relay using subinterfaces
- Verifying Frame Relay
- Troubleshooting Frame Relay
- Configuration example: Point-to-point Frame Relay using subinterfaces and OSPF
- Configuration example: Point-to-multipoint Frame Relay using subinterfaces and EIGRP

Configuring Frame Relay

Setting the Frame Relay Encapsulation Type

`Router(config)#interface serial 0/0/0`	Moves to interface configuration mode.
`Router(config-if)#encapsulation frame-relay`	Turns on Frame Relay encapsulation with the default encapsulation type of cisco.
Or	
`Router(config-if)#encapsulation frame-relay ietf`	Turns on Frame Relay encapsulation with the encapsulation type of ietf (RFC 1490). Use the ietf encapsulation method if connecting to a non-Cisco router.

Setting the Frame Relay Encapsulation LMI Type

`Router(config-if)#frame-relay lmi-type {ansi	cisco	q933a}`	Depending on the option you select, this command sets the LMI type to the ANSI standard, the Cisco standard, or the ITU-T Q.933 Annex A standard.

NOTE   As of Cisco IOS Software Release 11.2, the LMI type is auto-sensed, making
this command optional.

Setting the Frame Relay DLCI Number

Router(config-if)#**frame-relay interface-dlci 110**	Sets the DLCI number of 110 on the local interface and enters Frame Relay DLCI configuration mode
Router(config-fr-dlci)#**exit**	Returns to interface configuration mode
Router(config-if)#**exit**	Returns to global configuration mode
Router(config)#	

Configuring a Frame Relay map Statement

Router(config-if)#**frame-relay map ip 192.168.100.1 110 broadcast**	Maps the remote IP address (192.168.100.1) to the local DLCI number (110). The optional broadcast keyword specifies that broadcasts across IP should be forwarded to this address. This is necessary when using dynamic routing protocols.
Router(config-if)#**no frame-relay inverse arp**	Turns off Inverse ARP.

NOTE   Cisco routers have Inverse Address Resolution Protocol (IARP) turned on by
default. This means that the router will go out and create the mapping for you. If the
remote router does not support IARP, or you want to control broadcast traffic over the
permanent virtual circuit (PVC), you must statically set the DLCI/IP mappings and turn
off IARP.

You need to issue the **no frame-relay inverse-arp** command before you issue the **no
shutdown** command; otherwise, the interface performs IARP before you can turn it off.

Configuring a Description of the Interface (Optional)

Router(config-if)#**description Connection to the Branch office**	Optional command to allow you to enter in additional information such as contact name, PVC description, and so on

Configuring Frame Relay Using Subinterfaces

Subinterfaces enable you to solve split-horizon problems and to create multiple PVCs on
a single physical connection to the Frame Relay cloud.

Router(config)#**interface serial 0/0/0**	
Router(config-if)#**encapsulation frame-relay ietf**	Sets the Frame Relay encapsulation type for all subinterfaces on this interface

`Router(config-if)#frame-relay lmi-type ansi`	Sets the LMI type for all subinterfaces on this interface
`Router(config-if)#no ip address`	Ensures there is no IP address set to this interface
`Router(config-if)#no shutdown`	Enables the interface
`Router(config-if)#interface serial 0/0/0.102 point-to-point`	Creates a point-to-point subinterface numbered 102
`Router(config-subif)#ip address 192.168.10.1 255.255.255.0`	Assigns an IP address and netmask to the subinterface
`Router(config-subif)#frame-relay interface-dlci 102`	Assigns a DLCI to the subinterface
`Router(config-subif)#interface serial 0/0/0.103 point-to-point`	Creates a point-to-point subinterface numbered 103
`Router(config-subif)#ip address 192.168.20.1 255.255.255.0`	Assigns an IP address and netmask to the subinterface
`Router(config-subif)#frame-relay interface-dlci 103`	Assigns a DLCI to the subinterface
`Router(config-subif)#exit`	Returns to interface configuration mode
`Router(config-if)#exit`	Returns to global configuration mode
`Router(config)#`	

NOTE   There are two types of subinterfaces:

- **Point-to-point**, where a single PVC connects one router to another and each subinterface is in its own IP subnet.
- **Multipoint**, where the router is the middle point of a group of routers. All other routers connect to each other through this router, and all routers are in the same subnet.

NOTE   Use the **no ip split-horizon** command to turn off split-horizon commands on multipoint interfaces so that remote sites can see each other.

Verifying Frame Relay

`Router#show frame-relay map`	Displays IP/DLCI map entries
`Router#show frame-relay pvc`	Displays the status of all PVCs configured
`Router#show frame-relay lmi`	Displays LMI statistics
`Router#clear frame-relay counters`	Clears and resets all Frame Relay counters
`Router#clear frame-relay inarp`	Clears all Inverse ARP entries from the map table

TIP   If the **clear frame-relay inarp** command does not clear Frame Relay maps, you might need to reload the router.

Troubleshooting Frame Relay

Router#**debug frame-relay lmi**	Used to help determine whether a router and Frame Relay switch are exchanging LMI packets properly

Configuration Example: Point-to-Point Frame Relay Using Subinterfaces and OSPF

Figure 30-1 shows the network topology for the configuration that follows, which demonstrates how to use OSPF on a point-to-point Frame Relay network.

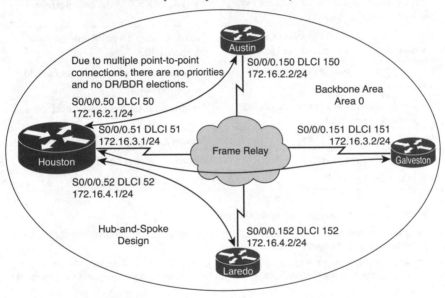

Figure 30-1   Network Topology for Point-to-Point Frame Relay Using Subinterfaces and OSPF

Houston Router

Router>**enable**	Moves to privileged mode.
Router#**configure terminal**	Moves to global configuration mode.
Router(config)#**hostname Houston**	Sets the router host name.
Houston(config)#**interface serial 0/0/0**	Enters interface configuration mode.
Houston(config-if)#**encapsulation frame-relay**	Enables Frame Relay encapsulation.
Houston(config-if)#**no shutdown**	Enables the interface.

Houston(config-if)#interface serial 0/0/0.50 point-to-point	Creates a subinterface.
Houston(config-subif)#description Link to Austin	Creates a locally significant description of the interface.
Houston(config-subif)#ip address 172.16.2.1 255.255.255.252	Assigns an IP address and netmask.
Houston(config-subif)#frame-relay interface-dlci 50	Assigns a DLCI to the subinterface.
Houston(config-subif)#exit	Returns to interface configuration mode.
Houston(config-if)#interface serial 0/0/0.51 point-to-point	Creates a subinterface.
Houston(config-subif)#description Link to Galveston	Creates a locally significant description of the interface.
Houston(config-subif)#ip address 172.16.3.1 255.255.255.252	Assigns an IP address and netmask.
Houston(config-subif)#frame-relay interface-dlci 51	Assigns a DLCI to the subinterface.
Houston(config-subif)#exit	Returns to interface configuration mode.
Houston(config-if)#interface serial 0/0/0.52 point-to-point	Creates a subinterface.
Houston(config-subif)#description Link to Laredo	Creates a locally significant description of the interface.
Houston(config-subif)#ip address 172.16.4.1 255.255.255.252	Assigns an IP address and netmask.
Houston(config-subif)#frame-relay interface-dlci 52	Assigns a DLCI to the subinterface.
Houston(config-subif)#exit	Returns to interface configuration mode.
Houston(config-if)#exit	Returns to global configuration mode.
Houston(config)#router ospf 1	Starts OSPF process 1.
Houston(config-router)#network 172.16.0.0 0.0.255.255 area 0	Read this line to say, "Any interface with an IP address of 172.16.x.x will be placed into area 0."
Houston(config-router)#exit	Returns to global configuration mode.
Houston(config)#exit	Returns to privileged mode.
Houston#copy running-config startup-config	Saves the configuration to NVRAM.

Austin Router

`Router>`**`enable`**	Moves to privileged mode.
`Router#`**`configure terminal`**	Moves to global configuration mode.
`Router(config)#`**`hostname Austin`**	Sets the router host name.
`Austin(config)#`**`interface serial 0/0/0`**	Enters interface configuration mode.
`Austin(config-if)#`**`encapsulation frame-relay`**	Enables Frame Relay encapsulation.
`Austin(config-if)#`**`no shutdown`**	Enables the interface.
`Austin(config-if)#`**`interface serial 0/0/0.150 point-to-point`**	Creates a subinterface.
`Austin(config-subif)#`**`description Link to Houston`**	Creates a locally significant description of the interface.
`Austin(config-subif)#`**`ip address 172.16.2.2 255.255.255.252`**	Assigns an IP address and netmask.
`Austin(config-subif)#`**`frame-relay interface-dlci 150`**	Assigns a DLCI to the subinterface.
`Austin(config-subif)#`**`exit`**	Returns to interface configuration mode.
`Austin(config-if)#`**`exit`**	Returns to global configuration mode.
`Austin(config)#`**`router ospf 1`**	Starts OSPF process 1.
`Austin(config-router)#`**`network 172.16.0.0 0.0.255.255 area 0`**	Read this line to say, "Any interface with an IP address of 172.16.$x.x$ will be placed into area 0."
`Austin(config-router)#`**`exit`**	Returns to global configuration mode.
`Austin(config)#`**`exit`**	Returns to privileged mode.
`Austin#`**`copy running-config startup-config`**	Saves the configuration to NVRAM.

Galveston Router

`Router>`**`enable`**	Moves to privileged mode.
`Router#`**`configure terminal`**	Moves to global configuration mode.
`Router(config)#`**`hostname Galveston`**	Sets the router host name.
`Galveston(config)#`**`interface serial 0/0/0`**	Enters interface configuration mode.
`Galveston(config-if)#`**`encapsulation frame-relay`**	Enables Frame Relay encapsulation.
`Galveston(config-if)#`**`no shutdown`**	Enables the interface.
`Galveston(config-if)#`**`interface serial 0/0/0.151 point-to-point`**	Creates a subinterface.
`Galveston(config-subif)#`**`description Link to Houston`**	Creates a locally significant description of the interface.
`Galveston(config-subif)#`**`ip address 172.16.3.2 255.255.255.252`**	Assigns an IP address and netmask.

`Galveston(config-subif)#frame-relay interface-dlci 151`	Assigns a DLCI to the subinterface.
`Galveston(config-subif)#exit`	Returns to interface configuration mode.
`Galveston(config-if)#exit`	Returns to global configuration mode.
`Galveston(config)#router ospf 1`	Starts OSPF process 1.
`Galveston(config-router)#network 172.16.0.0 0.0.255.255 area 0`	Read this line to say, "Any interface with an IP address of 172.16.x.x will be placed into area 0."
`Galveston(config-router)#exit`	Returns to global configuration mode.
`Galveston(config)#exit`	Returns to privileged mode.
`Galveston#copy running-config startup-config`	Saves the configuration to NVRAM.

Laredo Router

`Router>enable`	Moves to privileged mode.
`Router#configure terminal`	Moves to global configuration mode.
`Router(config)#hostname Laredo`	Sets the router host name.
`Laredo(config)#interface serial 0/0/0`	Enters interface configuration mode.
`Laredo(config-if)#encapsulation frame-relay`	Enables Frame Relay encapsulation.
`Laredo(config-if)#no shutdown`	Enables the interface.
`Laredo(config-if)#interface serial 0/0/0.152 point-to-point`	Creates a subinterface.
`Laredo(config-subif)#description Link to Houston`	Creates a locally significant description of the interface.
`Laredo(config-subif)#ip address 172.16.4.2 255.255.255.252`	Assigns an IP address and netmask.
`Laredo(config-subif)#frame-relay interface-dlci 152`	Assigns a DLCI to the subinterface.
`Laredo(config-subif)#exit`	Returns to interface configuration mode.
`Laredo(config-if)#exit`	Returns to global configuration mode.
`Laredo(config)#router ospf 1`	Starts OSPF process 1.
`Laredo(config-router)#network 172.16.0.0 0.0.255.255 area 0`	Read this line to say, "Any interface with an IP address of 172.16.x.x will be placed into area 0."
`Laredo(config-router)#exit`	Returns to global configuration mode.
`Laredo(config)#exit`	Returns to privileged mode.
`Laredo#copy running-config startup-config`	Saves the configuration to NVRAM.

Configuration Example: Point-to-Multipoint Frame Relay Using Subinterfaces and EIGRP

Figure 30-2 shows the network topology for the configuration that follows, which demonstrates how to use EIGRP on a point-to-multipoint Frame Relay network.

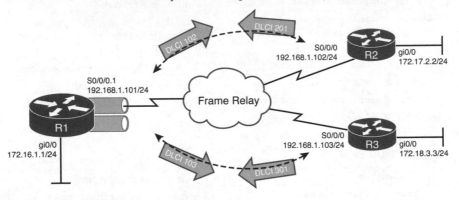

Figure 30-2   EIGRP over Frame Relay Using Multipoint Subinterfaces

R1 Router

`R1(config)#interface serial 0/0/0`	Enters interface configuration mode.
`R1(config-if)#no ip address`	Removes any previous IP address and mask information assigned to this interface. Address now has no address or mask.
`R1(config-if)#encapsulation frame-relay`	Enables Frame Relay on this interface.
`R1(config-if)#no frame-relay inverse-arp eigrp 100`	Turns off dynamic mapping for EIGRP 100.
`R1(config-if)#exit`	Returns to global configuration mode.
`R1(config)#interface serial 0/0/0.1 multipoint`	Enables subinterface configuration mode. Multipoint behavior is also enabled.
`R1(config-subif)#ip address 192.168.1.101 255.255.255.0`	Assigns IP address and mask information.
`R1(config-subif)#no ip splithorizon eigrp 100`	Disables split horizon for EIGRP on this interface. This is to allow R2 and R3 to have connectivity between their connected networks.
`R1(config-subif)#frame-relay map ip 192.168.1.101 101`	Maps the IP address of 192.168.1.101 to DLCI 101.
	NOTE The router includes this map to its own IP address so that the router can ping the local address from itself.

`R1(config-subif)#frame-relay map ip 192.168.1.102 102 broadcast`	Maps the remote IP address 192.168.1.102 to DLCI 102. The **broadcast** keyword means that broadcasts will now be forwarded as well.
`R1(config-subif)#frame-relay map ip 192.168.1.103 103 broadcast`	Maps the remote IP address 192.168.1.103 to DLCI 103. The **broadcast** keyword means that broadcasts will now be forwarded as well.
`R1(config-subif)#exit`	Returns to global configuration mode.
`R1(config)#router eigrp 100`	Creates routing process 100.
`R1(config-router)#network 172.16.1.0 0.0.0.255`	Advertises the network in EIGRP.
`R1(config-router)#network 192.168.1.0`	Advertises the network in EIGRP.

NOTE To deploy EIGRP over multipoint subinterfaces, no changes are needed to the basic EIGRP configuration.

R2 Router

`R2(config)#interface serial 0/0/0`	Moves to interface configuration mode.
`R2(config-if)#encapsulation frame-relay`	Enables Frame Relay on this interface.
`R2(config-if)#ip address 192.168.1.102 255.255.255.0`	Assigns IP address and mask information.
`R2(config-if)#frame-relay map ip 192.168.1.102 102`	Maps the local IP address 192.168.1.102 to DLCI 102. This map will allow the router to ping the local address from itself.
`R2(config-if)#frame-relay map ip 192.168.1.101 201 broadcast`	Maps the remote IP address 192.168.1.101 to DLCI 201. The broadcast keyword means that broadcasts will now be forwarded as well.
`R2(config-if)#no shutdown`	Enables the interface.
`R2(config-if)#exit`	Returns to global configuration mode.
`R2(config)#router eigrp 100`	Creates EIGRP routing process 100.
`R2(config-router)#network 172.17.2.0 0.0.0.255`	Advertises the network in EIGRP.
`R2(config-router)#network 192.168.1.0`	Advertises the network in EIGRP.
`R2(config-router)#exit`	Returns to global configuration mode.
`R2(config)#exit`	Returns to privileged EXEC mode.
`R2#copy running-config startup-config`	Saves the configuration to NVRAM.

R3 Router

R3(config)#**interface serial 0/0/0**	Moves to interface configuration mode.
R3(config-if)#**encapsulation frame-relay**	Enables Frame Relay on this interface.
R3(config-if)#**ip address 192.168.1.103 255.255.255.0**	Assigns IP address and mask information.
R3(config-if)#**frame-relay map ip 192.168.1.103 103**	Maps the local IP address 192.168.1.103 to DLCI 103. This map will allow the router to ping the local address from itself.
R3(config-if)#**frame-relay map ip 192.168.1.101 301 broadcast**	Maps the remote IP address 192.168.1.101 to DLCI 301. The **broadcast** keyword means that broadcasts will now be forwarded as well.
R3(config-if)#**no shutdown**	Enables the interface.
R3(config-if)#**exit**	Returns to global configuration mode.
R3(config)#**router eigrp 100**	Creates EIGRP routing process 100.
R3(config-router)#**network 172.18.3.0 0.0.0.255**	Advertises the network in EIGRP.
R2(config-router)#**network 192.168.1.0**	Advertises the network in EIGRP.
R2(config-router)#**exit**	Returns to global configuration mode.
R2(config)#**exit**	Returns to Privileged EXEC mode.
R2#**copy running-config startup-config**	Saves the configuration to NVRAM.

CHAPTER 31

Configuring Generic Routing Encapsulation (GRE) Tunnels

This chapter provides information and commands concerning the following topics:

- Configuring a GRE tunnel
- Verifying a GRE tunnel

Generic routing encapsulation (GRE) is a tunneling protocol that can encapsulate a wide variety of protocol packets inside IPv4 and IPv6 tunnels. GRE was developed by Cisco.

CAUTION GRE does not include any strong security mechanisms to protect its payload. To ensure a secure tunnel, you should use IPsec in conjunction with a GRE tunnel.

Configuring a GRE Tunnel

Figure 31-1 illustrates the network topology for the configuration that follows, which shows how to configure a GRE tunnel between two remote sites. This example shows only the commands needed to set up the GRE tunnel. Other commands are necessary to complete the configuration: host names, physical interfaces, routing, and so on.

Figure 31-1   GRE Tunnel Configuration

Branch Router

`Branch(config)#interface tunnel0`	Moves to interface configuration mode
`Branch(config-if)#tunnel mode gre ip`	Sets tunnel encapsulation method to GRE over IP
`Branch(config-if)#ip address` `192.168.1.101 255.255.255.224`	Sets IP address and mask information for interface
`Branch(config-if)#tunnel source` `10.165.201.1`	Maps tunnel source to Serial 0/0/0 interface
`Branch(config-if)#tunnel destination` `172.16.1.1`	Maps tunnel destination to HQ router

HQ Router

HQ(config)#**interface tunnel0**	Moves to interface configuration mode
HQ(config-if)#**tunnel mode gre ip**	Sets tunnel encapsulation method to GRE over IP
HQ(config-if)#**ip address** 192.168.1.102 255.255.255.224	Sets IP address and mask information for interface
HQ(config-if)#**tunnel source** 172.16.1.1	Maps tunnel source to Serial 0/0/0 interface
HQ(config-if)#**tunnel destination** 10.165.201.1	Maps tunnel destination to Branch router

Verifying a GRE Tunnel

Router#**show interface tunnel0**	Verifies GRE tunnel configuration.
Router#**show ip interface brief**	Shows brief summary of all interfaces, including tunnel interfaces.
Router#**show ip interface brief | include tunnel**	Shows summary of interfaces named tunnel.
Router#**show ip route**	Verifies a tunnel route between Branch and HQ routers. The path will be seen as directly connected (C) in the route table.

CHAPTER 32

Configuring Point-to-Point Protocol over Ethernet (PPPoE)

This chapter provides information and commands concerning the following topic:

- Configuring a DSL connection using PPPoE

The Point-to-Point over Ethernet (PPPoE) protocol is used to encapsulate PPP frames inside Ethernet frames. It is most often used when working with broadband communications such as digital subscriber line (DSL), a family of technologies that provides Internet access over the wires of a local telephone network.

Configuring a DSL Connection using PPPoE

Figure 32-1 shows an asymmetric digital subscriber line (ADSL) connection to the ISP DSL address multiplexer

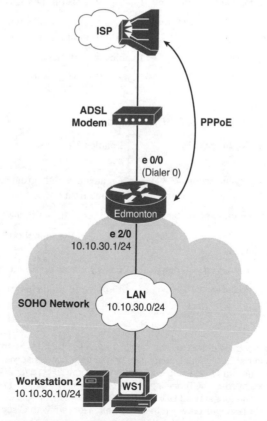

Figure 32-1 PPPoE Reference

The programming steps for configuring PPPoE on an Ethernet interface are as follows:

1. Configure PPPoE (external modem).

2. Configure the dialer interface.

3. Define interesting traffic and specify default routing.

4. Configure Network Address Translation (NAT) using an access control list (ACL).

5. Configure NAT using a route map.

6. Configure DHCP service.

7. Apply NAT programming.

8. Verify a PPPoE connection.

Step 1: Configure PPPoE (External Modem)

Edmonton(config)#**interface ethernet 0/0**	Enters interface configuration mode
Edmonton(config-if)#**pppoe enable**	Enables PPPoE on the interface
Edmonton(config-if)#**pppoe-client dial-pool-number 1**	Chooses the physical Ethernet interface for the PPPoE client dialer interface
Edmonton(config-if)#**no shutdown**	Enables the interface
Edmonton(config-if)#**exit**	Returns to global configuration mode

Virtual Private Dial-Up Network (VPDN) Programming

Edmonton(config)#**vpdn enable**	Enables VPDN sessions on the network access server
Edmonton(config)#**vpdn-group PPPOE-GROUP**	Creates a VPDN group and assigns it a unique name
Edmonton(config-vpdn)#**request-dialin**	Initiates a dial-in tunnel
Edmonton(config-vpdn-req-in)#**protocol pppoe**	Specifies the tunnel protocol
Edmonton(config-vpdn-req-in)#**exit**	Exits request-dialin mode
Edmonton(config-vpdn)#**exit**	Exits vpdn mode and returns to global configuration mode

NOTE VPDNs are legacy dial-in access services provided by ISPs to enterprise customers who chose not to purchase, configure, or maintain access servers or modem pools. A VPDN tunnel was built using Layer 2 Forwarding (L2F), Layer 2 Tunneling Protocol (L2TP), Point-to-Point Tunneling Protocol (PPTP), or Point-to-Point over Ethernet (PPPoE). The tunnel used UDP port 1702 to carry encapsulated PPP datagrams and control messages between the endpoints. Routers with Cisco IOS Release 12.2(13)T or earlier require the additional VPDN programming.

Step 2: Configure the Dialer Interface

`Edmonton(config)#interface dialer0`	Enters interface configuration mode.
`Edmonton(config-if)#ip address negotiated`	Obtains IP address via PPP/IPCP address negotiation.
`Edmonton(config-if)#ip mtu 1492`	Accommodates for the 6octet PPPoE header to eliminate fragmentation in the frame.
`Edmonton(config-if)#ip tcp adjust-mss 1452`	Adjusts the maximum segment size (MSS) of TCP SYN packets going through a router to eliminate fragmentation in the frame.
`Edmonton(config-if)#encapsulation ppp`	Enables PPP encapsulation on the dialer interface.
`Edmonton(config-if)#dialer pool 1`	Links the dialer interface with the physical interface Ethernet 0/1.
	NOTE The ISP defines the type of authentication to use.

For Password Authentication Protocol (PAP)

`Edmonton(config-if)#ppp authentication pap callin`	Uses PAP for authentication
`Edmonton(config-if)#ppp pap sent-username pieman password bananacream`	Enables outbound PAP user authentication with a username of pieman and a password of bananacream

For Challenge Handshake Authentication Protocol (CHAP)

`Edmonton(config-if)#ppp authentication chap callin`	Enables outbound CHAP user authentication
`Edmonton(config-if)#ppp chap hostname pieman`	Submits the CHAP username
`Edmonton(config-if)#ppp chap password bananacream`	Submits the CHAP password
`Edmonton(config-if)#exit`	Exits programming level

Step 3: Define Interesting Traffic and Specify Default Routing

`Edmonton(config)#dialer-list 2 protocol ip permit`	Declares which traffic will invoke the dialing mechanism
`Edmonton(config)#interface dialer0`	Enters interface configuration mode
`Edmonton(config-if)#dialer-group 2`	Applies the "interesting traffic" rules in dialer-list 2
`Edmonton(config)#ip route 0.0.0.0 0.0.0.0 dialer0`	Specifies the dialer0 interface as the candidate default next-hop address

Step 4: Configure NAT Using an ACL

Edmonton(config)#**access-list 1 permit 10.10.30.0 0.0.0.255**	Specifies an access control entry (ACE) for NAT.
Edmonton(config)#**ip nat pool NAT-POOL 192.31.7.1 192.31.7.2 netmask 255.255.255.0**	Defines the inside global (WAN side) NAT pool with subnet mask.
	NOTE When a range of public addresses is used for the NAT/PAT inside global (WAN) addresses, it is defined by an address pool and called in the NAT definition programming.
Edmonton(config)#**ip nat inside source list 1 pool NAT-POOL overload**	Specifies the NAT inside local addresses by ACL and the inside global addresses by address pool for the NAT process.
	NOTE In the case where the inside global (WAN) address is dynamically assigned by the ISP, the outbound WAN interface is named in the NAT definition programming.
Edmonton(config)#**ip nat inside source list 1 interface dialer0 overload**	Specifies the NAT inside local addresses (LAN) and inside global addresses (WAN) for the NAT process.

Step 5: Configure NAT Using a Route Map

Edmonton(config)#**access-list 3 permit 10.10.30.0 0.0.0.255**	Specifies the access control entry (ACE) for NAT.
	NOTE The **route-map** command is typically used when redistributing routes from one routing protocol into another or to enable policy routing. The most commonly used method for defining the traffic to be translated in the NAT process is to use an ACL to choose traffic and call the ACL directly in the NAT programming. When used for NAT, a route map allows you to match any combination of ACL, next-hop IP address, and output interface to determine which pool to use. The Cisco Router and Security Device Manager (SDM) uses a route map to select traffic for NAT.
Edmonton(config)#**route-map ROUTEMAP permit 1**	Declares route map name and enters route-map mode.
Edmonton(config-route-map)#**match ip address 3**	Specifies the ACL that defines the dialer "interesting traffic."
Edmonton(config-route-map)#**exit**	Exits route-map mode.
Edmonton(config)#**ip nat inside source route-map ROUTEMAP interface dialer0 overload**	Specifies the NAT inside local (as defined by the route map) and inside global (interface dialer0) linkage for the address translation.

Step 6: Configure DHCP Service

`Edmonton(config)#ip dhcp excluded-address 10.10.30.1 10.10.30.5`	Excludes an IP address range from being offered by the router's DHCP service.
`Edmonton(config)#ip dhcp pool CLIENT-30`	Enters dhcp-config mode for the pool CLIENT-30.
`Edmonton(dhcp-config)#network 10.10.30.0 255.255.255.0`	Defines the IP network address.
`Edmonton(dhcp-config)#default-router 10.10.30.1`	Declares the router's vlan10 interface address as a gateway address.
`Edmonton(dhcp-config)#import all`	Imports DHCP option parameters into the DHCP server database from external DHCP service.
	NOTE Any manually configured DHCP option parameters override the equivalent imported DHCP option parameters. Because they are obtained dynamically, these imported DHCP option parameters are not part of the router configuration and are not saved in NVRAM.
`Edmonton(dhcp-config)#dns-server 10.10.30.2`	Declares any required DNS server addresses.
`Edmonton(dhcp-config)#exit`	Exits dhcp-config mode.

Step 7: Apply NAT Programming

`Edmonton(config)#interface ethernet2/0`	Enters interface configuration mode
`Edmonton(config-if)#ip nat inside`	Specifies the interface as an inside local (LAN side) interface
`Edmonton(config)#interface dialer0`	Enters interface configuration mode
`Edmonton(config-if)#ip nat outside`	Specifies the interface as an inside global (WAN side) interface
`Edmonton(config-if)#end`	Returns to privileged EXEC mode

Step 8: Verify a PPPoE Connection

`Edmonton#debug pppoe events`	Displays PPPoE protocol messages about events that are part of normal session establishment or shutdown.
`Edmonton#debug ppp authentication`	Displays authentication protocol messages such as CHAP and PAP messages.
`Edmonton#show pppoe session`	Displays information about currently active PPPoE sessions.
`Edmonton#show ip dhcp binding`	Displays address bindings on the Cisco IOS DHCP server.
`Edmonton#show ip nat translations`	Displays active NAT translations.

CHAPTER 33

Managing Traffic Using Access Control Lists (ACL)

This chapter provides information and commands concerning the following topics:

- Access list numbers
- Using wildcard masks
- ACL keywords
- Creating standard ACLs
- Applying standard ACLs to an interface
- Verifying ACLs
- Removing ACLs
- Creating extended ACLs
- Applying extended ACLs to an interface
- The **established** keyword (optional)
- Creating named ACLs
- Using sequence numbers in named ACLs
- Removing specific lines in named ACLs using sequence numbers
- Sequence number tips
- Including comments about entries in ACLs
- Restricting virtual terminal access
- Tips for configuring ACLs
- ACLs and IPv6
- Configuration examples: ACLs

Access List Numbers

Although many different protocols can use access control lists, the CCNA vendor exams are concerned only with IPv4 ACLs. The following chart shows some of the other protocols that can use ACLs.

1–99 or 1300–1999	Standard IPv4
100–199 or 2000–2699	Extended IPv4
600–699	AppleTalk
800–899	IPX
900–999	Extended IPX
1000–1099	IPX Service Advertising Protocol

Using Wildcard Masks

When compared to an IP address, a wildcard mask identifies which addresses get matched to be applied to the **permit** or **deny** argument in an access control list (ACL) statement:

- A 0 (zero) in a wildcard mask means to check the corresponding bit in the address for an exact match.

- A 1 (one) in a wildcard mask means to ignore the corresponding bit in the address—can be either 1 or 0. In the examples, this is shown as x.

Example 1: 172.16.0.0 0.0.255.255

$$172.16.0.0 = 10101100.00010000.00000000.00000000$$
$$0.0.255.255 = 00000000.00000000.11111111.11111111$$
$$result = 10101100.00010000.xxxxxxxx.xxxxxxxx$$
$$172.16.x.x \text{ (Anything between 172.16.0.0 and 172.16.255.255 will match}$$
the example statement.)

TIP   An octet of all 0s means that the octet has to match exactly to the address. An octet of all 1s means that the octet can be ignored.

Example 2: 172.16.8.0 0.0.7.255

$$172.168.8.0 = 10101100.00010000.00001000.00000000$$
$$0.0.0.7.255 = 00000000.00000000.00000111.11111111$$
$$result = 10101100.00010000.00001xxx.xxxxxxxx$$
$$00001xxx = 00001000 \text{ to } 00001111 = 8–15$$
$$xxxxxxxx = 00000000 \text{ to } 11111111 = 0–255$$
Anything between 172.16.8.0 and 172.16.15.255 will match the example statement.

ACL Keywords

| **any** | Used in place of 0.0.0.0 255.255.255.255, will match any address that it is compared against |
| **host** | Used in place of 0.0.0.0 in the wildcard mask, will match only one specific address |

Creating Standard ACLs

NOTE Standard ACLs are the oldest type of ACL. They date back as early as Cisco IOS Release 8.3. Standard ACLs control traffic by comparing the source of the IP packets to the addresses configured in the ACL.

`Router(config)#access-list 10 permit 172.16.0.0 0.0.255.255`	Read this line to say, "All packets with a source IP address of 172.16.*x.x* will be permitted to continue through the internetwork."
`access-list`	ACL command.
`10`	Arbitrary number between 1 and 99, or 1300 and 1999, designating this as a standard IP ACL.
`permit`	Packets that match this statement will be allowed to continue.
`172.16.0.0`	Source IP address to be compared to.
`0.0.255.255`	Wildcard mask.
`Router(config)#access-list 10 deny host 172.17.0.1`	Read this line to say, "All packets with a source IP address of 172.17.0.1 will be dropped and discarded."
`access-list`	ACL command.
`10`	Number between 1 and 99, or 1300 and 1999, designating this as a standard IP ACL.
`deny`	Packets that match this statement will be dropped and discarded.
`host`	Keyword.
`172.17.0.1`	Specific host address.
`Router(config)#access-list 10 permit any`	Read this line to say, "All packets with any source IP address will be permitted to continue through the internetwork."
`access-list`	ACL command.
`10`	Number between 1 and 99, or 1300 and 1999, designating this as a standard IP ACL.
`permit`	Packets that match this statement will be allowed to continue.
`any`	Keyword to mean all IP addresses.

TIP An implicit **deny** statement is hard-coded into every ACL. You cannot see it, but it states "deny everything not already permitted." This is always the last line of any ACL. If you want to defeat this implicit **deny**, put a **permit any** statement in your standard ACLs or **permit ip any any** in your extended ACLs as the last line.

Applying Standard ACLs to an Interface

Router(config)#interface gigabitethernet 0/0	Moves to interface configuration mode.
Router(config-if)#ip access-group 10 in	Takes all access list lines that are defined as being part of group 10 and applies them in an inbound manner. Packets going into the router from gigabitethernet 0/0 will be checked.

TIP   Access lists can be applied in either an inbound direction (keyword **in**) or in an outbound direction (keyword **out**).

TIP   Not sure in which direction to apply an ACL? Look at the flow of packets. Do you want to filter packets as they are going *in* a router's interface from an external source? Use the keyword **in** for this ACL. Do you want to filter packets before they go *out* of the router's interface toward another device? Use the keyword **out** for this ACL.

TIP   Apply a standard ACL as close as possible to the destination network or device.

Verifying ACLs

Router#show ip interface	Displays any ACLs applied to that interface
Router#show access-lists	Displays the contents of all ACLs on the router
Router#show access-list access-list-number	Displays the contents of the ACL by the number specified
Router#show access-list name	Displays the contents of the ACL by the *name* specified
Router#show run	Displays all ACLs and interface assignments

Removing ACLs

Router(config)#no access-list 10	Removes *all* ACLs numbered 10

Creating Extended ACLs

NOTE   Extended ACLs were also introduced in Cisco IOS Release 8.3. Extended ACLs control traffic by comparing the source and destination of the IP packets to the addresses configured in the ACL. Extended ACLs can also filter packets using protocol/port numbers for a more granular filter.

`Router(config)#access-list 110 permit tcp 172.16.0.0 0.0.0.255 192.168.100.0 0.0.0.255 eq 80`	Read this line to say, "HTTP packets with a source IP address of 172.16.0.*x* will be permitted to travel to the destination address 192.168.100.*x*."
`access-list`	ACL command.
`110`	Number is between 100 and 199, or 2000 and 2699, designating this as an extended IP ACL.
`permit`	Packets that match this statement will be allowed to continue.
`tcp`	Protocol must be TCP.
`172.16.0.0`	Source IP address to be compared to.
`0.0.0.255`	Wildcard mask for the source IP address.
`192.168.100.0`	Destination IP address to be compared to.
`0.0.0.255`	Wildcard mask for the destination IP address.
`eq`	Operand, means "equal to."
`80`	Port 80, indicating HTTP traffic.
`Router(config)#access-list 110 deny tcp any 192.168.100.7 0.0.0.0 eq 23`	Read this line to say, "Telnet packets with any source IP address will be dropped if they are addressed to specific host 192.168.100.7."
`access-list`	ACL command.
`110`	Number is between 100 and 199, or 2000 and 2699, designating this as an extended IP ACL.
`deny`	Packets that match this statement will be dropped and discarded.
`tcp`	Protocol must be TCP protocol.
`any`	Any source IP address.
`192.168.100.7`	Destination IP address to be compared to.
`0.0.0.0`	Wildcard mask; address must match exactly.
`eq`	Operand, means "equal to."
`23`	Port 23, indicating Telnet traffic.

Applying Extended ACLs to an Interface

`Router(config)#interface gigabitethernet 0/0`
 	
`Router(config-if)#ip access-group 110 out`
	Moves to interface configuration mode and takes all access list lines that are defined as being part of group 110 and applies them in an outbound manner. Packets going out gigabitethernet 0/0 will be checked.

TIP   Access lists can be applied in either an inbound direction (keyword **in**) or in an outbound direction (keyword **out**).

TIP   Only one access list can be applied per interface, per direction.

TIP   Apply an extended ACL as close as possible to the source network or device.

The established Keyword (Optional)

`Router(config)#access-list 110 permit tcp`
`172.16.0.0 0.0.0.255 192.168.100.0 0.0.0.255 eq`
`80 established`
	Indicates an established connection

NOTE   A match will now occur only if the TCP datagram has the ACK or the RST bit set.

TIP   The **established** keyword will work only for TCP, not UDP.

TIP   Consider the following situation: You do not want hackers exploiting port 80 to access your network. Because you do not host a web server, it is possible to block incoming traffic on port 80 ... except that your internal users need web access. When they request a web page, return traffic on port 80 must be allowed. The solution to this problem is to use the **established** command. The ACL will allow the response to enter your network, because it will have the ACK bit set as a result of the initial request from inside your network. Requests from the outside world will still be blocked because the ACK bit will not be set, but responses will be allowed through.

Creating Named ACLs

`Router(config)#ip access-list extended serveraccess`	Creates an extended named ACL called serveraccess and moves to named ACL configuration mode.
`Router(config-ext-nacl)#permit tcp any host 131.108.101.99 eq smtp`	Permits mail packets from any source to reach host 131.108.101.99.

`Router(config-ext-nacl)#permit udp any host 131.108.101.99 eq domain`	Permits Domain Name System (DNS) packets from any source to reach host 131.108.101.99.
`Router(config-ext-nacl)#deny ip any any log`	Denies all other packets from going anywhere. If any packets do get denied, this logs the results for you to look at later.
`Router(config-ext-nacl)#exit`	Returns to global configuration mode.
`Router(config)#interface gigabitethernet 0/0` `Router(config-if)#ip access-group serveraccess out`	Moves to interface configuration mode and applies this ACL to the gigabitethernet interface 0/0 in an outbound direction.

Using Sequence Numbers in Named ACLs

`Router(config)#ip access-list extended serveraccess2`	Creates an extended named ACL called serveraccess2.
`Router(config-ext-nacl)#10 permit tcp any host 131.108.101.99 eq smtp`	Uses a sequence number 10 for this line.
`Router(config-ext-nacl)#20 permit udp any host 131.108.101.99 eq domain`	Sequence number 20 will be applied after line 10.
`Router(config-ext-nacl)#30 deny ip any any log`	Sequence number 30 will be applied after line 20.
`Router(config-ext-nacl)#exit`	Returns to global configuration mode.
`Router(config)#interface gigabitethernet 0/0`	Moves to interface configuration mode.
`Router(config-if)#ip access-group serveraccess2 out`	Applies this ACL in an outbound direction.
`Router(config-if)#exit`	Returns to global configuration mode.
`Router(config)#ip access-list extended serveraccess2`	Moves to named ACL configuration mode for the ACL serveraccess2.
`Router(config-ext-nacl)#25 permit tcp any host 131.108.101.99 eq ftp`	Sequence number 25 places this line after line 20 and before line 30.
`Router(config-ext-nacl)#exit`	Returns to global configuration mode.

TIP Sequence numbers are used to allow for easier editing of your ACLs. The preceding example used numbers 10, 20, and 30 in the ACL lines. If you had needed to add another line to this ACL, it would have previously been added after the last line—line 30. If you had needed a line to go closer to the top, you would have had to remove the entire ACL and then reapply it with the lines in the correct order. Now you can enter in a new line with a sequence number, placing it in the correct location.

NOTE The *sequence-number* argument was added in Cisco IOS Software Release 12.2(14)S. It was integrated into Cisco IOS Software Release 12.2(15)T.

Removing Specific Lines in Named ACLs Using Sequence Numbers

`Router(config)#ip access-list` `extended serveraccess2`	Moves to named ACL configuration mode for the ACL serveraccess2
`Router(config-ext-nacl)#no 20`	Removes line 20 from the list
`Router(config-ext-nacl)#exit`	Returns to global configuration mode

Sequence Number Tips

- Sequence numbers start at 10 and increment by 10 for each line.
- The maximum sequence number is 2147483647.
  - If you have an ACL that is so complex that it needs a number this big, I'd ask your boss for a raise.
- If you forget to add a sequence number, the line is added to the end of the list and assigned a number that is 10 greater than the last sequence number.
- If you enter an entry that matches an existing entry (except for the sequence number), no changes are made.
- If the user enters a sequence number that is already present, an error message of "Duplicate sequence number" displays. You have to reenter the line with a new sequence number.
- Sequence numbers are changed on a router reload to reflect the increment by 10 policy (see first tip in this section). If your ACL has numbers 10, 20, 30, 32, 40, 50, and 60 in it, on reload these numbers become 10, 20, 30, 40, 50, 60, 70.
- If you want to change the numbering sequence of your ACLs to something other than incrementing by 10, use the global configuration command ip **access-list resequence** *name/number start# increment#*:

```
Router(config)#ip access-list resequence serveracces 1 2
```

This resets the ACL named serveraccess to start at 1 and increment by steps of 2 (1, 3, 5, 7, 9, and so on). The range for using this command is 1 to 2147483647.

- Sequence numbers cannot be seen when using the Router#**show running-config** or Router#**show startup-config** command. To see sequence numbers, use one of the following commands:

```
Router#show access-lists
Router#show access-lists list name
Router#show ip access-list
Router#show ip access-list list name
```

Including Comments About Entries in ACLs

`Router(config)#access-list 10` `remark only Jones has access`	The **remark** command allows you to include a comment (limited to 100 characters).
`Router(config)#access-list 10` `permit 172.16.100.119`	Read this line to say, "Host 172.16.100.119 will be permitted through the internetwork."
`Router(config)#ip access-list` `extended telnetaccess`	Creates a named ACL called telnetaccess and moves to named ACL configuration mode.
`Router(config-ext-nacl)#remark` `do not let Smith have telnet`	The **remark** command allows you to include a comment (limited to 100 characters).

`Router(config-ext-nacl)#deny`
`tcp host 172.16.100.153 any eq`
`telnet`
	Read this line to say, "Deny this specific host Telnet access to anywhere in the internetwork."

TIP   You can use the **remark** command in any of the IP numbered standard, IP numbered extended, or named IP ACLs.

TIP   You can use the **remark** command either before or after a **permit** or **deny** statement. Therefore, be consistent in your placement to avoid any confusion as to which line the **remark** statement is referring.

Restricting Virtual Terminal Access

`Router(config)#access-list 2` `permit host 172.16.10.2`	Permits host from source address of 172.16.10.2 to telnet/SSH into this router based on where this ACL is applied.
`Router(config)#access-list 2` `permit 172.16.20.0 0.0.0.255`	Permits anyone from the 172.16.20.*x* address range to telnet/SSH into this router based on where this ACL is applied.
	The implicit **deny** statement restricts anyone else from being permitted to telnet/SSH.
`Router(config)#line vty 0 4`	Moves to vty line configuration mode.
`Router(config-line)#access-` `class 2 in`	Applies this ACL to all 5 vty virtual interfaces in an inbound direction.

TIP   When restricting access through Telnet, use the **access-class** command rather than the **access-group** command, which is used when applying an ACL to a physical interface.

CAUTION   Do not apply an ACL intending to restrict Telnet traffic on a physical interface. If you apply to a physical interface, *all* packets will be compared to the ACL before it can continue on its path to its destination. This scenario can lead to a large reduction in router performance.

Tips for Configuring ACLs

- The type of ACL determines what is filtered.

    — Standard filters only on source IP.

    — Extended filters on source IP, Destination IP, Protocol Number, Port Number

- Only one ACL per interface, per protocol, per direction.

- Place your most specific statements at the top of the ACL. The most general statements should be at the bottom of the ACL.

- The last test in any ACL is the implicit **deny** statement. You cannot see it, but it is there.

- Every ACL must have at least one **permit** statement. Otherwise, you will block everything.

- Place extended ACLs as close as possible to the source network or device.

- Place standard ACLs as close as possible to the destination network or device.

- You can use numbers when creating a named ACL. The 'name' you choose is the number: For example, **ip access-list extended 150** creates an extended ACL named 150.

- An ACL can filter traffic going through a router, or traffic to and from a router, depending on how the ACL is applied.

    — Think of yourself as standing in the middle of the router. Are you filtering traffic that is coming into the router toward you? Make the ACL an inbound one using the keyword **in**.

    — Are you filtering traffic that is going away from you and the router and toward another device? Make the ACL an outbound one using the keyword **out**.

- When restricting access through Telnet, use the **access-class** command rather than the **access-group** command, which is used when applying an ACL to a physical interface.

ACLs and IPv6

Although not part of the CCNA curriculum, ACLs can be created in IPv6. The syntax for creating an IPv6 ACL is limited to named ACLs.

`Router(config)#ipv6 access-list v6example`	Creates an IPv6 ACL called v6example and moves to IPv6 ACL configuration mode
`Router(config-ipv6-acl)#permit tcp 2001:db8:300:201::/32 eq telnet any`	Permits the specified IPv6 address to telnet to any destination
`Router(config-ipv6-acl)#deny tcp host 2001:db8:1::1 any log-input`	Denies a specific IPv6 host. Attempts will be logged
`Router(config-ipv6-acl)#exit`	Returns to global configuration mode

Router(config)#**interface gigabitethernet 0/0**	Moves to interface configuration mode
Router(config-if)#**ipv6 traffic-filter v6example out**	Applies the IPv6 ACL named v6example to the interface in an outbound direction

TIP   You use the **traffic-filter** keyword rather than the **access-group** keyword when assigning IPv6 ACLs to an interface.

TIP   You still use the **access-class** keyword to assign an IPv6 ACL to virtual terminal (vty) lines for restricting Telnet/SSH access, just like working with IPv4 ACLs.

Configuration Examples: ACLs

Figure 33-1 illustrates the network topology for the configuration that follows, which shows five ACL examples using the commands covered in this chapter.

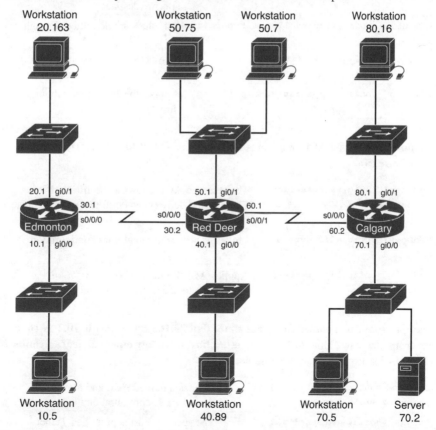

Figure 33-1   Network Topology for ACL Configuration

Example 1: Write an ACL that prevents the 10.0 network from accessing the 40.0 network but allows everyone else to.

`RedDeer(config)#access-list 10 deny 172.16.10.0 0.0.0.255`	The standard ACL denies complete network for complete TCP/IP suite of protocols.
`RedDeer(config)#access-list 10 permit any`	Defeats the implicit **deny**.
`RedDeer(config)#interface gigabitethernet 0/0`	Moves to interface configuration mode.
`RedDeer(config)#ip access-group 10 out`	Applies ACL in an outbound direction.

Example 2: Write an ACL that states that 10.5 cannot access 50.7. Everyone else can.

`Edmonton(config)#access list 115 deny ip host 172.16.10.5 host 172.16.50.7`	The extended ACL denies specific host for entire TCP/IP suite to a specific destination.
`Edmonton(config)#access list 115 permit ip any any`	All others are permitted through.
`Edmonton(config)#interface gigabitethernet 0/0`	Moves to interface configuration mode.
`Edmonton(config)#ip access-group 115 in`	Applies the ACL in an inbound direction.

Example 3: Write an ACL that states that 10.5 can Telnet to the Red Deer router. No one else can.

`RedDeer(config)#access-list 20 permit host 172.16.10.5`	The standard ACL allows a specific host access. The implicit deny statement filters everyone else out.
`RedDeer(config)#line vty 0 4`	Moves to virtual terminal lines configuration mode.
`RedDeer(config-line)#access-class 20 in`	Applies ACL 20 in an inbound direction. Remember to use access-class, not access-group.

Example 4: Write a named ACL that states that 20.163 can Telnet to 70.2. No one else from 20.0 can Telnet to 70.2. Any other host from any other subnet can connect to 70.2 using anything that is available.

`Calgary(config)#ip access-list extended serveraccess`	Creates a named ACL and moves to named ACL configuration mode.
`Calgary(config-ext-nacl)#10 permit tcp host 172.16.20.163 host 172.16.70.2 eq telnet`	The specific host is permitted Telnet access to a specific destination.

`Calgary(config-ext-nacl)#20 deny`
`tcp 172.16.20.0 0.0.0.255 host`
`172.16.70.2 eq telnet`
	No other hosts are allowed to telnet to the server.

`Calgary(config-ext-nacl)#30 permit` `ip any any`	Defeats the implicit **deny** statement and allows all other traffic to pass through.
`Calgary(config-ext-nacl)#exit`	Returns to global configuration mode.
`Calgary(config)#interface` `gigabitethernet 0/0`	Moves to interface configuration mode.
`Calgary(config)#ip access-group` `serveraccess out`	Sets the ACL named serveraccess in an outbound direction on the interface.

Example 5: Write an ACL that states that hosts 50.1–50.63 are not allowed web access to 80.16. Hosts 50.64–50.254 are. Everyone can do everything else.

`RedDeer(config)#access-list 101`
`deny tcp 172.16.50.0 0.0.0.63`
`host 172.16.80.16 eq 80`
	Creates an ACL that denies HTTP traffic from a range of hosts to a specific destination

`RedDeer(config)#access-list 101` `permit ip any any`	Defeats the implicit **deny** statement and allows all other traffic to pass through
`RedDeer(config)#interface` `gigabitethernet 0/0`	Moves to interface configuration mode
`RedDeer(config)#ip access-group` `101 in`	Applies the ACL in an inbound direction

Binary/Hex/Decimal Conversion Chart

The following chart lists the three most common number systems used in networking: decimal, hexadecimal, and binary. Some numbers you will remember quite easily, as you use them a lot in your day-to-day activities. For those other numbers, refer to this chart.

Decimal Value	Hexadecimal Value	Binary Value
0	00	0000 0000
1	01	0000 0001
2	02	0000 0010
3	03	0000 0011
4	04	0000 0100
5	05	0000 0101
6	06	0000 0110
7	07	0000 0111
8	08	0000 1000
9	09	0000 1001
10	0A	0000 1010
11	0B	0000 1011
12	0C	0000 1100
13	0D	0000 1101
14	0E	0000 1110
15	0F	0000 1111
16	10	0001 0000
17	11	0001 0001
18	12	0001 0010
19	13	0001 0011

Decimal Value	Hexadecimal Value	Binary Value
20	14	0001 0100
21	15	0001 0101
22	16	0001 0110
23	17	0001 0111
24	18	0001 1000
25	19	0001 1001
26	1A	0001 1010
27	1B	0001 1011
28	1C	0001 1100
29	1D	0001 1101
30	1E	0001 1110
31	1F	0001 1111
32	20	0010 0000
33	21	0010 0001
34	22	0010 0010
35	23	0010 0011
36	24	0010 0100
37	25	0010 0101
38	26	0010 0110
39	27	0010 0111
40	28	0010 1000
41	29	0010 1001
42	2A	0010 1010
43	2B	0010 1011
44	2C	0010 1100
45	2D	0010 1101
46	2E	0010 1110
47	2F	0010 1111
48	30	0011 0000
49	31	0011 0001
50	32	0011 0010
51	33	0011 0011
52	34	0011 0100
53	35	0011 0101
54	36	0011 0110

Decimal Value	Hexadecimal Value	Binary Value
55	37	0011 0111
56	38	0011 1000
57	39	0011 1001
58	3A	0011 1010
59	3B	0011 1011
60	3C	0011 1100
61	3D	0011 1101
62	3E	0011 1110
63	3F	0011 1111
64	40	0100 0000
65	41	0100 0001
66	42	0100 0010
67	43	0100 0011
68	44	0100 0100
69	45	0100 0101
70	46	0100 0110
71	47	0100 0111
72	48	0100 1000
73	49	0100 1001
74	4A	0100 1010
75	4B	0100 1011
76	4C	0100 1100
77	4D	0100 1101
78	4E	0100 1110
79	4F	0100 1111
80	50	0101 0000
81	51	0101 0001
82	52	0101 0010
83	53	0101 0011
84	54	0101 0100
85	55	0101 0101
86	56	0101 0110
87	57	0101 0111
88	58	0101 1000
89	59	0101 1001

Decimal Value	Hexadecimal Value	Binary Value
90	5A	0101 1010
91	5B	0101 1011
92	5C	0101 1100
93	5D	0101 1101
94	5E	0101 1110
95	5F	0101 1111
96	60	0110 0000
97	61	0110 0001
98	62	0110 0010
99	63	0110 0011
100	64	0110 0100
101	65	0110 0101
102	66	0110 0110
103	67	0110 0111
104	68	0110 1000
105	69	0110 1001
106	6A	0110 1010
107	6B	0110 1011
108	6C	0110 1100
109	6D	0110 1101
110	6E	0110 1110
111	6F	0110 1111
112	70	0111 0000
113	71	0111 0001
114	72	0111 0010
115	73	0111 0011
116	74	0111 0100
117	75	0111 0101
118	76	0111 0110
119	77	0111 0111
120	78	0111 1000
121	79	0111 1001
122	7A	0111 1010
123	7B	0111 1011
124	7C	0111 1100

Decimal Value	Hexadecimal Value	Binary Value
125	7D	0111 1101
126	7E	0111 1110
127	7F	0111 1111
128	80	1000 0000
129	81	1000 0001
130	82	1000 0010
131	83	1000 0011
132	84	1000 0100
133	85	1000 0101
134	86	1000 0110
135	87	1000 0111
136	88	1000 1000
137	89	1000 1001
138	8A	1000 1010
139	8B	1000 1011
140	8C	1000 1100
141	8D	1000 1101
142	8E	1000 1110
143	8F	1000 1111
144	90	1001 0000
145	91	1001 0001
146	92	1001 0010
147	93	1001 0011
148	94	1001 0100
149	95	1001 0101
150	96	1001 0110
151	97	1001 0111
152	98	1001 1000
153	99	1001 1001
154	9A	1001 1010
155	9B	1001 1011
156	9C	1001 1100
157	9D	1001 1101
158	9E	1001 1110
159	9F	1001 1111

Decimal Value	Hexadecimal Value	Binary Value
160	A0	1010 0000
161	A1	1010 0001
162	A2	1010 0010
163	A3	1010 0011
164	A4	1010 0100
165	A5	1010 0101
166	A6	1010 0110
167	A7	1010 0111
168	A8	1010 1000
169	A9	1010 1001
170	AA	1010 1010
171	AB	1010 1011
172	AC	1010 1100
173	AD	1010 1101
174	AE	1010 1110
175	AF	1010 1111
176	B0	1011 0000
177	B1	1011 0001
178	B2	1011 0010
179	B3	1011 0011
180	B4	1011 0100
181	B5	1011 0101
182	B6	1011 0110
183	B7	1011 0111
184	B8	1011 1000
185	B9	1011 1001
186	BA	1011 1010
187	BB	1011 1011
188	BC	1011 1100
189	BD	1011 1101
190	BE	1011 1110
191	BF	1011 1111
192	C0	1100 0000
193	C1	1100 0001
194	C2	1100 0010

Decimal Value	Hexadecimal Value	Binary Value
195	C3	1100 0011
196	C4	1100 0100
197	C5	1100 0101
198	C6	1100 0110
199	C7	1100 0111
200	C8	1100 1000
201	C9	1100 1001
202	CA	1100 1010
203	CB	1100 1011
204	CC	1100 1100
205	CD	1100 1101
206	CE	1100 1110
207	CF	1100 1111
208	D0	1101 0000
209	D1	1101 0001
210	D2	1101 0010
211	D3	1101 0011
212	D4	1101 0100
213	D5	1101 0101
214	D6	1101 0110
215	D7	1101 0111
216	D8	1101 1000
217	D9	1101 1001
218	DA	1101 1010
219	DB	1101 1011
220	DC	1101 1100
221	DD	1101 1101
222	DE	1101 1110
223	DF	1101 1111
224	E0	1110 0000
225	E1	1110 0001
226	E2	1110 0010
227	E3	1110 0011
228	E4	1110 0100
229	E5	1110 0101

Decimal Value	Hexadecimal Value	Binary Value
230	E6	1110 0110
231	E7	1110 0111
232	E8	1110 1000
233	E9	1110 1001
234	EA	1110 1010
235	EB	1110 1011
236	EC	1110 1100
237	ED	1110 1101
238	EE	1110 1110
239	EF	1110 1111
240	F0	1111 0000
241	F1	1111 0001
242	F2	1111 0010
243	F3	1111 0011
244	F4	1111 0100
245	F5	1111 0101
246	F6	1111 0110
247	F7	1111 0111
248	F8	1111 1000
249	F9	1111 1001
250	FA	1111 1010
251	FB	1111 1011
252	FC	1111 1100
253	FD	1111 1101
254	FE	1111 1110
255	FF	1111 1111

APPENDIX B

Create Your Own Journal Here